# Fodor's 92
# Boston

Fodor's Travel Publications, Inc.
New York and London

## Fodor's Boston

**Editor:** Susan M. Bain
**Area Editor:** Kimberly Grant
**Editorial Contributors:** Helena Bentz, Suzanne De Galan, Mary H. Frakes, Jane Holtz Kay, Kay Howe Scheller, William Scheller, Katherine Minton Tatum, Christina Tree
**Art Director:** Fabrizio La Rocca
**Cartographer:** David Lindroth
**Illustrator:** Karl Tanner
**Cover Photograph:** Owen Franken/Stock Boston

**Design:** Vignelli Associates

## Special Sales

Fodor's Travel Publications are available at special discounts for bulk purchases (100 copies or more) for sales promotions or premiums. Special editions, including personalized covers, excerpts of existing guides, and corporate imprints, can be created in large quantities for special needs. For more information write to Special Marketing, Fodor's Travel Publications, 201 East 50th St., New York, NY 10022; or call 800/800–3246. Inquiries from the United Kingdom should be sent to Fodor's Travel Publications, 20 Vauxhall Bridge Rd., London, England SW1 2SA.

MANUFACTURED IN THE UNITED STATES OF AMERICA
10 9 8 7 6 5 4 3 2 1

# Contents

## Maps

# Foreword

Perhaps no one today would speak of the Boston State House as "the hub of the solar system," as Oliver Wendell Holmes once did, yet Boston itself is very much at the heart of American history. Reminders of the American past are everywhere here, and visitors will come upon them frequently as they explore Boston, Cambridge, and the towns west and north of Boston to which this book takes the reader.

While every care has been taken to ensure the accuracy of the information in this guide, the passage of time will always bring change, and consequently the publisher cannot accept responsibility for errors that may occur.

All prices and opening times quoted here are based on information supplied to us at press time. Hours and admission fees may change, however, and the prudent traveler will avoid inconvenience by calling ahead.

Fodor's wants to hear about your travel experiences, both pleasant and unpleasant. When a hotel or restaurant fails to live up to its billing, let us know and we will investigate the complaint and revise our entries where the facts warrant it.

Send your letters to the editors of Fodor's Travel Publications, 201 E. 50th Street, New York, NY 10022.

# Highlights'92 and Fodor's Choice

# Highlights '92

While Massachusett's recent fiscal difficulties have been widely publicized and are the current talk of the town, on a practical level the impact on tourists visiting Boston is not that severe. Yes, some public facilities, like the ice skating rinks, have reduced hours. (It's best to double check times and fees for public services and institutions.) And yes, some development projects have slowed or even come to a grinding halt. But at the same time, many restaurants and hotels are offering attractive deals and packages to entice travelers. The new administration of Governor Weld recognizes and values the impact of tourism on the local economy, so decisions are being made with out-of-town visitors in mind. Ultimately, the national and international importance of Boston's historic and cultural offerings continues to be an overwhelming draw for tourists.

Because of the downturn in the economy, there are no major renovations scheduled at existing hotels, and there is only one new hotel defying Boston's "building bust." Harvard University expected to open **The Inn at Harvard,** a four-story, 113-room hotel for tourists and university-affiliated guests in the fall of 1991. Situated across from **Harvard Yard** on Massachusetts Avenue, architect Graham Gund designed the structure to echo typical 18th-century Georgian buildings on campus. Individual guest rooms will open onto corridor balconies overlooking an atrium.

Visitors to Boston in the spring of 1992 will find **Faneuil Hall** and the **Old State House** reopened after more than a year and $14.5 million-worth of structural restoration and interior renovations. At the Old State House, structural improvements include a stabilized roof and brick walls, which were previously connected to each other only by gravity and friction. At Faneuil Hall there will be new visitor information services, structural reinforcements, and a refurbishment of the 19th-century ventilation system. Restoration projects have a way of falling behind schedule, so if your trip to Boston revolves around either of these buildings, don't be disappointed; call ahead to make sure it will be open.

At the Charlestown Navy Yard, the USS *Constitution* is scheduled to go into dry dock for repairs in late 1992; officials plan to keep parts of the ship open while other parts are being repaired. In mid-1991 the **John F. Kennedy Library** opened two new facilities: a summertime cafe with indoor and outdoor seating, and the new Stephen Smith Center which is to be used as a public meeting place. Both southbound branches of the MBTA's Red Line now stop at the JFK Library on Columbia Point.

The ongoing reconstruction of the **Central Artery,** a massive public works project to depress and enlarge the main north-south highway cutting through Boston, should not impact visitors in 1992. The initial surface work is still in its infancy. The 7-mile-long project involves replacing the Artery with an underground highway eight to 10 lanes wide while keeping the elevated highway open throughout the construction. A seaport access road will be built from the end of the turnpike to the South Boston waterfront, and a four-lane tunnel will be constructed under the harbor from South Boston to Logan International Airport, connecting with Route 1A. Currently, the only visible aspect of the $4.3 billion Central Artery/Third Harbor tunnel project is the appearance of heavy machinery across the Charlestown Bridge and on the specially built South Boston Bypass Road. Traffic is not affected in either of these places. Regardless, strongly consider using public transportation while you're in and around Boston. There are always traffic delays and practically every hour seems to be "rush hour." As more and more construction gets under way, the resulting detours and delays are another *big* reason for tourists not to drive in Boston.

As part of **SAIL BOSTON '92,** the **Tall Ships** visit Boston July 11–16 in 1992 in celebration and commemoration of the Quincentennial Anniversary of Christopher Columbus's exploration of the Americas. Ships will be berthed at numerous piers around Boston Harbor including East Boston and Charlestown. Activities will be ongoing in the Marine Industrial Park, Fish Pier, Fan Pier, and the World Trade Center. North of Boston in the seaport of **Salem,** 1992 is also a big year for special events. It is the 300th anniversary of the infamous Witch Trials, and to commemorate the occasion, historical, educational, and haunted happenings are planned during the year.

The first phase of the **Prudential Center** restructuring is underway with the rebuilding of 225,000 square feet of retail space in arcades linking St. Botolph Street to the Back Bay Train Station and Copley Place to the Hynes Convention Center. Construction in 1992 should not hamper visitors in any way.

Over the river in Cambridge, Harvard's **Busch-Reisinger Museum,** specializing in Central and Northern European art, was to reopen its doors to the art world in a new building in the fall of 1991.

The **Women's Heritage Trail** celebrates the lives of 20 women who have contributed significantly to Boston and the nation. Based on the concept of the Freedom Trail and the Black Heritage Trail, the Women's Heritage Trail includes 12 downtown sites which will be mapped out on a walking trail. The project is managed by the Boston school system, but call the National Park Service for information.

# Fodor's Choice

No two people will agree on what makes a perfect vacation, but it's fun and helpful to know what others think. We hope you'll have a chance to experience some of Fodor's Choices yourself while visiting Boston. For detailed information about each entry, refer to the appropriate chapters within this guidebook.

## Favorite Sights

Commonwealth Avenue when the magnolia trees are in bloom

Louisburg Square under a blanket of newly fallen snow

The Public Garden at twilight on a clear winter's night

Boston from the top of the Prudential or the Hancock Tower

The first spring day the sculls and the sailboats are sighted on the Charles River

## Jazz

The Regattabar at the Charles Hotel

The *Boston Globe* jazz festival in the spring

## Works of Art

*The Spirit of '76* in Marblehead

Daniel Chester French's *Minuteman* statue in Concord

*Asaroton,* by Mags Harries, in the Haymarket

Titian's *Rape of Europa* in the Gardner Museum

All the Impressionist paintings in the Museum of Fine Arts

## Bars

The Hampshire House

The Ritz-Carlton

Jacob Wirth's

The revolving rooftop lounge of the Hyatt Regency at night

## Day Trips

Plum Island in Newburyport

Boston Harbor Islands

Rockport on the North Shore

**Favorite Walks**

Along the Esplanade

The Freedom Trail in the North End

From the Ritz-Carlton Hotel, down Newbury Street to Gloucester Street, right on Gloucester to Commonwealth Avenue, and right on Commonwealth to the Public Garden

Memorial Drive in Cambridge from MIT to Harvard

Anywhere in the Arnold Arboretum

**Hotels**

The Boston Harbor Hotel at Rowes Wharf *(Very Expensive)*

The Ritz-Carlton *(Very Expensive)*

The Copley Square Hotel *(Moderate)*

The Lenox Hotel *(Moderate)*

**Restaurants**

L'Espalier *(Very Expensive)*

Ristorante Toscano *(Expensive–Very Expensive)*

Biba *(Moderate–Expensive)*

Miyako *(Moderate)*

Ho Yuen Ting *(Inexpensive–Moderate)*

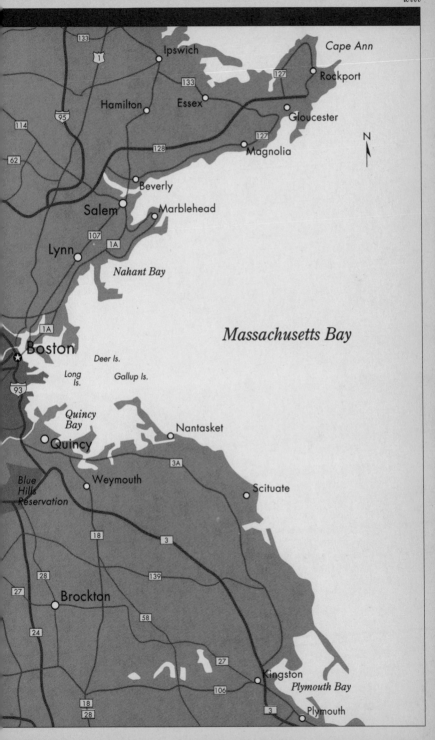

Ipswich

Cape Ann

133

1

127

Rockport

133

Hamilton

Essex

114

95

128

127

Gloucester

62

Magnolia

N

Beverly

Salem

Marblehead

107

Lynn

1A

*Nahant Bay*

1A

Boston

*Deer Is.*

*Massachusetts Bay*

*Long
Is.*

*Gallup Is.*

93

*Quincy
Bay*

Quincy

Nantasket

Blue
Hills
Reservation

Weymouth

3A

Scituate

18

3

28

27

139

Brockton

24

58

27

Kingston

*Plymouth Bay*

18

106

28

3

Plymouth

CAMBRIDGE

Hampshire St.
Webster St.
Willow St.
Cambridge St.
Otis St.
Scarappa St.
Norfolk St.
Union St.
Berkshire St.
8th St.
7th St.
Thorndike St.
3rd St.
Elm St.
Market St.
Portland St.
Fulkerson St.
6th St.
5th St.
Spring St.
Hurley St.
Harvard St.
Windsor St.
Clark St.
Charles St.
Bent St.
2nd St.
1st St.
Commercial St.
Washington St.
Rogers St.
Binney St.
Munroe St.
Broadway
State St.
Massachusetts Ave.
Main St.
Ames St.
Carleton St.
Wadsworth St.
Longfellow Br.
Albany St.
Vassar St.
Amherst St.
2A
3
Cambridge Pkwy.
Harvard Br.
Charles River Basin
1
Back St.
1/4 mile
0
0
250 meters
James J. Storrow Memorial Drive
Beacon St.
Dartmouth St.
Marlborough St.
Berkeley St.
BACK BAY
Fairfield St.
Commonwealth Ave.
Clarendon St.
Back St.
Hereford St.
Gloucester St.
Newbury St.
Exeter St.
Kenmore
Boylston St.
Blagden St.
Beacon St. Sq.
90
90
Ipswich St.
Ipswich
PRUDENTIAL CENTER
28
1
Dalton St.
Belvidere
9
Jersey St.
Van Ness St.
Hemenway
Massachusetts Ave.
Huntington Ave.
Columbus Ave.
Appleton St.
Boylston St.
Burbank St.
St. Botolph St.
Warren Ave.
THE FENS
Westland Ave.
Petersborough St.
Canton St.
Queensberry St.
St. Stephen St.
Pembroke St.
Tremont St.
Kilmarnock St.
Park Dr.
St. Gainsborough St.
Newton St.

# World Time Zones

Numbers below vertical bands relate each zone to Greenwich Mean Time (0 hrs.).
Local times frequently differ from these general indications,
as indicated by light-face numbers on map.

Algiers, **29**
Anchorage, **3**
Athens, **41**
Auckland, **1**
Baghdad, **46**
Bangkok, **50**
Beijing, **54**

Berlin, **34**
Bogotá, **19**
Budapest, **37**
Buenos Aires, **24**
Caracas, **22**
Chicago, **9**
Copenhagen, **33**
Dallas, **10**

Delhi, **48**
Denver, **8**
Djakarta, **53**
Dublin, **26**
Edmonton, **7**
Hong Kong, **56**
Honolulu, **2**

Istanbul, **40**
Jerusalem, **42**
Johannesburg, **44**
Lima, **20**
Lisbon, **28**
London (Greenwich), **27**
Los Angeles, **6**
Madrid, **38**
Manila, **57**

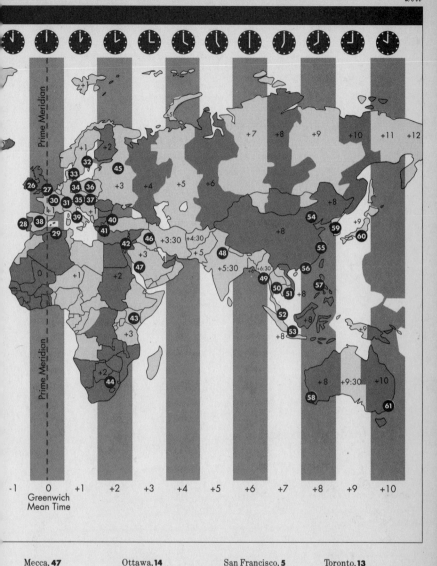

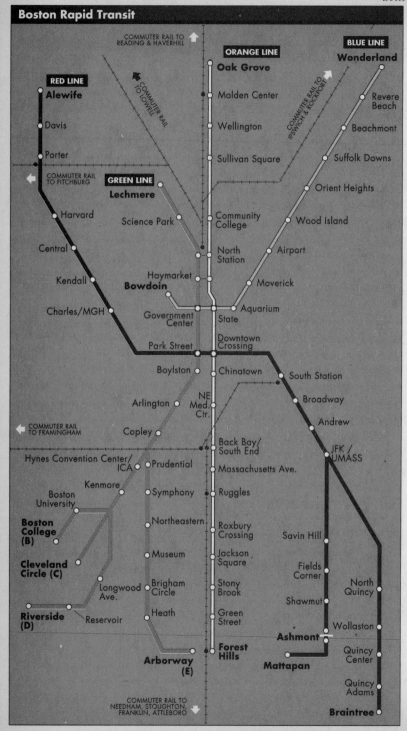

# Introduction

*by William G.
Scheller*

*The author of*
More Country
Walks Near
Boston *and* New
Hampshire:
Portrait of the
Land and Its
People, *William
Scheller
contributes
frequently to
national and
regional
publications.*

Two destinations named Boston occupy the clutch of irregularly shaped peninsulas at the westernmost recess of Massachusetts Bay. The tourist's Boston is the old city, soul and anchor of that peculiar thing called New England civilization and the cradle of American independence. Its most famous buildings are not merely civic landmarks but national icons; its great citizens are not the political and financial leaders of today but the Adamses, Reveres, and Hancocks who live at the crossroads of history and myth. This city is 360 years old, far older than the republic it helped to create in the days of its vigorous youth.

The other Boston, built no less by design than the original, is barely three decades old and every bit as young and vigorous as Paul Revere's town. This is the business traveler's destination, the new Boston created by high finance and higher technology as an answer to those who thought the city had become scarcely more than a museum. It is a place of granite and glass towers rising along what once had been rutted village lanes, dwarfing the commercial structures that stood as the city's largest just a generation ago. In this new city, Samuel Adams is the name of a premium beer, and John Hancock is an insurance company with a dramatic headquarters tower designed by I. M. Pei.

It is entirely possible to come to Boston intent on visiting either the Freedom Trail or the 48th floor of Amalgamated Software and to get exactly what you want out of the experience. With a little extra time and effort, though, you can appreciate both the old and the new Boston and understand why they are really one and the same American city.

Boston is where the Mystic and the Charles flow together to form the Atlantic Ocean. That's the old attitude, and it has been reinforced by local anecdotes, such as the one about the Boston lady who said she had driven to the West Coast "by way of Dedham," and the one about the two Bostonians who blamed a spate of hot San Francisco weather on the fact that the sea was 3,000 miles distant. "The Bostonian who leaves Boston ought to be condemned to perpetual exile," a character says in William Dean Howells's *The Rise of Silas Lapham;* years later, Leverett Saltonstall, the Brahmin senator, said that "the real New England Yankee is a person who takes the midnight train home from New York."

The sayings and stories reinforce the popular notion that Boston is an exceedingly self-important town. Yet Bostonians are not the only people who take the place so seriously. Boston, in reality and in myth, surely looms larger than any other settlement of 600,000 souls in the United States, with the possible exception of San Francisco. The reason for this is hard to come by, but it has to be more than merely the result of masterful self-promotion on the part of a city where "the Lowells speak only to the Cabots, and the Cabots speak only to God" and the common folk used to vote "often and early for James Michael Curley."

Boston has an odd combination of reputations to live up to. For years, the standard line was that it was staid, respectable, and quick to raise its eyebrows at anything or anyone smacking of impropriety. It was a town in which the Watch and Ward Society recommended the books and plays that ought to be banned, where the major social outlets were evenings at the Symphony and afternoons at the Club, and where the loudest noise was the sound of dust and interest collecting on old Yankee money. More recently, word has gone around that Boston's enormous population of undergraduate and graduate students, artists, academics, and smart young professionals who graduated and stayed on have made the town a haven for foreign movies, late-night bookstores, racquetball, sushi restaurants, unconventional politics, and progressive rock bands.

**N**either view is closer to the truth than the other, and neither will do on its own. Nor can the tempting but ultimately glib idea of homogenization prevail; for all its age and small physical size, Boston is one of the least socially homogeneous cities on earth. Sure, men with three last names sit in leather wing chairs at the Somerset Club, but in most of the city the prevailing idea of a club is the Holy Name Society or the Sons of Italy. Yes, you will see lampposts and litter barrels plastered with ads for performances by radical dance collectives, but Boston's big political concerns revolve around which shade of Democrat is running for high city office (a Republican would as soon swim to Provincetown) and how he will dispense help to the homeless, asphalt to the potholes, and goodwill to the hightech barons. Women stockbrokers with Harvard M.B.A.s eat *gelato* and play racquetball; at the same time, guys in South Boston eat potato chips and play the numbers. Despite its small size, Boston compartmentalizes itself so neatly that you can come here and find as staid or as hip a city as you desire, and effectively ignore the city you chose not to find—even if you stay around for years.

In considering the roots of the Boston image and the Boston reality, we have to recognize two overwhelming influences on the Boston we know today. The first is Anglo-Saxon, aka Yankee or Brahmin. The second is unquestionably Irish, despite the diversity of the races and nationalities that have disembarked on the wharves of Boston during the past 150 years. Though there may never have been much love lost between the two factions, Boston is their mutual creation.

Most of the Yankees' ancestors left England in the 17th or the 18th century on a wing and a prayer, with little more than the clothes on their backs and a willingness to apprentice or even indenture themselves to compatriots who had already become established. There was nothing aristocratic about them then, and there is nothing aristocratic about them today—assuming we encounter them as the unspectacular yeomen and urban-suburban *bourgeoisie* who constitute the base coat of New England's overlay of populations. In the 1700s and early 1800s, however, some of them began to acquire fortunes to go with their ancient lineage, and thus the Brahmin was born. The term was first used by Dr. Oliver Wendell Holmes in *The Autocrat of the Breakfast-Table:* "He comes of the Brahmin caste of New England. This is the harmless, inoffensive, untitled aristocracy." Holmes himself was a sterling example of a Brahmin, as was his son and namesake the Supreme Court justice. Although not spectacularly wealthy, the Holmeses were vastly learned and endowed with a sense of civic responsibility. When combined with pedigree, these qualities counted as much as money in establishing the Brahmin mystique.

Money counted less and less as the years separated the Brahmins from their merchant-prince and industrialist ancestors who provided them with their China-trade porcelain, Back Bay town houses, and summer homes in Nahant. It became something you had but didn't talk about, something you devoted no great amount of time to multiplying. One theory as to why Boston lost out to New York in the struggle for financial supremacy in post–Civil War America credits the practice of tying up family legacies in trusteeships so that potential venture capital was inaccessible to one's heirs. But the best explanation is probably the simplest: making money with gusto began to seem gauche, a frenetic activity best left to ostentatious New Yorkers. It was thought far better to husband your resources and live a seemly life.

At worst, this attitude created a race of "cold-roast Bostonians," thin-lipped and tight with a dollar, as conservative in the realm of social and aesthetic ideas as they were with their portfolios. At best, it produced an atmosphere in which people spent their energies on public beneficence and the cultivation of the life of the mind rather than on commerce. Organizations such as the Appalachian Mountain Club, the American Ornithological Union, and the Massachusetts Trustees of Public Reservations were talked into vigorous existence over sherry and biscuits in the homes of comfortable men. Colonel Henry Lee Higginson founded the Boston Symphony and financed it for years out of his own pocket. Scholars such as Francis Parkman and Samuel Eliot Morison, secure in social standing and without pressing material needs, worked as hard writing history as their ancestors had making money. And men like Thomas Appleton cultivated salons in which good conversation for its own sake was the prized commodity. Most important, the old Yankee money poured into education; the investment in scores of colleges and universities, more than anything else, has helped establish the region's present character.

Putting money into college endowments was the logical extension of the acute concern with education that the Puritans had brought to Boston in 1630 and that manifested itself during that first decade in John Harvard's donation of his library to form the cornerstone of Harvard College. Finally, it was the means by which the idea of cold-roast Boston as a stodgy, intolerant, and unchanging place was laid to rest. The strains of dynamism and liberality evident in the intellectual and economic climate of Boston today are owed to the tremendous influx of fertile minds that the great investment in education made possible. People come here for schooling and never go home. Scientific and humane inquiry have reached critical mass in Boston, and the reactions go on and on. In time they may reach even to Boston's public schools, whose largely poor and minority children are too easily forgotten when municipal budgets and priorities must be set.

As Boston is a city of colleges, it is also a city of neighborhoods. Neighborhoods are traditionally the bastions of continuity in a big city, places where a certain outlook and sense of parochial identity are preserved. Ironically, Boston's ethnic groups, the Irish in particular, have managed to maintain the conservative, tradition-minded neighborhood spirit cultivated by the Yankees when all Boston was the neighborhood. If any custom replaced beans and brown bread on Saturday night in the Back Bay, it was fish during Lent in Charlestown and Southie. The Irish, in this century, have been the keel of Boston.

The Irish began to arrive in the late 1840s, when the potato famine devastated their home island. Boston had never seen such an invasion of immigrants and was anything but ready. The famous "No Irish Need Apply" signs went up, although the rapid growth of the city made it necessary for the natives to give the Irish jobs. There were only so many farm girls willing to come to the city and enter domestic service, and few businesses during the boom time of the Civil War era could afford the Waltham Watch Company's "Yankees only" employment strictures.

The Irish found their way into jobs and into the social structure, and they found two avenues particularly appealing: the civil service, particularly in the police and fire departments, and local politics. The venture into politics was in large part a defensive maneuver, a means of consolidating power in municipal institutions when it was denied them in the social and economic spheres. The first Irish mayor was elected in 1886, and by 1906 John F. Fitzgerald, the legendary "Honey Fitz," held the office. He was fiercely Irish, the most flamboyant and assertive Boston politician, until

Mayor Curley himself appeared and defined big-city machine politics in a way only Chicago's Richard Daley—and, some say, retired Boston Mayor Kevin White—have surpassed.

The wresting of political power from the Yankees allowed the Irish and their more recently arrived ethnic allies to take care of their own, and loyalty and votes were the mortar in the agreement. Similarly, civil service and other relatively secure blue-collar positions were a path to the kind of security that translated itself into stable, parish-oriented neighborhoods made up of row upon row of triple-decker apartment buildings, the wooden monoliths known in Boston as "Irish battleships." While you are in the area, read one of Mike Barnicle's *Boston Globe* columns, which often recall the spirit of these neighborhoods. (Barnicle has long since decamped for the suburbs.)

The Irish and other ethnics, then, are the inheritors and guardians of the old Boston insularity and stability. It was neighborhood (not just Irish) discomfiture at the violation of this state of affairs that produced the terrible antagonisms associated with court-ordered school busing in the early 1970s. The new minorities—blacks, Hispanics, Orientals—often find themselves in a situation similar to that faced by the new arrivals in the last century.

**N**owadays working-class white enclaves and poor minority neighborhoods alike worry about the effects of gentrification, loosely defined as the migration of upper middle class, white-collar workers and professionals (yesterday's would-be suburbanites) into the core of the city, where there are town houses to be restored and apartments to be converted into condominiums. Boston was made to order for this implosion of the affluent because it has so much solid housing stock within walking distance of downtown. The prime gentrification areas are the South End, the Italian North End, Charlestown, and part of Dorchester. In Cambridge, the Central Square area is changing its tone. The South End, the most racially and ethnically homogenous Boston neighborhood, stands to lose some of its diversity as poorer residents are displaced by the new gentry. In Charlestown and the North End, the white working class and older citizens are most likely to suffer from the disruption. Many people can move to blue-collar suburbs such as Malden or Revere, and graduate students priced out of Cambridge can always go to Somerville; the situation is more difficult for the low-income minorities and pension-dependent elderly. The disappearance of inexpensive rental housing has led to an increase in homelessness in Boston.

A lot can be said for gentrification. Places like Union Park in the South End and some of the streets around the Bunker Hill Monument in Charlestown look better than they have in years, and the city can certainly use the tax base. New businesses flourish, often selling kiwi fruit and the *Wall Street Journal* across from *bodegas* (Hispanic groceries) and tired old luncheonettes. Yet there are people who insist that the reclaimed blocks are pretty but sterile and that the old neighborhood identities have gone. One thing is certain: We have not seen the end of this new movement, which is beginning to spill over into traditional working-class neighborhoods such as South Boston. The threat to supplies of affordable housing stock is real enough; of the thousands of condominium units created in Boston in recent years, only a handful have been in new buildings. The majority have represented an upscaling of older rental units.

The appearance of the new gentry is evidence of the success of Boston's 30-year attempt to redefine its place in New England and the world. By the 1950s, Boston was living on its past. The industrial base had eroded, the population had begun to decrease (it is still about 100,000 below its peak), and the high-tech era had yet to begin. To the successive mayors Hynes, Collins, and White, and to the fiscal nabobs who made up the private advisory group known as "the Vault," it seemed to make sense to play up the service aspects of the local economy and at the same time to launch vast tear-down-and-start-over projects like the Prudential Center, Government Center, and Charles River Park. By the 1970s the emphasis had shifted from new construction to recycling old buildings, except downtown, where office towers rose at a frantic pace during the boom years of the 1980s. Other new projects included Copley Place, in the Back Bay, and several adjoining Park Square in Boston and Harvard and Kendall squares in Cambridge. Whether the physical plant was to be new or recycled, the objective—especially during the 16-year tenure of Mayor Kevin White—was the same: Boston was going to be a "world city," divested of its provinciality and standing shoulder to shoulder with New York and San Francisco, Frankfurt and Paris. Hotels and restaurants began to multiply. Logan Airport expanded. Banking flourished; once the Athens of America, Boston now wanted to become the Zurich. To paraphrase Carl Sandburg, Boston would be a player with computers and the nation's data handler. And the universities would continue to provide both an intellectual patina and a steady stream of technical accomplishments.

To a significant degree the plan has worked, and the legions of condo buyers and town-house restorers are part of a new order only recently slowed by the recession of the early 90s. What remains are the questions of how the old neighborhoods will fit in, whether the public school system can be salvaged, and whether there will be a middle class of any size in Boston as the century draws to a close.

Given a population with such divergent antecedents, and one caught up in such a vast civic overhaul, it is difficult to

point to a "typical" Bostonian. We see a number of types—
Cambridge academics, North Shore Brahmin ladies in town
for the Friday afternoon symphony, business-suited young
women with rucksacks and running shoes—but generaliza-
tions fail us. Even the famous old Boston accent is hard to
pin down, beyond a few broad As and dropped Rs; there are
so many emigrants from other parts of the country that the
native speech has become hopelessly diluted. (One thing is
certain: *No one* talks like the Kennedys, who developed an
Irish Brahmin accent all their own.)

Your essential Bostonian does love sports and politics,
probably because both are vehicles for argument. And argument is an ancient Celtic pastime, one the Yankees cultivated when Calvinists and freethinkers went toe-to-toe.
The disputations could well be carried past recent Red Sox
trades and the City Council to questions of whether Boston
is on its way up or down, whether it is forward-thinking or
preoccupied with the past, whether the "world city" label
fits or not, whether Boston is fashionable or dowdy, progressive or conservative, wise to the world or just kidding
itself. Go into a bar (or into the Union Boat Club, if you're a
member) and pick your topic. You may well decide that it is
sheer contentiousness, often mixed with respectable intel-
ligence and more than a little rectitude, that put Boston on
the map.

**B**oston, at least north and east of Massachusetts Avenue, is a compact city whose neighborhoods can be
divided along precise lines. The city proper, at the
tip of the Shawmut Peninsula, consists of Beacon Hill, the
North End (largely Italian), the downtown retail and financial district, and Chinatown. Opposite the mouth of the
Charles is Charlestown, and across the inner harbor to the
north and east is East Boston and the airport. South Boston, much of it landfill, juts due east toward the outer harbor and its cluster of islands; it is not to be confused with
the South End, which hugs the Huntington Avenue flank of
the Back Bay and is bordered by Chinatown and Roxbury.

The Back Bay, with its orderly grid of streets, extends
along the Charles opposite Cambridge, ending at Kenmore
Square.

South of Kenmore Square are the Back Bay Fens; here are
clustered two important art museums and a much-loved
baseball park. Farther south is Roxbury, a largely black
neighborhood that merges along its eastern border with bi-
racial but poorly integrated Dorchester, and Jamaica Plain,
one of the first of the "streetcar suburbs" brought into existence by turn-of-the-century trolley lines. West of Kenmore
Square is the separate municipality of Brookline, which almost completely cuts off Allston and Brighton, two residential and industrial Boston neighborhoods, from the rest of
the city. Brookline, long home to many of the Boston area's

Jewish families, now shares with Allston and Brighton an increasing number of Asian residents.

Farther south still are West Roxbury, Roslindale, Hyde Park, and Mattapan, virtual suburbs within the city. People here are more likely to identify themselves as coming from these neighborhoods than as hailing from Boston itself. After all, parts of them are farther from Beacon Hill than Cambridge, Medford, or Winthrop.

**B**oston's neighborhoods and the surrounding suburbs have one thing in common aside from the Red Sox and zip codes beginning with 02. This is the Massachusetts Bay Transit Authority, or "T." The T's services are divided among conventional buses, buses that run like trolleys off overhead wires, real subway and elevated trains, and the Green Line, a trolley system that runs partly underground and partly at street level. The Green Line connects Lechmere Station, just across the Charles River from the Museum of Science, with Government Center, Park Street, and Copley Square; after Copley, it branches into lines serving Jamaica Plain, Boston College, Cleveland Circle, Brookline, and Newton. The Red Line, using conventional subway equipment, runs between Alewife Brook Parkway (in suburban Cambridge) and downtown by way of Harvard Square; from downtown, branches run to Mattapan by way of Dorchester, and to Braintree by way of Quincy. The Orange Line connects Malden (north of Boston) with downtown by way of Charlestown and continues along an all-new underground route through Roxbury to Forest Hills, Jamaica Plain. The Blue Line runs north from downtown to Logan Airport, East Boston, and Revere.

Few people speak well of any of these lines, although taking public transport is always better than driving. Better still, bring comfortable shoes or a bicycle.

# 1 Essential Information

# Before You Go

## Visitor Information

For general information and brochures, contact the **Greater Boston Convention and Visitors Bureau,** Box 490, Prudential Plaza, Boston, MA 02199 (tel. 617/536–4100).

For maps and brochures on Boston and the rest of Massachusetts, contact the **Massachusetts Office of Travel and Tourism,** 100 Cambridge St., 13th floor, Boston, MA 02202 (tel. 617/727–3201 or 800/624–6277).

## Tour Groups

Although you will have to march to the beat of a tour guide's drum rather than your own, taking a package tour is likely to save you money on airfare, hotels, and ground transportation. For the more experienced or adventurous traveler, a variety of special-interest and independent packages are available. Listed below is a sampling of available options. Consult your travel agent or the Boston Convention and Visitors Bureau (tel. 617/536–4100) for additional resources.

When considering a tour, be sure to find out (1) exactly what expenses are included (particularly tips, taxes, side trips, additional meals and entertainment); (2) ratings of all hotels on the itinerary and the facilities they offer; (3) cancellation policies for both you and the tour operator; and (4) if you are traveling alone, what the single supplement is. Most tour operators request that bookings be made through a travel agent, and there is no additional charge for doing so.

**Globus-Gateway** (150 S. Los Robles Ave., Suite 860, Pasadena, CA 91101, tel. 818/449–0919 or 800/556–5454) has an "Autumn Highlights" tour that takes you through Boston en route to scenic spots in the East during the fall foliage season. **Cosmos,** the budget affiliate, offers a similar tour at a lower price.

**Talmage Tours** (1223 Walnut St., Philadelphia, PA 19107, tel. 215/923–7100) offers an escorted Boston city package with an excursion to Newport.

**American Express Vacations** (Box 5014, Atlanta, GA 30302, tel. 800/241–1700 or 800/282–0800 in GA) teams Boston with the cities of New York, Washington, Montreal, Toronto, and Quebec in an "Eastern Highlights" tour.

**Domenico Tours** (751 Broadway, Bayonne, NJ 07002, tel. 201/823–8687 or 800/554–8687) will take you to Boston and, if you wish, on to Cape Cod and Martha's Vineyard.

**Casser Tours** (46 W. 43rd St., New York, NY 10036, tel. 212/840–6500 or 800/251–1411) follows the historic ride of Paul Revere through Lexington and Concord to Boston.

**Tauck Tours** (11 Wilton Road, Westport, CT 06881, tel. 800/168–2825 or 203/226–6911) has a number of fall foliage tours, all of which include a stop in Boston.

**Gadabout Tours** (700 E. Tahquitz Way, Palm Springs, CA 92262, tel. 619/325–5556) offers an 11-day tour of New England and Cape Cod.

## Package Deals for Independent Travelers

**American Fly AAway Vacations** (tel. 817/355–1234 or 800/433–7300) offers fly/drive packages with a choice of four hotels.
**Supercities** (7855 Haskell Ave., Van Nuys, CA 91406, tel. 818/988–7844 or 800/556–5660) has two-night and three-night packages with a choice of sightseeing trips.
**Americantours International East** (350 5th Ave., Suite 718, New York, NY 10018, tel. 212/695–2841) offers five-night and two-night Boston packages that include airport transfers, a dinner, and a city tour. The five-night package includes a nightclub admission.
**United Airlines** (800/328–6877) and **Continental Airlines** (800/634–5555) should be contacted about the availability of packages.

## Tips for British Travelers

**Tourist Information**
Contact the U.S. Travel and Tourism Administration (22 Sackville St., London W1X 2EA, England, tel. 071/439–7433) for useful touring tips.

**Passports and Visas**
You will need a valid 10-year passport (cost £15). You do not need a visa if you are staying for less than 90 days, have a return ticket, or are flying with a major airline and complete visa waiver Form I791, which is supplied at the airport of departure or on the plane. Ask your travel agent or ring the U.S. Embassy (071/499–3443) for more information.

**Customs**
Visitors 21 or over can take in 200 cigarettes or 50 cigars or 2 kilograms of smoking tobacco; 1 liter of alcohol; duty-free gifts to a value of $100. Do not try to take in meat or meat products, seeds, plants or fruits. Avoid illegal drugs like the plague.

Returning to Britain a traveler 17 or older may bring home: (1) 200 cigarettes or 100 cigarillos or 50 cigars or 250 grams of tobacco; (2) two liters of table wine with additional allowances for (a) one liter of alcohol over 22% by volume (38.8 proof, most spirits) or (b) two liters of alcohol under 22% by volume; (3) 60 milliliters of perfume and 250 milliliters of toilet water, and (4) other goods up to a value of £32 but no more than 50 liters of beer or 25 lighters.

**Insurance**
We recommend that you insure yourself to cover health and motoring mishaps with **Europ Assistance** (252 High St., Croydon, Surrey CRO 1NF, tel. 081/680–1234).

It is wise to take out insurance to cover loss of luggage (but see that this isn't already covered in an existing homeowner's policy). Trip-cancellation insurance is another wise buy. **The Association of British Insurers** (Aldermary House, 10–15 Queen St., London EC4N 1TT, tel. 071/248–4477) will give comprehensive advice on all aspects of vacation insurance.

**Tour Operators**
Among those who offer holidays in Boston are

**Albany Travel (Manchester) Ltd.** (Central Buildings, 211 Deansgate, Manchester M25QR, M3 MNW, tel. 061/833–0202).
**American Airplan** (Airplan House, Churchfield Rd., Walton-on-Thames, Surrey KT12 2TZ, tel. 0932/246347).
**Poundstretcher** (Atlantic House, Hazelwick Avenue, Three Bridges, Crawley, West Sussex RH10 1NP, tel. 0293/518022).

**Greyhound World Travel Ltd.** (Sussex House, London Road, East Grinstead, West Sussex RH19 1LD, tel. 0342/317317).
**Speedbird** (Pacific House, Hazelwick Ave., Three Bridges, Crawley, West Sussex RH10 1NP).
**Thomson Citybreaks** (Greater London House, Hampstead Road, London NW1 75D, tel. 071/387–6534).
**Trek America** (Trek House, The Bullring, Deddington, Oxford OX5 4TT, tel. 08/693–8777).

**Airfares** The wise traveler will explore the current scene for budget flight possibilities. The availability of standby service on the major airlines cannot be counted on, but there are APEX and other fares that offer a considerable saving over the full-price fare. At press time an APEX round-trip fare was between £423 and £590, depending on when you travel. Another good source of low-cost flights is the small ads of the daily and Sunday newspapers.

## When to Go

Where the weather is concerned, the best times to visit Boston are late spring and the months of September and October. Like other American cities of the northeast, Boston can be uncomfortably hot and humid in high summer and freezing cold in the winter. Yet the city is not without its pleasures in these seasons. In summer, there are Boston Pops concerts on the Esplanade, harbor cruises, and a score of sidewalk cafes. In winter, there is Christmas shopping on Newbury Street, the symphony, the theater, and college drama and music seasons. And a lot can be said for winter afternoon light on red brick.

Each September, Boston and Cambridge welcome thousands of returning students, along with the perennially wide-eyed freshmen beginning their four-year (or longer) stays in Boston. University life is a big part of the local atmosphere, and it begins to liven considerably as the days grow shorter.

Autumn is a fine time to visit the suburbs. The combination of bright foliage and white church steeples may have been photographed countless times, but it will never become clichéd. The shore routes are less crowded in spring and fall, nearly all the lodging places and restaurants are open, and the Atlantic is as dramatic as ever.

For a classic shore vacation, summer is the only time to go. Select your preference—sailing, swimming, surfcasting, or just lying in the sun—and make your reservations early in the year.

**Climate** What follows are the average daily maximum and minimum temperatures for Boston.

| Jan. | 36F | 2C | May | 66F | 19C | Sept. | 71F | 22C |
|------|-----|-----|------|-----|-----|-------|-----|-----|
|      | 20  | –7  |      | 49  | 9   |       | 55  | 13  |
| Feb. | 37F | 3C  | June | 75F | 24C | Oct.  | 62F | 17C |
|      | 21  | –6  |      | 58  | 14  |       | 46  | 8   |
| Mar. | 43F | 6C  | July | 80F | 27C | Nov.  | 49F | 9C  |
|      | 28  | –2  |      | 63  | 17  |       | 35  | 2   |
| Apr. | 54F | 12C | Aug. | 78F | 26C | Dec.  | 40F | 4C  |
|      | 38  | 3   |      | 62  | 17  |       | 25  | –4  |

**Weather Trak** provides information on more than 750 cities around the world, 450 of them in the United States. Dialing 900/

370–8728 will connect you to a computer, with which you can communicate by touch tone (cost: 95¢ per minute). A recording tells you to dial a three-digit access code for the destination you're interested in; the code is either the area code (in the United States) or the first three letters of the name of the foreign city. For a list of access codes, send a self-addressed stamped envelope to Cities, 9B Terrace Way, Greensboro, NC 27403, or call 800/247–3282.

## Festivals and Seasonal Events

Top seasonal events in Boston include Chinese New Year in January or early February, the Boston Marathon in April, the Cambridge River Festival in June, and Harborfest (Boston's Fourth of July celebration), which is followed by a Boston Pops concert and fireworks. For dates and details, request a Calendar of Events from the **Greater Boston Convention and Visitors Bureau** (Box 490, Prudential Plaza, Boston, MA 02199, tel. 617/536–4100).

**Jan. or early Feb. Chinese New Year** is celebrated in Boston's Chinatown, with special events at the Children's Museum, 300 Congress St., Museum Wharf, tel. 617/426–8855.

**Mid–Feb. The Boston Festival** spotlights the city as a major winter destination. Scheduled events include an ice skating party in the Public Garden and Valentine's Day parties. Tel. 617/536–4100.

**Early Mar. Annual Spring New England Flower Show** blooms at the Bayside Expo Center. Tel. 617/536–9280.

**Mar. 17. St. Patrick's Day Parade** is celebrated by many more than the city's substantial Irish population.

**April. Museum Goer's Month** means special exhibits at all of Boston's museums.

**Mid-Apr. (Patriot's Day). Boston Marathon** stretches from Hopkinton to Back Bay Boston. Boston Athletic Association, tel. 617/435–6905.

**Mid-May. Greater Boston Kite Festival** is a high-flying event at Franklin Park. Tel. 617/725–4000.

**Mid-May. Lilac Sunday** at the Arnold Arboretum, from sunrise to sunset, celebrates 400 varieties of lilac in bloom. Tel. 617/524–1718.

**Late May. Street Performers' Festival** includes everything from mimes to magicians at Faneuil Hall Marketplace. Tel. 617/523–3886.

**Early June. Cambridge River Festival** features numerous outdoor events off Memorial Drive along the Charles River. Tel. 617/349–4380.

**Mid-June. Bunker Hill Weekend** is an authentic reenactment of the Battle of Bunker Hill in Charlestown, culminating in a parade. Tel. 617/241–9511.

**Late June–July 4. Harborfest,** Boston's annual Fourth of July celebration, takes place on Boston Harbor and along the Waterfront. Tel. 617/227–1528.

**July 4. Boston Pops Concert and Fireworks Display** is an annual extravaganza of music at the Hatch Shell and fireworks on the Esplanade along the Charles River. Tel. 617/227–1528.

**July 4. USS** *Constitution* is turned around once a year. Tel. 617/227–1528.

**Early July. Chowderfest** takes place on the Harbor Terrace of the New England Aquarium on Central Wharf. Tel. 617/227–1528.

**Late Aug. Anniversary of Faneuil Hall Marketplace** means a variety of events. Tel. 617/523–2980.

**Late Aug. August Moon Festival** breaks out in the streets of Chinatown. Tel. 617/542–2574.

**Late Sept. Art Newbury Street/Fashion Newbury Street** is sponsored by the art galleries and boutiques along fashionable Newbury Street in Back Bay. Tel. 617/267–9416.

**Early Oct. Columbus Day Parade** moves from East Boston to the North End. Tel. 617/725–3952.

**Late Oct. Head of the Charles Regatta** draws college crew teams from all over and spectators with blankets and beer. Tel. 617/421–4356.

**Mid-Nov. Veterans Day Parade** follows a route from Back Bay to Boston Common. Tel. 617/725–3952.

**Early Dec. Holiday Lighting** of 25,000 bulbs takes place on Boston Common. Tel. 617/725–4033.

**Mid-Dec. Boston Tea Party Reenactment** takes place at the Boston Tea Party ship and museum at the Congress Street Bridge. Tel. 617/338–1773.

**Mid-Dec. Christmas Revels** in Cambridge celebrates the winter solstice with traditional dances, processionals, carols, and folk music. Tel. 617/621–0505.

**New Year's Eve. First Night Celebration** continues past midnight throughout the city. Tel. 617/536–4100 or 424–1699.

## What to Pack

Pack light because porters and luggage trolleys are hard to find. Luggage allowances on domestic flights vary slightly from airline to airline. In most cases, checked luggage cannot weigh more than 70 lbs. each or be larger than 62″ total dimensions (length + width + height). Carry-on luggage must fit under the seat, in the overhead luggage compartment, or in a closet on board. Most airlines allow two checked suitcases and two carry-on bags.

Boston is generally regarded as one of the "dressier" American cities, although standards and expectations vary from one part of town to another. In Cambridge it is perfectly acceptable, in all but the best restaurants, to dress like a reasonably neat student regardless of your age; jeans and a sports shirt will let you in almost anywhere. For downtown Boston, Beacon Hill, and the Back Bay, however, more conservative dress is in order, especially in the evening. Many restaurants require that men wear jacket and tie. Women can wear anything from business clothes to casual dresses and slacks outfits. Although elegant cocktail outfits are not required anywhere, there are plenty of restaurants where you can wear them and not feel overdressed. Winters are cold and snowy, so come prepared with heavy coats and sweaters, and take along snow boots or sturdy shoes with a good grip for those icy sidewalks.

## Cash Machines

Virtually all U.S. banks belong to a network of ATMs (Automatic Teller Machines) that dispense cash 24 hours a day in cities throughout the country. There are eight major networks in the United States, the largest of which are Cirrus, owned by

MasterCard, and Plus, affiliated with Visa. Some banks belong to more than one network. These cards are not issued automatically; you have to ask for them. Cards issued by Visa and MasterCard may also be used in the ATMs, but the fees are usually higher than the fees on bank cards (and there is a daily interest charge on the "loan" even when monthly bills are paid on time). Each network has a toll-free number you can call to locate its machines in a given city. The Cirrus number is 800/424–7787; the Plus number is 800/843–7587. Contact your bank for information on fees and the amount of cash you can withdraw on any given day.

Express Cash is not a cash advance service; only money already in the linked checking account can be withdrawn. Every transaction carries a 2% fee with a minimum charge of $2 and a maximum of $6. Apply for a PIN (Personal Identification Number) and link your accounts at least 2–3 weeks before departure. Call 800/CASH-NOW to receive an application or to locate the nearest Express Cash machine.

## Traveling with Film

If your camera is new, shoot and develop a few rolls of film before leaving home. Pack some lens tissue and an extra battery for your built-in light meter. Invest about $10 in a skylight filter and screw it onto the front of your lens; it will protect the lens and reduce haze.

Film doesn't like hot weather. When you're driving in summer, don't store film in the glove compartment or on the shelf under the rear window. Put it behind the front seat on the floor, on the side opposite the exhaust pipe.

On a plane trip, never pack unprocessed film in check-in luggage; if your bags are X-rayed, you can say goodbye to your pictures. Always carry undeveloped film with you through security and ask to have it inspected by hand. (It helps to isolate your film in a plastic bag, ready for quick inspection.) Inspectors at American airports are required by law to honor requests for hand inspection; abroad, you'll have to depend on the kindness of strangers.

The old airport scanning machines—still in use in some Third World countries—use heavy doses of radiation that can turn a family portrait into an early morning fog. The newer models used in all U.S. airports are safe for anything from five to 500 scans, depending on the speed of your film. The effects are cumulative; you can put the same roll of film through several scans without worry. After five scans, though, you're asking for trouble.

If your film is fogged and you want an explanation, send it to the National Association of Photographic Manufacturers, 550 Mamaroneck Ave., Harrison, NY 10528. They will try to determine what went wrong. The service is free.

## Traveling with Children

**Publications** *Family Travel Times* is an 8-to-12-page newsletter published 10 times a year by TWYCH (Travel with Your Children, 80 Eighth Ave., New York, NY 10011, tel. 212/206–0688). Subscription costs $35 and includes access to back issues and twice-weekly opportunities to call in for specific advice.

***Great Vacations with Your Kids: The Complete Guide to Family Vacations in the U.S.,*** by Dorothy Ann Jordon and Marjorie Adoff Cohen (E. P. Dutton, 2 Park Ave., New York, NY 10016; $12.95), details everything from city vacations to outdoor adventures and child-care resources.

***In and Out of Boston with (or without) Children,*** by Bernice Chesler (Globe Pequot Press, Box Q, Chester, CT 06412, tel. 800/243–0495 or 800/962–0973 in CT; 4th edition, $12.95 plus $2 postage).

***Boston Parents Paper*** (Box 1777, Boston, MA 02130, tel. 617/522–1515), a monthly newspaper that has events and resource listings, is available free at such places as libraries, supermarkets, museums, children's shops, and nursery schools.

**Hotels**  **The Four Seasons Hotel Boston** (200 Boylston St., Boston, MA 02116, tel. 617/338–4400) welcomes families with a host of amenities: a family packet of brochures and advice, cookies and milk before bedtime, magic kits, food to feed the ducks in the Public Garden, and, on request, complimentary copies of Robert McCloskey's *Make Way for Ducklings*.

**Saunders Hotels,** which owns The Boston Park Plaza Hotel & Towers (50 Park Plaza at Arlington St., Boston, MA 02117, tel. 617/426–2000), The Lenox Hotel (710 Boylston St., Boston, MA 02116, tel. 617/536–5300), and The Copley Square Hotel (47 Huntington Ave. at Copley Place, Boston, MA 02116, tel. 617/536–9000), allows children 16 and under to stay free with their parents, provides them with complimentary Swan Boat tickets, and offers children's menus in restaurants.

**The Ritz-Carlton** (15 Arlington St., Boston, MA 02117, tel. 617/536–5700) provides family amenities that include an etiquette course, a Teddy Bear Tea, and children's coloring book menus; Nintendo and small robes are provided in the children's "Presidential Suite."

**Home Exchange**  Exchanging homes is a surprisingly low-cost way to enjoy a vacation. **Vacation Exchange Club, Inc.** (P.O. Box 820, Haleiwa, HI 96712, tel. 800/638–3841) specializes in home exchanges. The club publishes three directories a year, in February, April, and August, and updated late listings throughout the year. Annual membership, which includes your listing in one book, a newsletter, and copies of all publications (mailed first class) is $50. **Loan-a-Home** (2 Park La., Apt. 6E, Mount Vernon, NY 10552, tel. 914/664–7640) is popular with the academic community on sabbatical and businesspeople on temporary assignment. There's no annual membership fee or charge for listing your home, but one directory and a supplement costs $35.

**Getting There**  On domestic flights, children under 2 not occupying a seat travel free. Various discounts apply to children 2–12. To be sure your infant is secure and traveling in his or her own safety seat, you must buy a separate ticket and bring your own infant car seat. (But check with the airline in advance; certain seats aren't allowed.) Some airlines allow babies to travel in their own car seats at no charge only when a spare seat is available; otherwise safety seats must be stored and the child held by a parent. (For the booklet *Child/Infant Safety Seats Acceptable for Use in Aircraft,* contact the Federal Aviation Administration, APA-200, 800 Independence Ave. SW, Washington, DC 20591, tel. 202/267–3479.) When holding your baby on your lap, keep the infant outside your seatbelt so that he or she won't be crushed in case of a sudden stop. Inquire, too, about special children's meals or snacks; "TWYCH's Airline Guide," in the February 1990 and 1992 issues of *Family Travel Times*, lists children's services offered by 46 airlines.

**Baby-sitting Services**  Make your child-care arrangements with the hotel concierge or housekeeper. One local agency is **Parents in a Pinch** (45 Bartlett Crescent, Brookline, MA 02146, tel. 617/739-5437).

## Hints for Disabled Travelers

**The Information Center for Individuals with Disabilities** (Fort Point Place, 27–43 Wormwood St., Boston, MA 02210, tel. 617/727-5540 or TDD 617/727-5236 for the hearing impaired) provides referral and problem-solving assistance weekdays 8:30–4:30.

**Moss Rehabilitation Hospital Travel Information Service** (1200 West Tabor Rd., Philadelphia, PA 19141–3009, tel. 215/456-9600; TDD 215/456-9602) provides information on tourist sights, transportation, and accommodations at destinations around the world for a small fee.

**Mobility International USA** (Box 3551, Eugene, OR 97403, tel. 503/343-1284) is an internationally affiliated organization with 500 members. For a $20 annual fee, it coordinates exchange programs for disabled people around the world and offers information on accommodations and organized study programs.

**The Society for the Advancement of Travel for the Handicapped** (26 Court St., Penthouse Suite, Brooklyn, NY 11242, tel. 718/858-5483) offers access information. Annual membership costs $45, or $25 for senior travelers and students. Send $1 and a stamped, self-addressed envelope.

*The Itinerary* (Box 2012, Bayonne, NJ 07002, tel. 201/858-3400) is a bimonthly travel magazine for the disabled.

*Access to the World: A Travel Guide for the Handicapped,* by Louise Weiss, offers tips on travel and accessibility around the world. It is available from Henry Holt & Co. for $12.95 (tel. 800/247-3912; order number 0805001417).

**Greyhound Lines** (tel. 800/752-4841; TDD 800/345-3109) will carry a disabled person and companion for the price of a single fare. **Amtrak** (tel. 800/USA-RAIL) requests 24-hour notice to provide redcap service, special seats, and a 25% discount.

## Hints for Older Travelers

The **American Association of Retired Persons** (AARP, 1909 K St. NW, Washington, DC 20049, tel. 202/662-4850) has two programs for independent travelers: (1) The Purchase Privilege Program offers discounts on hotels, airfare, car rentals, and sightseeing, and (2) The AARP Motoring Plan offers emergency aid and trip routing information for an annual fee of $33.95 per couple. The AARP also arranges group tours, including apartment living in Europe, through American Express Vacations (Box 5014, Atlanta, GA 30302, tel. 800/241-1700 or 800/637-6200 in GA). AARP members must be 50 or older. Annual dues are $5 per person or couple.

When using an AARP or other identification card, ask for a reduced hotel rate at the time you make your reservation, not when you check out. At participating restaurants, show your card to the maître d' before you're seated, since discounts may be limited to certain set menus, days, or hours. When renting a car, be sure to ask about special promotional rates which might offer greater savings than the available discount.

**Elderhostel** (75 Federal St., 3rd floor, Boston, MA 02110–1941, tel. 426–8056) is an innovative educational program for people 60 and older. Participants usually live in dorms on some 1,200 campuses around the world. Mornings are devoted to lectures and seminars, afternoons to sightseeing and field trips. Domestic trips begin at $255 without transportation. Fees for two- to three-week trips—including room, board, tuition, and round-trip transportation—range from $1,800 to $4,500.

**Travel Industry and Disabled Exchange** (TIDE, 5435 Donna Ave., Tarzana, CA 91356, tel. 818/368–5648) is an industry-based organization with a $15 per person annual membership fee. Members receive a quarterly newsletter and information on travel agencies and tours.

**National Council of Senior Citizens** (925 15th St. NW, Washington, DC 20005, tel. 202/347–8800) is a nonprofit advocacy group with 5,000 local clubs across the country. Annual membership is $12 per couple. Members receive a monthly newspaper with travel information and an ID card for reduced rates on hotels and car rentals.

**Mature Outlook** (6001 N. Clark St., Chicago, IL 60660, tel. 800/336–6330), a subsidiary of Sears Roebuck & Co., is a travel club for people over 50, with hotel and motel discounts and a bimonthly newsletter. Annual membership is $9.95 per couple. Instant membership is available at participating Holiday Inns.

**Golden Age Passport** is a free lifetime pass to all parks, monuments, and recreation areas run by the federal government. People 62 and over should pick them up in person at any national park that charges admission. A driver's license or other proof of age is required.

**Saga International Holidays** (120 Boylston St., Boston, MA 02116, tel. 800/343–0273) specializes in group travel for people over 60 and has a variety of tour packages at various prices.

## Further Reading

The classic Boston books are Louisa May Alcott's *Little Women*, Henry James's *The Europeans* and *The Bostonians*, William Dean Howells's *A Modern Instance* and *The Rise of Silas Lapham*, and George Santayana's *The Last Puritan*.

Individual histories are recounted in Gerald Green's *The Last Angry Man*, Edwin O'Connor's *The Last Hurrah*, Sylvia Plath's *The Bell Jar*, May Sarton's *Faithful Are the Wounds*, Anthony J. Lukas's *Common Ground*, and Scott Turow's *One L*.

Several other good reads are Alice Adams's *Superior Women*, James Carroll's *Mortal Friends*, Jean Stafford's *Boston Adventure*, and John Updike's *Couples*.

The mystery writers Jane Langton and Robert B. Parker locate the action of their novels in the Boston area.

# Arriving and Departing

## By Plane

When booking a flight, air travelers will want to keep in mind the distinction between *nonstop flights* (your destination is the only scheduled stop), *direct flights* (one or more stops are scheduled before you reach your destination), and *connecting flights* (you'll stop and change planes before you reach your destination).

More than 50 major airlines fly to Boston's Logan International Airport from principal cities in North America and around the world. In addition, several regional airlines link the Boston area with smaller cities and vacation areas throughout New England. Many of these regional airlines come and go with each season, so it's best to consult a local travel agent. Currently, **New England Flyers Air Service** (tel. 508/922–2220) offers air taxi service from Beverly Airport in Beverly, and **Bar Harbor Airlines** (tel. 617/567–9034) operates between Boston and Bar Harbor.

**Smoking**    The Federal Aviation Administration has banned smoking on all scheduled flights within the 48 contiguous states; within the states of Alaska and Hawaii; to and from the U.S. Virgin Islands and Puerto Rico; and on flights of under six hours to and from Alaska and Hawaii. The rules apply to both domestic and foreign carriers. When necessary, a request for a seat in a nonsmoking section should be made at the time you make your reservation.

**Carry-on Luggage**    Passengers aboard major U.S. carriers are usually limited to two carry-on bags. Bags stored under the seat must not exceed 9″ × 14″ × 22″. Bags hung in a closet can be no larger than 4″ × 23″ × 45″. The maximum dimensions for bags stored in an overhead bin are 10″ × 14″ × 36″. Any item that exceeds the specified dimensions will generally be rejected as a carryon and handled as checked baggage. Keep in mind that an airline can adapt these rules to circumstances; on an especially crowded flight, you may be allowed to bring only one carry-on bag aboard.

In addition to the two carryons, passengers may bring aboard: a handbag, an overcoat or wrap, an umbrella, a camera, a reasonable amount of reading material, an infant bag, and crutches, braces, a cane, or other prosthetic device upon which the passenger is dependent. Infant/child safety seats can also be brought aboard if parents have purchased a ticket for the child or if there is space in the cabin.

**Checked Luggage**    Luggage allowances vary slightly among airlines. Many carriers allow three checked pieces; some allow only two. It is best to consult with the airline before you go. In all cases, checked luggage cannot weigh more than 70 pounds per piece or be larger than 62 inches (length + width + height).

**Lost Luggage**    Airlines are responsible for lost or damaged property only up to $1,250 per passenger on domestic flights; $9.07 per pound (or $20 per kilo) for checked baggage on international flights; and up to $400 per passenger for unchecked baggage on international flights. When you carry valuables, either take them with you on the airplane or purchase additional insurance for lost luggage. Some airlines will issue additional luggage insurance when you check in, but many do not. American Airlines is one that does. Its additional insurance is for both domestic and international flights; rates are $2 for every $100 valuation, with a maximum of $5,000 valuation per passenger. Hand luggage is not included.

Insurance for lost, damaged, or stolen luggage is available through travel agents or from various insurance companies. Two that issue luggage insurance are Tele-Trip, a subsidiary of Mutual of Omaha, and The Travelers Corporation.

**Tele-Trip** (tel. 800/228–9792) operates sales booths at airports and issues insurance through travel agents. Tele-Trip will insure checked or hand luggage through its travel insurance packages. Rates vary according to the length of the trip.
**The Travelers Corporation,** (Ticket and Travel Dept., 1 Tower Sq., Hartford, CT 06183, tel. 203/277–0111 or 800/243–3174) will insure checked or hand luggage for $500 to $2,000 valuation per person, for a maximum of 180 days. For 1–5 days, the rate for a $500 valuation is $10; for 180 days, $85. The two companies offer the same rates on both domestic and international flights. Consult the travel pages of your Sunday newspaper for the names of other companies that insure luggage. Before you travel, itemize the contents of each bag in case you need to file an insurance claim. Be certain to put your home address on each piece of luggage, including carry-on bags. If your luggage is stolen and later recovered, the airline will deliver the luggage to your home free of charge.

**From the Airport to Downtown Boston**  Only three miles—and Boston Harbor—separate Logan International Airport from downtown, yet it can seem like 20 miles when you're caught in one of the many daily traffic jams at the two tunnels that go under the harbor. Boston traffic is almost always heavy, and the worst conditions prevail during the morning (6:30–9) and evening (3:30–7) rush hours.

A 24-hour toll-free ground transport number provides information on parking and bicycle access, as well as schedules for Logan Express buses and the Airport Water Shuttle (tel. 800/235–6426). A call between 9 AM and 5 AM will receive personalized ground transportation assistance.

*By Taxi*  Cabs can be hired outside each terminal. Fares should average about $15, including tip, assuming that the driver follows the direct Summer Tunnel route, there are no major traffic jams, and you go no farther than the downtown business district. Call MASSPORT (tel. 617/561–1769) for cab information.

*By Water Shuttle*  **The Airport Water Shuttle** (tel. 800/235–6426) operates year-round and takes approximately seven minutes to cross Boston Harbor. It goes from Logan Airport to Rowes Wharf every 15 minutes, Monday through Friday, 6 AM–8 PM. On Saturday and Sunday it leaves every 30 minutes, noon–8:00 PM. A free shuttle bus operates between the airport ferry dock and all airline terminals. Connecting boats are available from Boston to Quincy, Hingham, and Hull. The shuttle leaves Rowes Wharf for Logan Airport Monday through Friday (except major holidays), every 15 minutes, 6 AM–8 PM. On Saturday and Sunday it leaves every 30 minutes, noon–8 PM. The one-way fare is $7 adults, children under 12 and senior citizens free.

By Subway  The **MBTA Blue Line** to Airport Station is one of the fastest ways to reach downtown from the airport. Free shuttle buses connect the subway station with all airline terminals (tel. 800/235–6426 or 617/561–1800 for Logan Airport Public Information).

By Car  Car rentals may be arranged at the ground level of all passenger terminals. The following rental firms are represented at Logan:

**Avis** (tel. 617/561–3500 or 800/331–1212)
**Budget** (tel. 617/569–4000 or 800/527–0700)
**Dollar** (tel. 617/569–5300 or 800/421–6868)
**Hertz** (tel. 617/569–7272 or 800/654–3131)
**National** (tel. 617/569–6700 or 800/227–7368).

If you are driving from Logan to downtown Boston, the most direct route is by way of the Sumner Tunnel ($1 toll inbound; no toll outbound). When there is a serious traffic delay in the tunnel, one alternative is to take Route 1A north to Route 16, then to the Tobin Bridge and into Boston.

**The Airport Handicapped Van** (tel. 617/561–1769) provides free service between terminals daily, 8 AM–8:30 PM. During off-peak hours contact the bus supervisor for service (tel. 617/561–1990).

## By Car

New England's major highways are spokes leading to the Hub of Boston. I–95 connects New York with Boston and continues north into New Hampshire and Maine. I–93, reached by I–89, is the major feeder from Canada and northwestern New England. The Massachusetts Turnpike (toll) runs east-west across the state and links up with the New York Thruway south of Albany.

## Car Rentals

Boston's public transportation system is fine for reaching all historic and entertainment sites in the city, but renting a car gives you easy access to the North Shore, Lexington, Concord, Plymouth, and Cape Cod. Logan International Airport can be five minutes from downtown Boston; major companies with airport and downtown locations include Hertz (tel. 800/654–3131), Avis (tel. 800/331–1212), Budget (tel. 800/527–0700) and Thrifty (tel. 800/367–2277). American International (tel. 800/527–0202) and Rent-A-Wreck (tel. 617/282–8200) offer some of the city's lowest rates; you might also check the local budget companies advertising in the weekly *Boston Phoenix*. The major rental companies charge $35–$50 per day for a subcompact, often with a daily allowance of just 75 free miles.

Getting the best rate may involve reserving a car at least seven and sometimes 14 days in advance. Get a car reservation number from whatever agency you use. Find out what the collision damage waiver (usually $8.95–$11.95 daily) covers and whether you must pay for a full tank of gas whether you use it or not. Ask about the number of free miles you get daily and the extra mileage charge. And inquire about seasonal and weekend specials. Drivers 25 and older receive better rates.

More than in any other eastern city, looking at a map *first* and having one with you at all times is essential in Boston. "We have lots of one-way streets and streets with the same names," a city spokesperson admitted cheerfully. "It's not an easy city to drive in, but it's worth it."

## By Train

Boston is the northern terminus of Amtrak's Northeast Corridor. **South Station** (Atlantic Ave. and Summer St., tel. 617/482-3660 or 800/872-7245) sees frequent trains arriving from and departing for New York, Philadelphia, and Washington, DC, with connections to all points in the nationwide Amtrak system. South Station is also an eastern terminus of Amtrak's Lake Shore Limited, which travels daily between Boston and Chicago by way of Albany, Rochester, Buffalo, and Cleveland. Amtrak's new New England Express, serving the Boston to New York route twice daily departs from here; reservations are required and travel time is just under 4 hours.

Boston's **North Station** (Causeway and Friend Sts., tel. 617/227-5070) is used by commuter trains serving points in Massachusetts north and west of the city.

## By Bus

**Greyhound/Trailways Lines** (St. James St., Park Sq., tel. 617/423-5810) serves Boston with direct trips or connections to all major cities in North America. **Peter Pan Bus Lines** (Atlantic Ave. opposite South Station, tel. 617/426-7838) connects Boston with cities elsewhere in Massachusetts, Connecticut, New Hampshire, and New York.

# Staying in Boston

## Important Addresses and Numbers

**Tourist Information**

**Boston Common Information Kiosk.** A multilingual staff provides maps, brochures, and information about ongoing events. *Tremont St., where the Freedom Trail begins. Tel. 617/536-4100. Open daily 8:30-5.*

**Greater Boston Convention & Visitors Bureau.** Maps and foreign-language informational materials are available here. *800 Boylston St., in the Prudential Plaza, tel. 617/536-4100. Open weekdays 8:30-6, weekends 9-5.*

**Massachusetts Tourism Office.** The state tourism office has information on all Massachusetts cities and towns and on day trips. *Saltonstall Bldg., 13th floor, 100 Cambridge St., tel. 617/727-3201. Open weekdays, 9-5.*

**National Park Service Visitor Center.** The center shows an eight-minute slide show on Boston's historic sites and provides maps and directions. *15 State St., across from the Old State House, tel. 617/242-5642. Open weekdays 8-5, weekends 9-5 in winter; weekdays 8-6, weekends 9-6 in summer. Closed major holidays.*

**Traveler's Aid Society** (17 East St., tel. 617/542-7286) will help to solve the problems of the distressed traveler, weekdays 9-4:45. The society has several "outreach booths" (manned by volunteers, so the hours vary); Greyhound Bus Terminal at St.

James Place; Logan Airport Terminal A (tel. 617/569–6284); and Logan Airport Terminal E (tel. 617/567–5385).

**Emergencies**  Police, fire, ambulance (tel. 911); Massachusetts General Hospital (tel. 617/726–2000); Dental emergency (tel. 508/651–3521); Poison control (tel. 617/232–2120); Rape crisis center (tel. 617/492–7273).

*24-Hour Pharmacy*  **Phillips Drug Store** (155 Charles St., Boston, tel. 617/523–1028 or 617/523–4372).

## Getting Around

Boston is a walker's city. You are likely to move faster, and see more, anywhere in downtown, the North End, Beacon Hill, and the Back Bay when you stay on foot. Should you tire, the MBTA's bus, trolley, and subway system is efficient and economical.

**By Bus**  Bus, trolley, and subway service in Boston and surrounding cities and towns is provided by the Massachusetts Bay Transportation Authority (MBTA). The MBTA bus routes crisscross the metropolitan area and extend farther into the suburbs than those of the subways and trolleys. (Some suburban schedules are designed primarily for commuters.) Current fares on MBTA local buses are 50¢ adults, 25¢ children 5–11, free under 5. An extra fare is required for the longer suburban bus trips. For general travel information, tel. 617/722–3200 or 800/392–6100 or TDD 617/722–5146, weekdays 6:30 AM–11 PM, weekends 9–6; for 24-hour recorded service information, tel. 617/722–5050; for customer relations, tel. 617/722–5125; for MBTA police emergency, tel. 617/722–5151.

A free map of the entire public transportation system is available at the Park Street Station information stand (street level), open daily 7 AM–10 PM.

**By Subway and Trolley**  The MBTA, or "T," operates subways, elevated trains, and trolleys along four connecting lines. The **Red Line** has two points of origin at Braintree and Mattapan to the south; the routes join near South Boston and proceed to Harvard and to suburban Arlington. The **Green Line** is a combined underground and elevated surface line, originating at Cambridge's Lechmere and heading south through Park Street to divide into four major routes; Boston College (Commonwealth Avenue), Cleveland Circle (Beacon Street), Riverside, and Arborway. Green Line trains are actually trolleys that travel major streets south and west of Kenmore Square and operate underground in the central city. The **Blue Line** runs from Bowdoin Square (near Government Center) to the Wonderland Racetrack in Revere, north of Boston. The **Orange Line** runs from Oak Grove in north suburban Malden to Forest Hills nears the Arnold Arboretum. Park Street Station (on the Common) is the major downtown transfer point for Red and Green Line trains; the Orange and Blue Lines intersect at State Street. Trains operate from about 5:30 AM to about 12:30 AM. Current fares on subways and trolleys are 75¢ adults, 35¢ children 5–11, free under 5. An extra fare is required for the distant Green Line stops. Visitor travel passes ($8 for 3 days, $16 for 7 days) are available from the MBTA (tel. 617/722–5657).

**By Car** Those who cannot avoid bringing a car into Boston should be able to minimize their frustration by keeping to the main thoroughfares and by parking in lots—no matter how expensive—rather than on the street. Parking on Boston streets is a tricky business. Some neighborhoods have residents-only rules, with just a handful of two-hour visitor's spaces; others have meters (25¢ for 15 minutes, two hours maximum). The meter maids are ruthless, and repeat offenders who don't pay fines may find the boot (an immovable steel clamp) secured to one of their wheels by the police. In other words, if you do get parking tickets, pay them if you expect to come back to town.

The major public parking lots are at Government Center and Quincy Market; beneath Boston Common (entrance on Charles Street); beneath Post Office Square at the Prudential Center; at Copley Place; and off Clarendon Street near the John Hancock Tower. Smaller lots are scattered through the downtown area. Most are expensive, especially the small outdoor lots; a few city garages are a bargain at about $6–$10 a day.

**By Taxi** Cabs are not easily hailed on the street, except at the airport; if you need to get somewhere in a hurry, use a hotel taxi stand or telephone for a cab. Companies offering 24-hour service include **Checker** (tel. 617/536–7000), **Independent Taxi Operators Association** or ITOA (tel. 617/426–8700), **Green Cab Association** (tel. 617/628–0600 or 617/623–6000), **Town Taxi** (tel. 617/536–5000), and, in Cambridge, **Cambridge Taxi** (tel. 617/876–5000). The current rate is about $1.20 per mile; traffic patterns (one-way streets) often make circuitous routes necessary and add to the cost.

**By Train** The MBTA runs commuter trains to points south, west, and north of Boston. Trains to Framingham, Needham, Franklin, Providence (RI), and Stoughton leave from **South Station** (tel. 617/722–3200 or 800/882–1220). Trains to Gardner, Lowell, Haverhill, Ipswich, and Rockport operate out of **North Station** (tel. 800/392–6099).

**By Commuter Boat** **Mass Bay Lines** (60 Rowes Wharf, tel. 617/542–8000) operates commuter service between Rowes Wharf in downtown Boston and Hewitt's Cove, off Route 3A in Hingham on the South Shore. Boats leave every 15 minutes during rush hours; the first boat leaves Hingham at 6 AM, and the last boat leaves Boston at 8 PM. Massport operates a ferry shuttle between the airport and downtown that is in service from late spring to early fall (tel. 800/235–6426).

## Opening and Closing Times

**Banks** are generally open weekdays 9–4. Some branches are open Sat. 9–noon or 9–1.

**Museums** are generally open Mon.–Sat. 9 (or 10)–5 (or 6), Sun. noon–5. Many are closed Mon.

**Post Offices.** Hours vary for post offices throughout Boston. Most are generally open weekdays 8–5, Sat. 9–12, and some close Thurs. afternoon. The General Post Office (25 Dorchester Ave., behind South Station, tel. 617/654–5225) is open weekdays 8–8, Sat. 8–5. A self-service machine is available 24 hours.

**Public Buildings** are open weekdays 9–5.

**Boston Public Library.** The main branch (Copley Sq., tel. 617/536–5400) is open Mon.–Thur. 9–9, Fri.–Sat. 9–5.

**Shops** and stores are generally open Mon.–Sat. 9 (or 9:30)–6 (or 7). Many stay open later toward the end of the week. Some, particularly those in malls or tourist areas, are open Sun. noon–5.

## Guided Tours

When it comes to touring Boston and environs, today's visitor has the same two options the British had when they struck out at the Middlesex hinterland; by land or by sea. There are several good bus and harbor boat tours, any one of which will whet your appetite for further exploration.

**Orientation Tours** A guided bus tour is an excellent way for visitors to get their
*By Land* bearings, both historically and geographically. The in-depth Brush Hill and Gray Line tours are specifically designed for first-time visitors.

**Brush Hill Transportation Company** (439 High St., Randolph, tel. 617/986–6100 or 800/343–1328). Buses leave from several downtown hotels twice daily from late April to early November for 3½-hour "Boston Adventure" tours of Boston and Cambridge, with stops at the USS *Constitution* and the Tea Party Ship. Winter tours are pared down and leave once a day.

**The Gray Line** (275 Tremont St., tel. 617/426–8805). A three-hour tour of Greater Boston, departing from several downtown hotels, includes the Freedom Trail, the USS *Constitution,* and the Boston Tea Party ship. Another three-hour tour takes in Lexington, Concord, and Cambridge. A seven-hour tour combines the two tours with a visit to Sudbury. For those who want to explore further, there are trips to Plymouth, Cape Cod, Salem, Gloucester, Martha's Vineyard, and Old Sturbridge Village. In autumn the fall foliage tours take passengers along the coast, to western Massachusetts, and to northern New England. There are no tours offered from October 30 through early Spring.

**Old Town Trolley** (329 W. 2nd St., tel. 617/269–7010). The trolley takes you on a 1½-hour narrated tour of Boston or an hour-long tour of Cambridge. You can catch the trolley at major hotels, Boston Common, Copley Place, or in front of the New England Aquarium on Atlantic Avenue.

*By Water* **AC Cruise Line** (28 Northern Ave., tel. 617/426–8419). From Memorial Day through Labor Day, the cruise to Gloucester departs daily at 10 AM from Pier 1 at the Northern Avenue Bridge.

**Boston Harbor Cruises** (1 Long Wharf, tel. 617/227–4320). Harbor sightseeing tours operate from mid-April to early September; ferry service to Georges Island operates from June 1 (and weekends in May if weather permits) to early September.

**Bay State Cruise Co.** (ticket office at 67 Long Wharf, tel. 617/723–7800). Harbor trips to Georges Island are scheduled to depart three times daily during the week and four times daily on weekends.

**Special-Interest** **Beacon Hill Garden Club Tours** (tel. 617/227–4392). Every
**Tours** year, on a day in mid-May, the Garden Club sponsors a tour of Beacon Hill's hidden gardens. Tickets may be purchased (in advance or on the day of the tour) at several locations on Beacon Hill and in the Back Bay. Ticket proceeds go toward civic improvements.

*The Boston Globe* (135 Wm. T. Morrissey Blvd., tel. 617/929–2000). The city's largest newspaper gives tours, by appointment, Tuesday–Thursday. Tours are free, but participants must be at least 12 years old. Call a few days in advance.

**Commonwealth Brewing Company** (138 Portland St., tel. 617/ 523–8383). This tiny brewery, which began operations in 1986, makes English-style ales and stouts by traditional methods. The brewery tour is Saturday and Sunday at 3:30. In the summer a horse-drawn omnibus usually takes passengers to the brewery from the Government Center side of Faneuil Hall, Saturday 11–3. After the tour, you might want to have a sandwich or a light entree and sample one of the many beers at the brewery restaurant.

**Federal Reserve Bank** (600 Atlantic Ave., tel. 617/973–3451). Tours are scheduled two Fridays a month, by reservation. Visitors will see money counted, checks processed, the computer and currency departments, and a slide program on the function and purpose of the Federal Reserve Bank.

**Make Way for Ducklings Tours** (Historic Neighborhoods Foundation, 2 Boylston St., tel. 617/426–1885). Tours for children five and older, accompanied by adults, are held on Saturdays in late spring, on Friday and Saturday from July 4 to Labor Day. The path begins at Boston Common and follows the route taken by the ducks in Robert McCloskey's popular children's book, *Make Way for Ducklings*.

**Whale Watches.** *A. C. Company* (28 Northern Ave., tel. 617/ 426–8419) has whale watch cruises Wednesday to Sunday at 10, mid-April to mid-October ($20 adults, $12 children). The *New England Aquarium* (Central Wharf, off Atlantic Ave., tel. 617/ 973–5277) sponsors five-hour cruises weekdays at 10 and weekends at 8 and 2, May to early October ($23 adults, $18.50 senior citizens and students, $16 children 4–15).

**Walking Tours**   **Bay Colony Historical Tours** (Box 9186, Boston 02203, tel. 617/ 523–7303). The motorcoach tours of historic areas of Boston are narrated in English and other languages. Custom-designed special-interest tours, walking tours of the Freedom Trail geared to high school students, and senior citizen tours are available.

**Black Heritage Trail** (tel. 617/742–5415). A 90-minute walk explores the history of Boston's 19th-century black community. The route passes 14 sites of historical importance on Beacon Hill, including the African Meeting House and the Robert Gould Shaw and 54th Regiment Memorial honoring the North's first black regiment. Guided tours are available by appointment. Maps and brochures can be obtained for self-guided tours.

**Boston by Foot** (77 North Washington St., tel. 617/367–2345). A variety of guided walks, available from May to October, includes the Freedom Trail, Copley Square, Beacon Hill, and the North End. Special tours are given once a month. "Boston By Little Feet," an hour-long tour for children 6–12 accompanied by an adult, is held weekly.

**Freedom Trail.** The mile-and-a-half Freedom Trail is marked in the sidewalk by a red line that winds its way past 16 of Boston's most important historic sites. The walk begins at the Freedom Trail Information Center on the Tremont Street side of Boston Common, not far from the MBTA Park Street station. Sites along the Freedom Trail include the State House, Park Street Church, Old Granary Burial Ground, King's Chapel and burying ground, Globe Corner Bookstore, Old State House, Boston Massacre Site, Faneuil Hall, Paul Revere House, Old North

Church, Copp's Hill Burying Ground, and the USS *Constitution*, with a side trip to the Bunker Hill Monument.

**Boston Walkabouts.** A dramatized 64-minute cassette tape tour of the Freedom Trail, in English, French, German, Spanish, and Japanese versions, is available for $10.95 at most Boston hotels and some gift shops and bookstores. Some locations will rent cassette players with two headsets.

**Harborwalk.** Maps are available at the Boston Common Information kiosk for a self-guided tour that traces Boston's maritime history. The walk begins at the Old State House (206 Washington St.) and ends on the Congress Street Bridge near the Boston Tea Party ship and museum.

**Historic Neighborhoods Foundation** (2 Boylston St., tel. 617/426–1885) is a nonprofit educational foundation that offers a variety of informal and informative guided walking tours, from April through November, covering the North End, Chinatown, Beacon Hill, and the waterfront. A Sunset Stroll through Beacon Hill takes place on Thursday from late April to late August. Tours are Wednesday–Saturday, one neighborhood a day, on a rotating schedule. Ticket prices average $5, and groups are limited to 15 people. Call for the schedule.

**New England Sights** (358 Chestnut Hill Ave., Brookline, MA 02146, tel. 617/232–1130). These tours are custom-tailored by multilingual guides to include historic, cultural, educational, and outdoor activities.

**Uncommon Boston** (437 Boylston St., 4th floor, tel. 617/731–5854) will make all arrangements for a specific tour or for your entire stay in the city, including meeting you at the airport. The group acts as meeting planners and convention coordinators and coordinates scheduled tours throughout the year—such as "Graveyards and Goodies" at Halloween. Call or write for the calendar.

**Victorian Society in America** (Gibson House Museum, 137 Beacon St., tel. 617/354–0539, evenings only). This organization sponsors a number of walking tours centered on specific Boston sites, neighborhoods, and architecture representative of the Victorian era.

# 2 Portraits of Boston

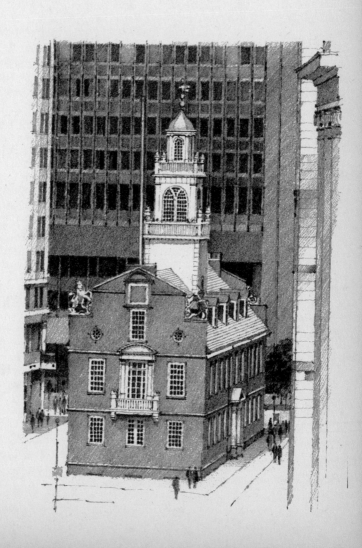

# Lobster, Clams, Beans, and Other Favorite Viands of Boston

*by Kay Howe Scheller*

*A freelance writer, Kay Howe Scheller serves also as an advertising consultant specializing in small businesses.*

**M**y moment of truth came not in a bullring in Madrid but at a restaurant in Boston. At the stolidly self-righteous age of 12 I had just become a full-fledged vegetarian when, on a family outing to Anthony's Pier 4, my uncle ordered me my first lobster.

It came artfully arranged on a large platter, its tail jutting playfully in the air, its eyes practically level with mine. And, oh, those eyes. Small, hard, as black as the ocean floor at 300 feet, they stared right into my soul, mutely challenging my every humanitarian conviction.

My uncle reached over, cracked open the tail, tore out an enormous chunk of white meat, dredged it in a bowl of hot melted butter, and popped it into my mouth. I knew then that the battle was lost.

After that, whenever we journeyed to Boston from our little landlocked town to the west, I would head for the nearest restaurant that served lobster. It took me years to explore its many variations: baked stuffed lobster, lobster thermidor, lobster pie, lazy man lobster, lobster newburg. I went to Chinatown to sample lobster Cantonese and to the North End to find lobster *fra diavolo*. I ate lobster boiled in seawater, lobster boiled in beer, lobster boiled in champagne.

When I moved to Boston to attend Boston University, I had time to visit the piers along Atlantic Avenue and to see the incredible variety of fish that were hauled in from the Atlantic Ocean by commercial fishermen every day: tuna, bluefish, flounder, haddock, squid, striped bass, tilefish, monkfish, sand dab, mako shark, and of course the sacred cod, a source of great debate among locals and great confusion to tourists. (Schrod, or scrod, denotes a filet taken from the large-flake, white-meat, mildly flavored young cod or haddock.) I discovered that in Boston, while everyone seems to have a different opinion about which fish is the tastiest, most people agree on the best way to cook it: broiled. If you want to go to hell with yourself, add a dab of butter. The theory is that fresh fish needs no disguise (and if it's not fresh, don't eat it).

Once I had sampled every kind of fish available, I became a connoisseur of the clam, a New England food that dates back to the Indians. I learned that there are two kinds of clams: soft-shell or steamer, named for the way they are generally served, steamed until their soft, brittle shells open to expose the meat (overcooking will make them tough), and hard-shell or quahog (pronounced *co-hog)*, which come in two sizes, littleneck (the smallest) and cherrystone. I made a pilgrimage to Woodman's in Essex, where the fried clam was invented, to taste them fried lightly in batter with their bellies intact, and I realized that the clam strips at Howard Johnson's were a poor imitation indeed.

I bought a clam rake and went out on the mud flats of the Parker River to dig up some of the littlenecks for which the river is famous. After steaming them just until they opened, I removed the meat from its shell, peeled away the dark, inedible membrane, swished the clam in hot clam broth to wash away the sand, dipped it in melted butter, and let 'er slide. I can describe the taste only as what it must be like to eat a candied ocean wave on a hot summer day. The holy lobster had at last found some competition. The larger quahogs from Cape Cod tasted brinier; with the addition of light cream, salt pork, and potatoes, they made the most wonderful chowder imaginable.

It took me some time to try a raw clam. When I looked at one, shimmering pristinely in its half shell, I understood the saying that "the bravest man in the world is the one who ate the first raw clam." Nevertheless, ever committed, I mustered my courage, dabbed the clam with lemon and Tabasco, scooped it from its shell with my teeth, and let it slide down my throat—and it was good!

Oysters are not as popular in Boston as clams, but I bought them whenever I saw them, and I am hard pressed to say which makes the tastier meal.

Small, delicate, sweet scallops from Cape Cod Bay, broiled to perfection or marinated in lime juice and added to a summer salad; sea scallops, harvested from the cold waters off Gloucester, fried to a golden brown and served with homemade tartar sauce; tiny sweet shrimp or fresh mussels from Maine, sauteed with white wine, garlic, and parsley: Exploring the variations and complexities of New England seafood took me right through my college years.

At the same time, I was fascinated with other specialties of the Boston area. I learned about baked beans from my neighbor, Allie Taylor, a died-in-the-wool Yankee who, like her mother before her, has been cooking them in her special stone crock every Friday night for 50 years. She explained that salt pork, molasses, and hours of slow cooking give the beans their distinctive smoky flavor and rich, sweet taste. (I also learned that very few restaurants make their own; the Ritz, Locke-Ober's, and Durgin Park are three that still do.) When Allie brought over a pot of beans, she would bring along a big chunk of brown bread "to chase 'em down." Brown bread is made with cornmeal, sour milk or buttermilk, and dark molasses; like the beans, it cooks for hours. Baked beans and brown bread have been a traditional Boston dinner since the pilgrims learned how to grow corn, and judging by the way the two go together, I expect they'll be a New England favorite for generations to come.

Another bread that has been around since the days of the pilgrims—and is a popular staple at traditional New England restaurants such as Durgin Park and the Union Oyster House—is cornbread. Aficionados can rave for hours about the delicious grainy texture and the sweet, nutty taste. Those, like myself, who are less enthusiastic are convinced that one of its main ingredients is sawdust.

Cornmeal is the principal ingredient in one of the region's most popular desserts, Indian pudding. Cornmeal, molasses, sugar, butter, milk, eggs, and spices are baked in a stone crock for hours, until the sugar caramelizes, the cornmeal swells, and the pudding takes on the density of a foggy night on the coast of Maine. This is another of those dishes that inspires either great loyalty or a loud raspberry. Yet it's easy to understand how the Pilgrims, fortified with a meal of baked beans, brown bread, and Indian pudding, were able to clear the wilderness without chain saws or Rototillers. (Or perhaps it's difficult to understand how they could stand up after such a repast.) I much prefer to finish my meal with another New England tradition, the apple pandowdy, a cobbler made with spiced apples in a biscuit dough crust.

When you come to Boston in search of traditional New England fare, look for me at the nearest restaurant that's holding a clambake over an open wood fire. You can't be more traditional than steamers, broth and butter, lobster, corn on the cob, hot dogs, and watermelon. Or perhaps I'll be trying to find the perfect Yankee pot roast or scouring the lobster pounds of Rockport for a four-pounder. The one sure bet is that I won't be out shopping for vegetarian hot dogs.

# The Buildings of Boston

*by Jane Holtz Kay*

*Architecture critic for* The Nation *and a contributor to* Progressive Architecture *and the* Boston Globe, *Jane Holtz Kay is the author of* Lost Boston *and* Preserving New England.

The "destination" building, the star of picture post-cards, the familiar structure that draws pilgrims and makes architects' lists, is not a common feature in Boston. The buildings of Boston are less renowned for their solo performance than for their place in a corps. It is the city's overall urban design—the relationship of splendid but neighborly buildings to their community—that gives Boston and its architecture a remarkable identity.

Boston's architecture of ensemble came about almost naturally as the city coped with the features of the landscape in its need to grow. The city founded by the Puritan John Winthrop in 1630 was a place of wetlands and mud flats crowned by three hills. Much smaller than Boston today, the original Boston of 783 acres soon seemed too small. The expansion that followed over three centuries demanded the cutting down of the hills to fill in the coves, a heroic process of transforming topography that called on an army of planners and builders, excavators and architects. Beacon Hill was shaved, the Back Bay formed on the mud flats, and Boston architecture became necessarily a product of collaboration.

Even the city's most renowned architects, Charles Bulfinch and H. H. Richardson, contributed more than their solitary masterpieces. Bulfinch, the city's Federalist architect-hero, not only designed the handsome State House and Faneuil Hall but shaped entire architectural enclaves and framed the city's parks. Richardson, America's most famous architect in the 19th century, created America's best known building in that century, Trinity Church, and also designed bridges on a vast park system from the city to the suburbs.

The city-making—the ultimate act of architecture—began slowly. A town whose economy was dependent on seafaring commerce, Boston needed more land to dock its sailing ships and warehouse the goods of its merchants. Moving outward from the crowded shores of the Shawmut peninsula, the city's builders "wharfed out" the town: Layer upon layer of fill topped by brick wharf buildings gradually fingered out to the sea in the 17th and 18th centuries. The North End, with its compact, medieval configuration of houses and streets, became the commercial end of the town. As time passed, builders filled the space between these digits of commerce to create the fist of the 19th century.

At the close of the Revolution, the once slumbering Colonial city again needed to expand, and the city fathers accelerated the ruthless enterprise of growth. The first Boston had grown up around its three hills, Beacon, Copp's, and Fort—the peaks of the old "Tramount" or "Tri-mountain," remembered in today's Tremont Street. (Early portraits depict the three hills serenely overlooking the rocky landscape and watery prospect of Boston.) As the population of postrevolutionary Boston swelled, land-hungry Bostonians simply carved their peaks. The earth from Copp's and Beacon was used to fill the North End's mill pond. Atop the pared down Beacon Hill, the grand dome of Bulfinch's State House was constructed. Copp's Hill became a burying ground. Fort Hill was leveled altogether; today's High Street in the downtown business district is the memento of its vanished height, just as Dock Square commemorates the first life of today's landlocked site.

More than filling in marshy soil to increase the land mass, the planners soon made a distinctly architectural move: They fitted in new structures on the land between isolated buildings. Where lone mansions had sat atop Beacon Hill, builders began to join them, first into duplexes and then into rows. Soon the single homes stretched into streets of row houses, and a new manner of building was born.

Charles Bulfinch oversaw the construction not only as architect but as ranking politician and planner. Beginning late in the 18th century, the master architect brought the look of Georgian London to an expanding Boston. His own row house projects have not survived—the Tontine Crescent, a semicircular enclave of 1793, was flattened into the Victorian buildings on Franklin Street, and the Pemberton Square row houses, carved around a park, were replaced by the grandiose courthouse that stands there today—yet the influence of this row house world endured. While Faneuil Hall and the Harrison Gray Otis houses are prominent among the works of Bulfinch that we see today, the row houses that line Beacon and Park streets reflect his design. And the curving collections of brick buildings around parks, emulated in Louisburg Square and throughout the city, show how he imported the urban style and elegant line of Robert Adam's England to create Boston's distinctive architecture of place.

The heyday of the seemly row lasted for a century. Varying in detail, the rows dominate the architectural landscape of the inner city to this day. The graceful conformity of the Beacon Street houses of this period—"the sunny street that holds the sifted few," in the words of Oliver Wendell Holmes—created a handsome bank of masonry. With their swelling fronts, their elegant wrought-iron trim, and their symmetrical entries, they set the style. Looser and more flowing than the row houses of other cities, rolling over the streets of the hilly peninsula, they became an orderly procession of residences built individually for the merchant princes of the 19th century. Made of brick and stone for the most part, their simple dignity could be copied by architects who lacked Bulfinch's finesse. If the carpenter-builders of Boston could not quite replicate the sweep of the master architect's staircase, the oval dining rooms, the Adamesque details, or the purity and balance of Bulfinch's poised facades, they might nevertheless stamp civilized copies across the Federalist landscape.

The bowfront, that curving bay on the face of the building, added to the elegance of the row house design. Pinched and narrow a row house might appear beside a single house, yet this swell in the facade would expand the view and enlarge the sense of space. Sometimes limited to a mere bay or a one-story oriel window, the projections did more than animate the exterior; they also enlivened the interior, releasing residents from the confines of a constricted space by giving them a more ample outlook. The expanded views to east and west widened the prospect from within and caught the sun as it moved across the sky. From the outside, too, the bow relieved architectural tedium. However relentless the long masonry wall of a row house street, the bowfront made a shifting surface that caught the light and created a chiaroscuro across the row.

**F**urther stylistic variations appeared as the Victorians who followed Bulfinch textured every inch of the face of their houses, applying ornament from a pastrycart of styles as the city became more affluent.

Yet the significance of the row house went beyond style: The upstairs-downstairs mode of the row house came to dominate the city's larger urban development. Able to accommodate more people in a more compact space, Boston could become a walkable city, it could add mass transit, it could shape the rowlike forms around its parks and promenades to come.

As the 19th century advanced, Boston felt again the press of its mounting numbers, and again a crowded city looked beyond its core, this time to the south. City planners saw a new space for the burgeoning population in the South End. By 1850, the old narrow neck to the south of Boston had become the viaduct to a new and splendid zone of row house architecture.

Once again, no single architect of stature but countless carpenter-builders and designers shaped America's largest Victorian district. As the tree-shaded Louisburg Square on Beacon Hill had determined the arrangement of the rows of mansions framing it, so the centerpieces of the South End's Rutland and Concord squares dictated the design of the curved brick enclaves of row houses around them. Nameless architects and builders brought high stoops and handsome bowfronts to fill in the new blocks. More renowned designers added the churches, schools, and hospitals that enriched the community with landmark buildings.

One more site, the "mournful and inodorous Lake Asphaltics—Back Bay, with its mud, its creeks, and its occasionally good shooting," needed tending to, and by the time the

Civil War had ended, the work on the Back Bay was at hand. Because Boston was now a more cosmopolitan city, France, not Bulfinch's England, provided the model.

Following the design of Baron Haussmann's Paris, Boston planners fashioned a ribbon of greenery, a mall 200 feet wide, along Commonwealth Avenue. Vistas or long corridors of row houses (rather than the South End's organic cluster of parks and buildings) lined this space. As the new railroad carried in dirt from suburban Needham to fill the mud flats, Boston architects drew up the specifications. In 1857 Arthur Gilman set the district's spatial limits and the buildings' setbacks and design silhouettes. Boston architects as renowned as Richardson and as humble as the carpenter-builder placed their row houses within these frames.

**N**otching their buildings westward from the newly planted Public Garden, the architects shaped bays, designed the proportions of windows, and chose masonry materials to dictates as orderly as the alphabetical street names of the Back Bay's grid from A (Arlington) to H (Hereford). The embroidery they attached to their facades was high style; in the five decades that followed, the flamboyant work of such architects as Peabody and Stearns, Sturgis and Brigham, and Charles Follen McKim was affixed to the basic row house. The details of the designs record the chronology of shifting styles as construction moved west.

The architects made certain that the interiors of their five-story Back Bay mansions displayed the utmost elegance. Within the row house's 25-foot width, the carved handrails swept upward, the ornate ceilings topped elegant chambers studded with carved fireplaces and laid with parquet floors. The exteriors, too, boasted rich designs. Whether of brownstone or brick, trimmed in limestone or tile, lidded by steeply pitched mansard roofs of slate or hooded by elaborate doorways, they were the ultimate in fashion, the trendsetters of their time.

Copley Square, a distinctly nonsquare space created on the southern edge of the Back Bay, filled slowly with stately buildings to transform the old wasteland between the South End and the Back Bay. At its eastern end, the new Trinity Church gave a 34-year-old architect with good connections the chance to prove himself the genius of his time. Winning a competition to design the church, Henry Hobson Richardson created a superb work of Victorian architecture. The powerful stone building beneath the peaked red tile roof incorporated the arts of the stained-glass maker John La Farge and the sculptor Augustus Saint-Gaudens into a model of the Cathedral of Salamanca. Atop the piles sunk into the fresh soil of the old Back Bay, the Romanesque masterpiece broadcast to the nation a new style and provided a handsome focus for the infant square.

The closing in of Copley Square with buildings of majesty and diversity culminated in the completion of the Boston Public Library in 1895. McKim, Mead and White created Boston's "people's palace," with murals by John Singer Sargent and bronze doors by Daniel Chester French. The Boston Public Library was the most substantial building of the latest mode, the Classical Revival; its imposing symmetries and the grandeur of its cool white facade helped stamp the Beaux Arts style on late 19th-century America.

Boston would undergo one more topographical transformation, and H. H. Richardson and McKim, Mead and White would share in the final act of city-making only a mile or so from Copley Square. Boston's "Emerald Necklace," beginning at the western border of the Back Bay, was the consequence of the same ecological urgency that gave rise to the Back Bay: the "noxious" condition of the Fens. Again, a single planner determined the layout of the new land and individual architects created major buildings. Yet this time the planner had a somewhat different outlook.

Frederick Law Olmsted was the first to bear the title of landscape architect. The inventor of the term and the creator of parks from Central Park to Yosemite, Olmsted came to Boston at Richardson's behest and spent much of his life in the city shaping just such space. America's greatest parkmaker took the polluted backwaters of the Fens and transformed them into an ordered ring of greenery punctuated by Richardson's handsome bridges and enriched by a chain of plantings along its waterway. Stretching from the edge of the Back Bay Fens to Franklin Park in West Roxbury, punctuated with small waterways and the superb space of the Arnold Arboretum, the Emerald Necklace became the site for the city's last great architecture of the late 19th and early 20th centuries: the Museum of Fine Arts, the Isabella Stewart Gardner Museum, Harvard Medical School, and nearby residential structures.

Until World War II, Boston conditioned its development with respect for the previous 100 years of construction: Architecture and surroundings remained intact. Even as fashions changed, and architects designed replacements in Deco or other modern modes along the stately rows of the Back Bay's Commonwealth Avenue and Newbury, Beacon, and Marlborough streets, the basic context stayed the same. Then, after World War II, the scope of change expanded. Copley Square lost its civilized height of 90 feet to a gargantuan invader, the 890-foot sleek glass tower of the John Hancock, which not only broke through the height barrier but shook Trinity Church to its foundations. In the inner city, the medieval contours of downtown established in the first wharfing out of the city crumbled under the onslaught of asphalt-wrapped towers; at the outer limits, Olmsted's landscape languished.

Finally, preservationists began to be heard. In residential areas of the city, historic or architecturally significant districts appeared; first in the Back Bay and Beacon Hill and later in the South End, the city established rules to guarantee that the style and scale of Boston's row house world would survive. No more would such intrusions as the New Brutalist concrete Boston Architectural Center of the 1960s be allowed. Copley Square supporters held another competition to shape the ungainly space into a more civilized enclave. The state provided funds to restore Olmsted's neglected ring of greenery.

Elsewhere in the city the building boom had greater consequence for the work of Boston's early placemakers. The medieval street pattern of downtown succumbed to glass and stone monoliths. Starting in 1962 with the Prudential Center, the city's efforts to rouse itself from an economic depression saw the replacement of congenial low-scale buildings and carefully contoured streets by isolated towers and wraparound roads. The old brick West End was flattened for luxury apartments and the filing-cabinet architecture of Government Center. Fine neighborhoods were reduced to rubble, to be succeeded by structures of less considerate design.

**T**oday the urban renewal of the late 1950s and the onrush of oversize modern architecture has abated somewhat. Gridded slabs no longer rise on windy plazas, and Boston's architects have begun to look to their heritage. Some 7,000 of the city's 120,000 buildings have been designated historic landmarks by the city. Architects have learned to excel at clinging to historic form by mastering the art of recycling; they have refurbished old architecture, and born-again buildings abound throughout the city. Adapting the old city to new ways, architects have placed enough fern and butcher block inside renovated buildings to qualify them for certification as the official state flora.

Quincy Market sets the national standard for transformations of this kind. Designed in a Greek Revival style by Alexander Parris in 1826, the market was long a Boston landmark, central to the city's identity as a working seaport. Then it declined in the 20th century, and by the 1970s the threat of the bulldozer was at hand. But the city rallied, a developer was found, and the vintage marketplace was remade in 1976 as the first of the festival markets that now stud the continent. Renamed Faneuil Hall Marketplace, the three buildings, each 555 feet long, are now a contemporary food emporium in a zone of gentrification, the epitome of a new architecture of recreation.

The reclaimed architecture of Lewis and Commercial wharves and the updated Charlestown Navy Yard with its new buildings typify a trend that has extended to Salem and Newburyport and moved across the country. Recycling is the cities' latest architectural solution. An Institute of

Contemporary Art springs up in a police station. Alarm clocks now awaken commuters who make their homes in the recycled churches, schools, and mills where bells once signaled the start of services, classes, and work.

**M**eanwhile, new attention is being paid to the city's open spaces. Designers have recognized that they are as essential to the quality of Boston architecture as the green parks and corridors that gave definition to the row house. Thus the spaces-in-between have become new oases. From small and singular vest-pocket parks to larger swaths of space, planners and landscape architects are recouping the amenities. Harborwalk, which will edge 45 miles of the inner city, has already shaped a pedestrian path along the waterfront; inching by the old wharves and new buildings, the thoroughfare has begun to bring the architecture into the ensemble in which Boston has always excelled. At Post Office Square downtown, on the site of a former garage, a replacement garage will be built below ground, a new park above.

Architects and planners have become adroit at maximizing minimal environments. Tucked into alleys, bricked over between buildings, packed with benches, bollards, and other adornments, these scraps of space are a delight. Find a fragment of leftover land—at Central Wharf, Winthrop Square, or Union Street—and you find an exercise in the artistry of shaping elegant outdoor space.

In an age of entrepreneurial greed and private affluence, the public art of architecture that transformed a few muddy acres crowded with hills endures. Three hundred fifty years after John Winthrop sought to establish his community of souls, the best of Boston's architects still strive for that sense of community in the linking of today's architecture with that of the past.

# 3 Exploring Boston

Boston can be seen as a series of concentric circles, with the oldest and most famous attractions clustered within easy walking distance of the State House. Many attractions are on the well-marked Freedom Trail; none is far off the track. You might draw an arbitrary line across the peninsula, stretching from, say, the Arthur Fiedler Footbridge (at the Charles River near Beacon and Arlington streets) to South Station, explore everything north of it—with a side trip west into the Back Bay—and truthfully say that you had "seen Boston." In fact, that is all many visitors ever see. This remarkable compactness is a boon to the pedestrian explorer (in central Boston there should be no other kind), and it assures a virtually complete education in the earliest history of the town. But just as Boston outgrew its cramped peninsular quarters, so too must the serious traveler's curiosity extend beyond our random demarcation. We begin our tour at the heart of things, in Boston Common, and follow the circles outward to Charlestown, the Back Bay, and beyond.

## Tour 1. Boston Common and Beacon Hill

*Numbers in the margin correspond with points of interest on the Boston Common and Beacon Hill map.*

**❶** Nothing is more central to Boston than the **Boston Common,** the oldest public park in the United States and undoubtedly the largest and most famous of the town commons around which all New England settlements were once arranged. Boston Common is not "made land," like the adjacent Public Garden; nor is it the result of 19th-century park planning, as is Olmsted's Fens and Franklin Park. It is simply the Common: 50 acres where the freemen of Boston could graze their cattle. It is as old as the city around it. No building of substance ever stood here, and until such time as codfish walk and the Red Sox move to Phoenix, it is safe to say that none ever will.

Start your walk at the **Park Street Station,** on the corner of Park and Tremont streets. This is the original eastern terminus of the first subway in America, opened in 1897 against the warnings of those who believed it would make the buildings along Tremont Street collapse. The copper-roof kiosks are national historic landmarks. The line originally ran only as far as the present-day Boylston stop. The area around the two subway kiosks is noisy with the hustle of commuters, newspaper and fruit vendors, street musicians, and partisans of causes and beliefs ranging from Irish nationalism to Krishna Consciousness. The general dither—and, sad to say, a considerable amount of litter—are more characteristic of the Common's Tremont Street borders than they are of the Beacon Street side.

As you stand at the Park Street Station, you are within a few steps of two historic churches and a burying ground. The **❷** Congregationalist **Park Street Church,** designed by Peter Banner and erected in 1809–1810, occupies the corner of Tremont and Park streets. The date may seem incongruous with the architecture, for the church is Georgian in character, perhaps the last major Georgian church built in the area before the Colonial revival of the early 20th century. Here, on July 4, 1831, Samuel Smith's hymn "America" was first sung, and here in 1829 William Lloyd Garrison began his long public campaign for the abolition of slavery. *Open to visitors last week in June–third week*

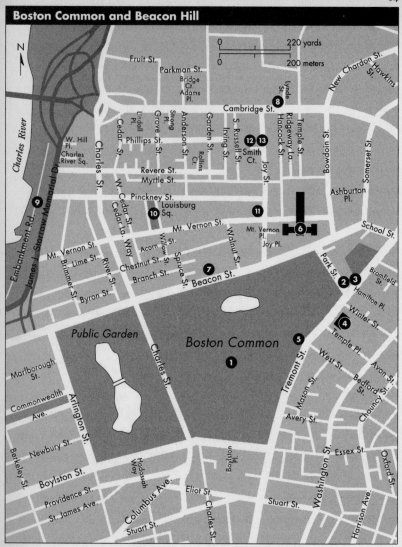

# Boston Common and Beacon Hill

African Meeting House, **12**

Appleton Mansions, **7**

Boston Common, **1**

Esplanade, **9**

First Otis House, **8**

Louisburg Square, **10**

Museum of Afro-American History, **13**

Nichols House, **11**

Old Granary Burial Ground, **3**

Park Street Church, **2**

State House, **6**

St. Paul's Cathedral, **4**

Visitor Information Booth (Boston Common), **5**

*in Aug., Tues.–Sat. 9:30–3:30. Closed July 4. Year-round Sun. services 10:30 and 6.*

**❸** Next to the church is the **Old Granary Burial Ground,** named after the public granary that stood on the church site in the 1700s (the sails of the USS *Constitution* were made in the granary loft). Note the winged hourglasses carved into the stone gateway of the burial ground; they are a 19th-century addition, made more than 150 years after this small plot began receiving the remains of Colonial Bostonians. The most famous individuals interred here are heroes of the Revolution: Samuel Adams, John Hancock (the precise location of his grave is not certain), James Otis, and Paul Revere. Here, too, are the graves of the philanthropist Peter Faneuil, Benjamin Franklin's parents (Franklin is buried in Philadelphia), and the victims of the Boston Massacre. *Open daily 8–4:30.*

**❹** **St. Paul's Cathedral** (Episcopal), the massive and severe Greek Revival structure on your right as you cross Tremont Street, was built 10 years after the Park Street Church. Even a cursory comparison of the two churches underscores the difference between 18th and early 19th century architectural aesthetics as they applied to large public buildings. Notice the uncarved entablature above St. Paul's pillars; as with New York's Metropolitan Museum of Art, similarly adorned with uncut blocks of stone, the money ran out before carvers could be employed. *Open Sun.–Fri. noon–5. Sun. services at 9 and 11; daily services at noon and 5; Holy Eucharist in Chinese at 12:30.*

Across Tremont Street from St. Paul's and a little to your left is
**❺** a **visitor information booth,** adjacent to the Common's **Parkman Plaza** with its bronzes extolling study, toil, and prayer. The monuments to the Puritan ethic make an ironic contrast to the seedy indolence of many of the characters who frequent this part of the Common. The information booth serves as the starting point for the Freedom Trail; guide booklets are available at no charge. For now, we'll head in the opposite direction from the trail and walk past the **Parkman Bandstand.**

The once handsome bandstand is seldom used and has been left to the care of spray-paint vandals. Musical events on the Common (apart from the buskers who work near Park Street Station) are now held within a stockadelike wooden enclosure erected near here each summer for the Concerts on the Common series, which features big-name acts and paid admission.

The **Central Burying Ground** may seem an odd feature for a public park, but remember that in 1756, when it was set aside, this was a lonely corner of the Common. Here are buried Gilbert Stuart, the portraitist most famous for his paintings of George and Martha Washington, and scores of British casualties of the Battle of Bunker Hill.

Walk back toward the bandstand, turn left, and head for the Common's highest ground, once called **Flagstaff Hill** and now surmounted by the **Soldiers and Sailors Monument** honoring those who fought in the Civil War. It was along the slope between the monument and Charles Street that thousands gathered for Pope John Paul II's outdoor mass in October 1979. A granite marker near Charles Street commemorates the event.

Immediately below and to the north is the **Frog Pond,** a tame and frogless concrete depression used as a children's wading pool during the summer and as a skating rink in winter. The site is that of an original pond after which Edgar Allan Poe called Bostonians "Frogpondians" and which was the focal point for the inauguration of Boston's municipal water system in 1848, when a gushing fountain of piped-in water was arranged for the occasion.

From the Frog Pond, walk uphill to the Joy Street steps. Head toward the State House (again, uphill) on the Common side of Beacon Street to reach the splendidly restored **Robert Gould Shaw Memorial,** executed in deep-relief bronze by Augustus Saint-Gaudens. It commemorates the 54th Massachusetts Regiment, a Civil War unit made up of free blacks led by the Young Brahmin Robert Gould Shaw. Colonel Shaw died with nearly half of his troops in an assault on South Carolina's Fort Wagner. The monument figures in works by the modern poets John Berryman and Robert Lowell, both of whom lived on the north slope of Beacon Hill in the 1940s.

Here at the corner of Beacon and Park streets is where Beacon Hill, the Common, and downtown Boston converge. If you head down Park Street along the Common, you will pass the **Ticknor Mansion,** a much altered structure of 1804 designed by Charles Bulfinch that now houses an antiques shop and offices; the exclusive **Union Club;** the Roman Catholic **Paulist Center;** and the offices of the venerable Boston publishing house of **Houghton Mifflin.** The block ends at the Park Street Church.

**Time Out**   II Dolce Momento (30 Charles St.), with its homemade gelato and pastries and freshly made gourmet sandwiches, is a perfect stop for a meal, a light snack, or a late-night espresso.

**❻** Charles Bulfinch's magnificent **State House** stands at the summit of Beacon Hill, which over the years has been vastly reduced from its original height. Beacon Hill, the seat of the Commonwealth's government and of Brahmin Boston itself, was called "Tremont" or "Trimount" by the early colonists. It had three summits, Cotton Hill, Beacon Hill, and Mount Vernon. Beacon, the highest, was named for the warning light (at first an iron skillet filled with tallow and suspended from a mast) set on its peak in 1634. The location of the old beacon was directly behind the State House, on land now occupied by the building's 19th-century additions. In 1790 it was replaced by a brick and stone column, designed by Bulfinch to commemorate American independence.

Neither monument nor hill was destined to stand for long. In 1793 the state bought the summit and the surrounding lands for the new State House. Much of the parcel had been pasture belonging to the estate of John Hancock, whose fine stone mansions stood until 1864 just to the west of the State House. Construction of Bulfinch's masterpiece began in 1795, accompanied by the carving away of Beacon Hill. By 1820 its summit was some 60 feet lower. The soil and gravel removed (and carried off by one of America's first "railroads," run by gravity and horsepower) was used not to fill the Back Bay but to fill the area where Charles Street now stands and to make dry land in the old North Cove (near present-day North Station). To visualize the original terrain, try to think of the Common sloping north to a knoll just behind the State House and reaching just as high as its dome.

While civic expansiveness leveled Beacon Hill, private entre-preneurship tamed and flattened Mount Vernon. Much of this land once belonged to the painter John Singleton Copley, who followed his Tory sympathies and removed himself to Britain as the Revolution approached. After the war, his estate was pur-chased by a syndicate called the Mount Vernon Proprietors and made the site of the planned suburban development that evolved into today's Beacon Hill neighborhood. As we will see when we walk the streets of the hill, little remains of the origi-nal plans for freestanding mansions and grassy squares, for even at the beginning of the 19th century the pressures of popu-lation density made row houses inevitable. Mount Vernon, too, was flattened by about 60 feet, the displaced earth being used to push the shores of the Charles even farther back. (Cotton Hill was leveled after 1835, and Pemberton Square replaced it.)

The **State House** is arguably the most architecturally distin-guished of American seats of state government; it was built well before the trend toward designs based on the Capitol in Washington. (Charles Bulfinch later held the position of archi-tect of the U.S. Capitol.) The design is neoclassical, poised be-tween Georgian and Federal; its finest features are the delicate Corinthian columns of the portico, the graceful pediment and window arches, and the vast yet visually weightless golden dome. The dome is sheathed in copper from the foundry of Paul Revere; the gilding was added in 1874. During World War II, the entire dome was painted gray so that it would not reflect moonlight during blackouts and offer a target to the Axis bombers (that never showed up).

Bulfinch's work would have stood splendidly on its own, but the growth of the state bureaucracy necessitated additions. The yellow brick annex extending to the rear is clumsily ostenta-tious, but at least it is invisible from Beacon Street. The light stone wings added to either side of the original early in this century serve no aesthetic purpose.

Inside the State House are Doric Hall, with its statuary and portraits, a part of the original structure; the chambers of the General Court (legislature) and Senate, including the carved wooden *Sacred Cod* that symbolizes the state's maritime wealth; and the Hall of Flags. *Tel. 617/727-3676. Admission free. Open weekdays 10-4. Research library (free) open week-days 9-5.*

Take the traditional path of retiring governors down the front steps of the State House and onto Beacon Street, turning right to explore Beacon Hill. The walk can take between two hours and an entire day, depending on one's thoroughness and pow-ers of resistance to the shops on and around Charles Street. Since a specific itinerary would require a complex retracing of steps, we'll concentrate instead on the gaslit highlights of the Hill, clustered in the several small but distinct neighborhoods that quilt its slopes.

Beacon Hill is the area bounded by Cambridge Street on the north, Beacon Street on the south, the Charles River Espla-nade on the west, and Bowdoin Street on the east. Within these borders, residents distinguish three informal districts: the flat side (the area west of Charles Street), the south side (the area east of Charles Street and south of Pinckney Street), and the north side (the area east of Charles Street and north of Pinckney Street).

No sooner do you put the State House behind you than you encounter the classic face of Beacon Hill: brick row houses, nearly all built between 1800 and 1850 in a style never far divergent from the early Federal norm. Even the sidewalks are brick, and they shall remain so; in the 1940s, residents staged an uncharacteristic sit-in to prevent conventional paving. Since then, public law, the Beacon Hill Civic Association, and the Beacon Hill Architectural Commision have maintained tight controls over everything from the gas lamps to the color of front doors. Beacon Hill was finished quite nicely a century and a quarter ago, and as the Yankees say, "If it ain't broke, don't fix it."

At the corner of Beacon and Joy streets is the headquarters of **Little, Brown,** another mainstay of Boston's publishing trade. **❼** Farther down Beacon, past Walnut Street, are the twin **Appleton Mansions** built by the pioneer textile family and now occupied by the Women's City Club of Boston. Taking a tour will give you the rare opportunity to look out through the famed purple panes of Beacon Hill; only a few buildings have them, and they are as valuable as an ancestor in the China Trade. The color was the result of the action of sunlight on the imperfections in a shipment of glass sent to Boston around 1820. *39 and 40 Beacon St., tel. 617/227–3550. Admission free. Tours of 40 Beacon St. by appointment.*

Adjacent to the Women's City Club is the private **Somerset Club** (42 Beacon St.). The older of the two buildings (the newer was built to match) was erected in 1819 by David Sears to a design by Alexander Parris, the architect of Quincy Market. It represents a rare intrusion of the granite Greek Revival into Beacon Hill.

The American Meteorological Society occupies 45 Beacon Street, the last of three houses built by Charles Bulfinch for Harrison Gray Otis, who was one of the Mount Vernon **❽** Proprietors, a Boston mayor, and a U.S. senator. The **First Otis House,** at 141 Cambridge Street, is now the headquarters of the Society for the Preservation of New England Antiquities (SPNEA), an organization that owns and maintains dozens of historic properties throughout the region. The society has restored the Otis House and opened two floors of it as a museum. The furniture, textiles, wall coverings, and even the interior paint, specially mixed to match old samples, are faithful to the Federalist era, c. 1790–1810. Visitors will be surprised to see how bright and vivid were the colors favored in those days and to learn that closets had not quite made their appearance. The dining room is laid out as though Harry Otis were about to come in and have a glass of Madeira; one gets the feeling he would have been good company. *Tel. 617/227–3956. Admission: $3. Open Tues.–Fri. for tours at noon, 1, 2, 3, and 4; Sat. tours hourly, 10–4.*

The **Second Otis House,** built in 1802 at 85 Mount Vernon Street, is today a private home. Otis moved into the **Third Otis House** at 45 Beacon Street in 1805 and stayed there until his death in 1848. His tenure thus extended from the first days of Beacon Hill's residential development almost to the time when many of the Hill's prominent families decamped for the Back

Bay, which was just beginning to be filled at the time of Otis's death.

Not all the families left; enough remained that the south slope of the Hill—where you are now—never lost its Brahmin character and at worst fell into a dowdy yet respectable eclipse. By the middle of the present century natives and newcomers alike began to realize that here was prime territory for the new urban gentry. In what other city can one live so elegantly within 10 minutes' walk from the central office district? Thus the unchanged facades of Beacon Hill are more and more likely to conceal condominiums and expensive apartments rather than four-story, single-family dwellings. They survive, too, but at prices in excess of a million dollars. Similarly, the people who live here are more likely to be young stockbrokers married to lawyers than DAR matrons whose fathers knew Justice Holmes.

One old family that stayed was that of Admiral Samuel Eliot Morison, the sailor-historian who lived his entire life at 44 Brimmer Street on the "flat side" of the Hill, the part separated from the slope by Charles Street. (This was land reclaimed with fill from the State House excavation; the oldest houses here are in the granite-faced 1828 block on Beacon between Charles and Brimmer streets.) Morison's family home was nearly new when he was born there in 1887, and the river bank was across the street. When he died in 1976, the river was on the other side of Storrow Drive and the Esplanade. His house has since been divided into condos.

Morison, the quintessential Boston gentleman scholar, did not have to look far to find the material for his Harvard dissertation; the papers of a prominent ancestor had been stashed at 44 Brimmer. The ancestor's name was Harrison Gray Otis. In Boston, that is known as being well connected.

**❾** If you continue toward the river, you can cross over to the **Esplanade** on the Arthur Fiedler Footbridge, named for the late maestro who conducted the Boston Pops for 50 years. Many of his concerts were given right here, in the **Hatch Memorial Shell,** where the Pops plays each summer. More than a pleasant place for a stroll, a run, or a picnic, the Esplanade is home port for the fleet of small sailboats that dot the Charles River Basin. They belong to Community Boating, which offers membership on a monthly or seasonal basis. Here, too, is the **Union Boat Club Boathouse,** private headquarters for the country's oldest rowing club. The boathouse was built at the turn of the century. If you come here with children, bring a few leftover rolls from breakfast; the ducks are always hungry.

**Time Out**  If you, too, are hungry, stop at **Romano's Bakery and Coffee Shop** (89 Charles St.) for fresh coffee, homemade blueberry muffins, cheese danish, croissants, quiche, sandwiches, and hearty soup.

Heading back to the Hill from the river, you will cross **Charles Street.** With a few exceptions, other streets in the area lack commercial establishments, and Charles Street makes up for it. Here is Boston's antiques district (the side streets on the flat side have some good shops, too) and an assortment of bookstores, leather goods shops, small restaurants, and vintage clothing boutiques. Dollhouse furniture, Italian ice cream, fresh fruit, and hardware are within steps of one another. The activity would be a curious sight to the elder Oliver Wendell Holmes, the publisher James T. Fields, and others who lived here when the neighborhood belonged to the establishment literati. Charles Street sparkles at dusk from gas street lamps making it a romantic place for an evening stroll.

**Chestnut** and **Mt. Vernon,** two of the loveliest streets in America, are distinguished not only for the history and style of their individual houses but for their general atmosphere and character as well. **Mt. Vernon Street** is the grander of the two, its houses set back farther and rising taller; it even has a free-standing mansion, the Second Otis House. Mt. Vernon opens out on **Louisburg Square,** an 1840s model for town-house development that was never repeated on the Hill because of space restrictions. The little green belongs collectively to the owners of the homes facing it. The statue at the north end of the green is of Columbus; the one at the south end is of Aristides the Just; both were a gift in 1850 of a Greek merchant in Boston, who lived on the square. The houses, most of which are now divided into apartments and condominiums, have seen their share of famous tenants: William Dean Howells at 4 and 16; the Alcotts at 10; and in 1852 the singer Jenny Lind was married in the parlor of 20.

There is no water in Louisburg Square today, and the ground level is some 60 feet below the height of the original hill, yet the legend long persisted that this was the location of the Rev. William Blackstone's spring. Blackstone was the original Bostonian, having come here to live with his books and his apple trees four or five years before the arrival of the Puritans in 1630. It was he who invited them to leave Charlestown and come to where the water was purer, he who sold them all but six acres of the peninsula he had bought from the Indians. He left for Rhode Island not long after, seeking greater seclusion; a plaque at 50 Beacon Street commemorates him. (The name "Boston" given by the Puritans comes from Boston, England, originally St. Botolph's Town.)

At 55 Mt. Vernon Street is the **Nichols House,** an early side-entrance home built in 1804 and attributed to Bulfinch. This was the lifelong residence of Rose Standish Nichols, a philanthropist, peace advocate, and one of the first women to practice the profession of landscape gardening. Although Nichols's life spanned the latter years of the 19th and the first half of the 20th centuries, few of the furnishings in her home date from later than the mid-Victorian era. The deep window seat with a view down Mt. Vernon Street is straight out of a Henry James novel. The house gives a pervasive impression of how a Brahmin lady of means and modesty lived among the rich and comfortably aging possessions of her forebears. Nichols arranged in her will for her home to become a museum, and visitors have been calling since her death more than a quarter of a century ago. *55 Mt. Vernon St., tel. 617/227–6993. Admission: $3. Open Tues.– Sat. 1–5. (summer); Mon., Wed., Sat. 1–5 (spring and fall); Sat. 1–5 (winter).*

Around the corner at 5 Joy Street, in a later bowfront mansion, is the headquarters of the **Appalachian Mountain Club,** a source of useful information on outdoor recreation, both nearby and in New England's North Country. *Tel. 617/523–0636. Open Mon., Fri., 8:30–5:30.*

**Chestnut Street** is more modest than Mt. Vernon, yet in its trimness and minuteness of detail it is perhaps even more fine. Delicacy and grace characterize virtually every structure, from the fanlights above the entryways to the wrought-iron boot scrapers on the steps. Francis Parkman lived here, as did Julia Ward Howe, Richard Henry Dana, and Edwin Booth. Booth's sometime residence at 29A, dating to 1800, is the oldest home on the south slope of the Hill.

Running parallel to Chestnut and Mt. Vernon streets, half a block down Willow Street from Louisburg Square, is **Acorn Street,** a narrow span of cobblestones lined on one side with almost toylike row houses and on the other with the doors to Mt. Vernon's hidden gardens. These were once the houses of artisans and small tradesmen; today they are every bit as prestigious as their larger neighbors. Acorn Street may be the most photographed street of its size in Boston.

There is another side to Beacon Hill: the north slope. Until just a few years ago it was not uncommon to hear the south slope called "the good side," with obvious connotations for the streets north of Pinckney. There are still a fair number of relatively low-cost apartments here in turn-of-the-century apartment buildings popular with students, new young professionals, and a handful of older blue-collar families. (There are also blocks and cul-de-sacs that would be perfectly at home in the vicinity of Chestnut and Mt. Vernon.) But gentrification is setting in, and yesterday's modest apartments are today's condos.

The north slope of the Hill was built up long before the Mount Vernon Proprietors set to work, although almost all its old wooden houses are gone now. Exceptions may be found at 5 and 7 Pinckney, near the corner of Joy, where a structure of 1791 stands. Joy Street beyond this point was a black neighborhood during the late 18th and early 19th centuries. The **African Meeting House** at 8 Smith Court (near Joy and Myrtle), built in 1806, is the oldest black church building still standing in the United States. It was constructed almost entirely with black labor, using funds raised in both the white and the black communities. The facade is an adaptation of a design for a town house published by the Boston architect Asher Benjamin. The school for colored children moved into the basement in 1808. In 1832 the New England Anti-Slavery Society was formed here under the leadership of William Lloyd Garrison. Daily tours are offered from the Museum of Afro-American History across the street.

Opposite the Meeting House is the home (1799) of **William Nell,** a black crusader for school integration active in Garrison's circle. These sites and others are part of a **Black Heritage Trail,** a walking tour that explores the history of the city's black community during the 19th century. The recently established **Museum of Afro-American History** provides information on the trail and on black history throughout Boston. *46 Joy St., tel. 617/742–1854. Admission free. Open daily 9–5. Information on the Trail can also be obtained from the National Park Service Visitor Center, 15 State St., tel. 617/742–5415. Admission free. Open weekdays 9–5.*

A visit to the north slope of the Hill should include a walk down Revere Street and glances into Rollins Place, Phillips Court, and Bellingham Place. These trim residential courts all dead-end at a hidden cliff; the shuttered white clapboard house at the blind end of Rollins Place is not a house at all but a false front masking a small precipice.

## Tour 2. The Old West End

*Numbers in the margin correspond with points of interest on The Old West End map.*

Cambridge Street draws the line between Beacon Hill proper and the old West End. Little remains of the West End—a few brick tenements, nothing more—since blocks of old structures were razed in the 1960s to make way for the Charles River Park apartment and retail development. The only survivors in this ❶ area having any real history are two public institutions, **Massachusetts General Hospital** and the **Suffolk County (or Charles Street) Jail.** Both are near the Charles Street Circle, where the Longfellow Bridge (called the Salt and Pepper Shaker Bridge for obvious reasons) begins its reach across the Charles to Cambridge. The jail is interesting chiefly for its central building of 1849, designed by Gridley Bryant at the close of Boston's Granite Age. That makes it terribly old for a jail and all the more crowded and miserable; the courts have been trying for years to get the county to close it.

Far more humanitarian associations are attached to the nearly adjacent hospital, usually called **Mass General,** which was incorporated in 1811. Seven years later work began on the domed granite **Bulfinch Pavilion,** which today stands at the center of a complex of modern buildings. The amphitheater beneath the dome was for many years the hospital's main operating room, where scholarly audiences learned the latest surgical techniques. It was here, on October 16, 1846, that Dr. John Collins Warren first performed an operation on a patient rendered senseless to pain by ether. You may visit the amphitheater today (use the hospital's North Grove Street entrance) and see a display describing this discovery that made modern surgery possible. *Admission free. Open 9–5 when no meeting is in session.*

Mass General was once the home of the Harvard Medical School, and it was in a laboratory here around Thanksgiving 1849 that one of Boston's most celebrated murders took place. Dr. George Parkman, a wealthy landlord and Harvard benefactor, was bludgeoned to death by Dr. John Webster, a Harvard medical professor and friend who supposedly became exasperated by demands that he repay a personal loan. After several days of mystery over Parkman's disappearance, Webster's doom was sealed when part of the victim's jaw was discovered in the laboratory stove. Other grisly evidence turned up in the cesspool beneath Webster's privy. The professor was hanged and buried in an unmarked grave on Copp's Hill in the North End.

Boston's original science museum, the Society of Natural History, was located in the spacious mansionlike structure at Berkeley and Newbury streets. Its successor institution, the ❷ **Museum of Science,** occupies the modern compound of buildings that stand north of Mass General, on a site astride the Charles River Dam and its boat locks. The museum's collections date to 1830; its development as a tremendously successful edu-

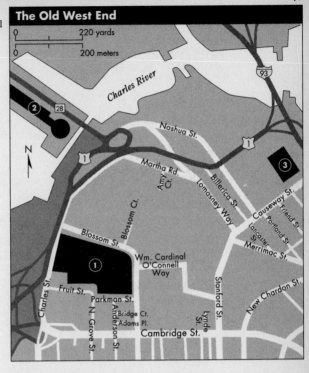

**The Old West End**

cational resource was largely accomplished under the recent directorship of the explorer, mountaineer, and mapmaker Bradford Washburn. More than 400 exhibits cover astronomy, astrophysics, anthropology, progress in medicine, computers, the organic and inorganic earth sciences, and much more. Washburn and his curators made the Museum of Science a leader in hands-on education; many exhibits invite the participation of children and adults. The Transparent Woman's organs light up as their functions are described, newborn chicks hatch in an incubator, and a powerful generator produces controlled indoor lightning flashes. The museum has three restaurants and a gift shop. *Tel. 617/723–2500 (for recorded information, tel. 617/523–6664). Admission: $6 adults, $4.50 students, $4.50 children, free under 4 and senior citizens. Open Tues.–Sun. 9–5, Fri. until 9. Closed Mon. except May 1–Labor Day and Mon. holidays, Thanksgiving, and Christmas; free Wed. 1-5.*

The **Hayden Planetarium,** located in the Museum of Science, features the $2 million Zeiss planetarium projector and New England's most sophisticated multi-image system that combine to produce exciting programs on astronomical discoveries. Laser light shows, using a new visual technology complete with brilliant laser graphics and computer animation, are scheduled Friday–Sunday evenings. *Tel. 617/589–0270. Admission for each: $6 adults, $4.50 children and senior citizens.*

The **Mugar Omni Theater** in the Museum of Science features state-of-the-art film projection and sound systems. The 76-foot, four-story domed screen wraps around and over you, and 27,000 watts of power drive the sound system's 84 loudspeakers. *Tel. 617/523–6664. Admission: $6 adults, $4.50 senior citizens and children 4–14, under 4 not admitted. Afternoon shows weekdays, evening shows Tues.–Sun. Reduced price combination tickets are available for the museum, planetarium and Omni Theater.*

Behind Mass General and the sprawling Charles River Park apartment complex is a small grid of streets recalling an older Boston. Here are furniture and electric supply stores, a good discount camping supply house (Hilton's, on Friend Street), and the Commonwealth Brewery and Tavern on Portland Street (*see* Tours). The main drag here is Causeway Street, **❸** home of the **Boston Garden,** where the Celtics (basketball) and the Bruins (hockey) play their home games. For the past few years there has been talk of either modernizing the old Garden or razing it (a new federal office building has already risen next to the Garden). We can probably expect another decade of debate; meanwhile, trains to the North Shore still run out of North Station, behind the Garden, while upstairs Larry Bird shows mere mortals how his game is played.

If you head up Cambridge Street, away from Charles Street Circle and the river, you will pass on your right the **Old West Church** and the first **Harrison Gray Otis House.** Built in 1806 to a design of the great builder and architect Asher Benjamin, the church stands along with Otis's house as a reminder of the days when the West End near Bowdoin Square was a fashionable district. Forty years ago, when the Church served as a public library and polling place, Congressman John F. Kennedy voted here. *Open Mon.–Sat. 9–4:30. Sun. service at 11.*

---

## Tour 3. Government Center and the North End

*Numbers in the margin correspond with points of interest on the Government Center and the North End map.*

Just where the old West End meets downtown Boston stands **❶ Government Center,** one of the most ambitious of the city's self-transformations of the 1960s. It completely obliterated the raffish, down-at-heels Scollay Square, a bawdy, raucous place where sailors would go when they came into port, famous for its burlesque houses and the sort of ambience that is always remembered more fondly as the years go by. (A small plaque in the square behind the Crescent Building marks the site of the Howard Theater's stage.) The **Center Plaza,** only six stories high, separates Tremont Street (Cambridge becomes Tremont here) from the higher ground of Pemberton Square, site of the old and "new" courthouses. Across Tremont stands the much older **Sears Crescent,** a curving commercial block that the new building sought to imitate.

The single most arresting structure in Government Center is **❷ City Hall,** an upside-down ziggurat set within a vast sloping plaza of red brick. The design by Kallman, McKinnell, and Knowles relegates administrative functions to the upper floors and places offices that deal with the public on street level. Despite the democratic intentions, the building is not much loved, though that may have less to do with its architecture than with its being the place you can't fight. And there has been criticism of the absence of intimacy and verdure in the surrounding 10 acres of brick.

# Government Center and the North End

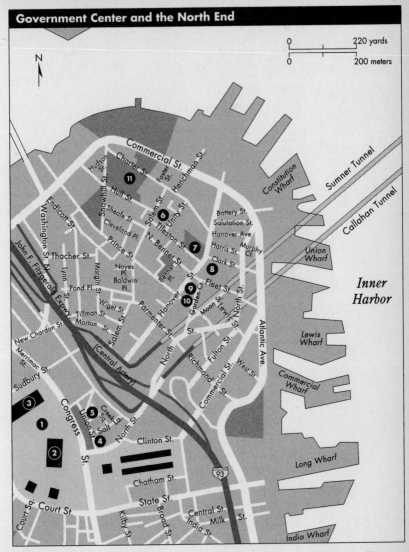

0       220 yards

0       200 meters

N

Commercial St.

Hudson St.

Charter St.

Hull St.

Foster St.

Henchman St.

Constitution Wharf

Sumner Tunnel

Callahan Tunnel

Snowhill St.

Sheafe St.

Cleveland Pl.

Salem St.

Tileston St.

Unity St.

Battery St.

Salutation St.

Hanover Ave.

Harris St.

Murphy Ct.

Union Wharf

Endicott St.

Washington St.

Thacher St.

Prince St.

N. Bennet St.

Clark St.

Inner Harbor

John F. Fitzgerald Expwy.

Lynn St.

Margin St.

Noyes Pl.

Baldwin Pl.

Bennet Pl.

Fleet St.

Garden Ct.

Lewis Wharf

Pond Pl.

Wiger St.

Parmenter St.

Hanover St.

Moon St.

Lewis St.

North St.

Atlantic Ave.

New Chardon St.

Tillman St.

Morton St.

Salem St.

Commercial Wharf

Merrimac St.

Sudbury St.

(Central Artery)

North St.

Richmond St.

Fulton St.

Commercial St.

West St.

Congress St.

Creek Sq.

Union St.

Salt St.

North St.

Clinton St.

Long Wharf

Chatham St.

93

State St.

Court Sq.

Court St.

Kilby St.

Broad St.

Central St.

Milk St.

India St.

India Wharf

Boston Stone, 5
City Hall, 2
Copp's Hill Burying Ground, 11
Government Center, 1
John F. Kennedy Federal Office Building, 3
Old North Church, 6

Paul Revere House, 9
Paul Revere Mall, 7
Pierce-Hichborn House, 10
St. Stephen's Church, 8
Union Oyster House, 4

**❸** The twin towers adjacent to City Hall Plaza constitute the **John F. Kennedy Federal Office Building,** designed by the Bauhaus founder Walter Gropius, who lived and taught in the Boston area toward the end of his life. Gropius's home, which he designed in textbook Bauhaus style, is in nearby suburban Lincoln; it is on the property roster of SPNEA and is open to visitors (inquire at SPNEA, 141 Cambridge St.).

Behind City Hall, past a small thatch of streets that survived urban renewal and an overhead expressway that will not, stands the oldest neighborhood in Boston and one of the oldest in the New World. Men and women walked the narrow streets of the North End when Shakespeare was not yet 20 years dead and Louis XIV was new to the throne of France. The town of Boston bustled and grew rich here for a century and a half before American independence. In the 17th century the North End *was* Boston, for much of the rest of the peninsula was still under water or had yet to be cleared of brush.

The North End visible to us today is almost entirely a creature of the late 19th century, when brick tenements began to fill with European immigrants. The Irish and the Jews both had their day here, but the Italians, more recent arrivals, have stayed. For more than 60 years the North End has been Italian Boston, so much so that one wonders whether the Puritan shades might scowl at the Mediterraneans' verve, volubility, and Roman Catholicism. This is not only a district of Italian restaurants (there are dozens) but of Italian groceries, bakeries, churches, social clubs, cafes, festivals honoring saints and food, and street-corner debates over soccer games.

Since the mid-1970s, change has been in the air. The conversion of wharves along the nearby waterfront to apartments, condos, and boutiques has brought pressures that have breached the boundaries of this neighborhood in which it was once hard to find an apartment unless you knew someone. Now it is a rare block in which one or more tenements have not gotten the exposed brick and track-lighting treatment; "gentrification" is a word that makes some of the old guard nervous (the others sell). It is unlikely that the North End will soon fall to being Italian in name and menu only; the people with Abruzzese accents that you see on Salem and Hanover streets are not paid actors, and they are not all going to move away tomorrow. However, the Italian population here is aging, and a recent estimate indicates that its numbers have dwindled to about half of the neighborhood total.

To get to the North End, walk down the steps at the rear of City Hall Plaza and cross New Congress Street. Faneuil Hall and the statue of Samuel Adams are off to your right. Closer at hand, in the vest-pocket park framed by New Congress Street and Dock Square, are two less conventional bronze statues, one seated on a bench and the other standing eye to eye with passersby. Both represent James Michael Curley, mayor, governor, congressman, and model for all urban bosses. It is well that he has no pedestal; he was much more a man than an idol.

**❹** Turn left and walk past the **Union Oyster House.** The building was first the residence and shop of Hopestill Capen in 1714, and in 1771–1775 Isaiah Thomas published the *Massachusetts Spy* here. The city's oldest restaurant, the Union Oyster House has been operating on this site since 1826. Follow Marshall Street

**⑤** behind the Oyster House and past the **Boston Stone**, set into
the brick wall of the gift shop of the same name. This was a
paint-mixing stone, older than the 1737 date the inscription
suggests, that was long used as milepost zero in measuring dis-
tances from Boston. Marshall Street leads into Blackstone
Street, where on weekends pushcart vendors sell fish, fruit,
and vegetables. This is commonly called the Haymarket,
though the Haymarket Square bus and subway stop is farther
down New Congress Street, behind the big parking garage.

**Time Out**    You are near the **Pizzeria Regina** (11½ Thatcher St.) and what
many consider the best pizza in Boston, if not in America: It's
thin-crusted, oily, and wonderful. There are branches, but this
is the one to go to. Ask for directions; the North End can be a
maze.

As you cross Blackstone Street on your way to the passage beneath the Fitzgerald Expressway (named for John Kennedy's
grandfather, Mayor John "Honey Fitz" Fitzgerald), look down
at the bronze sculptures of everyday garbage embedded in the
pavement. This was done in 1976 in whimsical reproduction
of a typical afternoon's debris. The work of Mags Harries,
*Asaroton* takes its name from the Greek word for unswept
floors.

The **Fitzgerald Expressway** appears to be not long for this
earth. After years of wrangling, federal funding has been ap-
proved for replacing the structure with an underground central artery that will carry a larger volume of traffic. Along with
the planned third harbor tunnel to Logan Airport, the project
is expected to take nearly until the end of the century to complete. In the meantime we may expect traffic tie-ups as the job
proceeds.

Opposite the pedestrian tunnel beneath the expressway is the
beginning of Salem Street, an ancient and constricted thoroughfare of meat markets, kitchen-supply shops, barrels of olives and *baccala* (salt cod), and one or two stores selling
furniture that makes the late Rococo look staid. It is an agreeable old street filled with fine smells, especially as you reach the
coffee and spice shop at the corner of Parmenter Street. A few
steps to the right on Parmenter will take you to the North End
branch of the **Boston Public Library**, where a bust of Dante ac-
knowledges local cultural pride. (There is no corresponding
bust of Yeats or Joyce in the South Boston branch.)

Stay on Salem Street beyond the point where the stores thin
out; up ahead is the church famous for two lanterns that glim-
mered from its steeple on the night of April 18, 1775. Christ
**⑥** Church, the **Old North Church** (1723), the oldest church building in Boston, was designed by William Price from a study of
Christopher Wren's London churches. It is best known for the
tower from which the signal lanterns of Paul Revere flashed
warning to Charlestown of British troop movements. (The
original tower blew down in 1804; the present one was put up in
1954 after yet another gale). But the Old North, still the home
of an active Episcopal congregation (including members of the
Revere family), is an impressive building in its own right. Inside, note the graceful layout of pews (reserved in Colonial
times for the families that rented them) and gallery; the bust of
George Washington, pronounced by the Marquis de Lafayette

to be the best likeness of the general he ever saw; the brass chandeliers, made in Amsterdam in 1700 and installed here in 1724; and the clock, the oldest still running in an American public building. Try to visit when changes on the bells are scheduled to be rung; recently restored and rehung, they bear the inscription, "We are the first ring of bells cast for the British Empire in North America." The work of the English bell foundry of Abel Rudhall, the bells today sound as sweet as when the boy Paul Revere rang them on Sabbath mornings. A small museum next to the church houses such artifacts as a musket from the battle of Lexington and a vial of tea decanted from the boots of a participant in the Boston Tea Party. *Tel. 617/523–6676. Open daily 9–5. Sun. services at 9, 11, and 4. Closed Thanksgiving.*

**7** Immediately behind the Old North Church and across Unity Street is the **Prado, or Paul Revere Mall,** lined with bronze plaques that tell the stories of famous North Enders and centering on Cyrus Dallin's equestrian statue of Paul Revere. It may surprise visitors who are largely familiar with Revere through Longfellow's "Midnight Ride" and statues such as this to know that the man was stocky and of medium height; whatever dash he possessed was in his eyes rather than his physique. That physique served him well enough, for he lived to be 83 and buried nearly all his revolutionary comrades.

The **Ebenezer Clough House** (not open to the public), built in 1712 and now the only local survivor of its era aside from the Old North, stands at 21 Unity Street. This spot requires an exercise in imagination: Picture the streets lined with houses such as this, with an occasional grander Georgian mansion and modest wooden survivors of old Boston's many fires, and you will come to an approximation of what the North End looked like when Paul Revere was young.

**8** The Prado opens onto Hanover Street, named for the ruling dynasty of 18th-century England. Almost directly opposite is **St. Stephen's,** the only Bulfinch church still standing in Boston. A rebuilding in 1802 of an earlier structure, it has served as a Catholic parish since 1862. *Open daily 8:30–5. Sun. services at 8:30 and 11; daily services at 7:30 PM.*

A left turn at St. Stephen's will take you to the harbor end of Hanover Street and the Boston headquarters of the U.S. Coast Guard (not open to visitors); a right turn at the Coast Guard Station takes you to the waterfront park and the restored wharves off Atlantic Avenue. A right turn at the church takes you through the business blocks of Hanover Street, thick with pastry shops and Italian espresso houses.

**Time Out** | **Caffe Vittoria** (296 Hanover St.) specializes in cappuccino and special coffee drinks; its Old World cafe ambience makes it a great spot at any hour. Next door, **Mike's Pastry** (300 Hanover St.) has fresh ricotta, cannoli, and other Italian pastries.

Beyond Hanover Street, by way of Fleet Street and Garden Court, is North Square. Here is the oldest house in Boston, the **9** **Paul Revere House,** built nearly a hundred years before Revere's 1775 midnight ride through Middlesex County. He owned it from 1770 until 1800, although he and his wife (Rachel Revere, for whom the facing park is named) rented it out during the later part of that period. The house was restored about

1905, after a century of disrepair; pre-1900 photographs show it as a shabby warren of storefronts and apartments. The clapboard sheathing is a replacement, but 90% of the framework is original. The downstairs is furnished as it would have been in the 17th century, while the second floor reflects the time of Revere's occupancy (although few of the articles are his own). The self-guided tour makes use of explanatory notes mounted on the railings that extend through the rooms. Attendants are available to answer questions. *19 North Sq., tel. 617/523–1676. Admission: $2 adults, 75¢ children 5–17, $1.50 senior citizens and college students. Open Apr. 15–Oct. 31, daily 9:30–5:15; other times until 4:15. Closed holidays and Mon. Jan–Mar.*

**⑩** Next door is the brick **Pierce-Hichborn** (or Hitchborn) **House,** one of the city's oldest brick buildings, once owned by relatives of Revere's mother. *29 North Sq., tel. 617/523–1676. Admission: $2 adults, 75¢ children 5–18, $1.50 senior citizens and college students. Combined admission for the Paul Revere and Pierce-Hichborn houses: $3.25 adults, $1 children 5–18, $2.25 senior citizens and college students. Open daily for guided tours only at 12:30 and 2:30.*

Most of the North End's historic sites are to be found east of Salem Street in the area we have just been exploring, and we must backtrack across Salem into the steep and narrow residential streets to savor the old Italian flavor of the neighbor-
**⑪** hood. Keep walking uphill and you will reach the **Copp's Hill Burying Ground,** which incorporates four cemeteries established between 1660 and 1819. Near the Charter Street gate is the tomb of the Mather family, the dynasty of divines (Cotton and Increase were the most famous sons) who held sway in Boston during the heyday of the old theocracy. Many headstones were chipped by practice shots fired by British soldiers during the occupation of Boston, and a number of the musketball pockmarks can still be seen. Of all Boston's early cemeteries, Copp's Hill seems most to preserve an ancient and melancholic air. *Open daily 9–4.*

## Tour 4. Charlestown

*Numbers in the margin correspond with points of interest on the Charlestown map.*

The view from Copp's Hill to the north encompasses the mouth of the Charles and much of Charlestown, and it is dominated by the spars and rigging of the USS *Constitution* and the spare granite obelisk of the Bunker Hill Monument. Both ship and monument, and the Charlestown neighborhoods that adjoin them, can be reached via the Charlestown Bridge; from Copp's Hill, turn left on Charter Street, descend to Commercial Street, and turn left again to reach the bridge.

The USS *Constitution,* nicknamed Old Ironsides for the strength of its oaken hull, not because of any iron plating, is the oldest commissioned ship in the U.S. Navy. As such, the men and women who look after her are regular Navy personnel. She
**❶** is moored at a national historic site, the **Charlestown Navy Yard,** one of six established to build warships. For 174 years, as wooden hulls and muzzle-loading cannon gave way to steel ships and sophisticated electronics, the yard evolved to meet the changing needs of a changing navy.

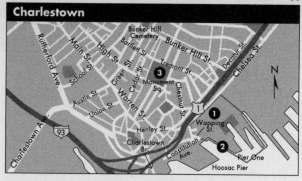

You come upon the entrance almost immediately after alighting
from the Charlestown Bridge (the No. 93 bus from Haymarket
Square, Boston, stops three blocks from the entrance, and in
summer there are boats from Long Wharf, Boston). In addition
to the *Constitution*, visitors may tour the USS *Cassin Young*, a
World War II destroyer typical of the ships built here during
that era; the museum; the commandant's house; and the collections of the Boston Marine Society. The Yard itself is a virtual
museum of American shipbuilding for almost her entire history. Here are early 19th-century barracks, workshops, and offi-
cers' quarters; a ropewalk (an elongated building for making
rope) designed in 1834 by the Greek Revival architect Alexander Parris and used by the Navy to turn out cordage for more
than 125 years; and one of the two oldest dry docks (the one
nearer the entrance) in the United States. The *Constitution*
was first to use this dry dock (in 1833), and in late 1992 the ship
will enter Dry Dock I for repairs in preparation for her 200th
birthday in 1997. *Tel. 617/242–5670. Admission free to the Constitution. Open daily 9–5.*

**2** *The* **USS** *Constitution* was launched in Boston, where Constitution Wharf now stands, in 1797. Her principal service was during Thomas Jefferson's campaign against the Barbary pirates,
off the coast of North Africa, and in the War of 1812. She never
lost an engagement. Sailors show visitors around the ship, taking them below decks to see the impossibly cramped living
quarters and the places at the guns where the desperate and
difficult work of naval warfare under sail was carried out. *Tel.
617/426–1812. Admission to the museum: $2.50 adults, $1.50
senior citizens and children 6–16. Open winter, Mon.–Fri.
9–4, Sat. and Sun. 9–5; spring and fall, daily 9–5; summer,
daily 9–6.*

The phrase "Battle of Bunker Hill" is one of America's most famous misnomers. The battle was fought on Breed's Hill, and
that is where Solomon Willard's 220-foot shaft of Quincy granite stands. The monument, for which the Marquis de Lafayette
laid the cornerstone in 1825, rises from the spot occupied by the
southeast corner of the American redoubt on the hot afternoon
of June 17, 1775. That was the day on which a citizen's militia,
commanded by Colonel William Prescott not to fire "till you see
the whites of their eyes," inflicted more than 1,100 casualties
on the British regulars (who eventually seized the hill). It was a
Pyrrhic victory for the British; the brave American defense
greatly boosted Colonial morale. Among the dead were the

brilliant young American doctor and political activist Joseph Warren, recently commissioned as a major general but fighting as a private, and the British Major Pitcairn, who two months before had led the redcoats into Lexington. Pitcairn is buried in the crypt of the Old North. Warren lay in a shallow grave on Breed's Hill until the British evacuation of Boston, when his remains were disinterred and buried ceremoniously in the Old Granary. How was the body identified? Warren's dentist recognized his handiwork in a pair of false teeth secured with silver wire. The "dentist" was Paul Revere, a jack and master of many trades, who made the teeth's silver springs.

**3** Ascend the **Bunker Hill Monument** (Main Street to Monument Street, then straight uphill) by a flight of 295 steps. There is no elevator, but the views from the observatory are worth the climb. At the base, four dioramas tell the story of the battle; ranger programs are given hourly. (Another Bunker Hill presentation, the multimedia show "Whites of Their Eyes," is shown in a pavilion near the Navy Yard entrance.) If you are in Boston on June 17, go to the hill to see a full-scale historical demonstration. *Admission free. Lodge open daily 9–5, monument until 4:30. Closed Thanksgiving, Christmas, and New Year's Day.*

The blocks around the Bunker Hill Monument are a good illustration of a neighborhood in flux. Elegantly restored Federal and mid-19th-century town houses stand cheek by jowl with working-class quarters of similar vintage but more modest recent pasts. Nearby Winthrop Square also has its share of interesting houses. Farther north along Main Street is City Square, Charlestown's main commercial district. On Phipps Street you'll find the grave of John Harvard, a young minister who in 1638 bequeathed his small library to the fledgling Cambridge College, which was to be renamed in his honor. The precise location of the grave is uncertain, but a monument of 1828 marks its approximate site. John Harvard is also commemorated in the nearby Harvard Mall, a vest-pocket park.

## Tour 5. Downtown Boston

*Numbers in the margin correspond with points of interest on the Downtown Boston map.*

The financial district—what Bostonians usually refer to as "downtown"—is off the beaten track for visitors who are concentrating on following the Freedom Trail, yet there is much to see in a walk of an hour or two. There is little logic to the streets here; they are, after all, village lanes that only happen to be lined with 40-story office towers. Just as the great fire of 1872 swept the old financial district clear, the downtown construction of the past two decades has obliterated many of the buildings where Boston businessmen of Silas Lapham's day sat at their rolltop desks.

The area is anchored at one end by Faneuil Hall and Quincy Market, at the other by South Station and Chinatown. It is bordered by Tremont Street and the Common on the west, by the harbor wharves on the east. Natives may be able to navigate the tangle of thoroughfares in between, but few of them manage to give intelligible directions when asked, and you will be better off trusting to a map. The area may be confusing, but it is mercifully small.

Just south of Government Center, at the corner of Tremont and
❶ School streets, stands **King's Chapel,** built in 1754 and never
topped with the steeple that the architect Peter Harrison had
planned. The first chapel on this site was erected in 1688, when
Sir Edmund Andros, the royal governor whose authority tem-
porarily replaced the original Colonial charter, appropriated
the land for the establishment of an Anglican place of worship.
This rankled the Puritans, who had left England to escape An-
glicanism and had until then kept it out of the colony. (In the
1780s King's Chapel became the first American church to em-
brace a new threat to congregationalist orthodoxy called Uni-
tarianism.)

It took five years to build the solid Quincy granite structure. As
construction proceeded, the old church continued to stand
within the walls of the new, to be removed in pieces when the
stone chapel was completed. The builders then went to work on
the interior, which remains essentially as they finished it, a
masterpiece of elegant proportions and Georgian calm. The
chapel's bell is Paul Revere's largest and, in his opinion, his
sweetest-sounding. *Open Tues.–Sat. 10–4, Sun. 1–4. Sun.
service at 11. Music program Tues. 12:15–12:45.*

The adjacent **King's Chapel Burying Ground,** the oldest in the
city, contains the remains of the first Massachusetts governor,
John Winthrop, and several generations of his descendants.
Here, too, are many other tombs of Boston worthies of three
centuries ago. Two markers recall individuals famous for less
conventional reasons. Take the path to the right from the entrance and then left by the chapel to the gravestone (1704) of
Elizabeth Pain, the model for Hester Prynne in Hawthorne's
*The Scarlet Letter.* The prominent slate monument near the entrance to the yard tells (in French) the story of the Chevalier de
Saint-Sauveur, a young officer who was part of the first French
contingent that arrived to help the rebel Americans in 1778. He
was killed in a riot that began when hungry Bostonians were
told they could not buy the bread the French were baking for
their men with their own wheat—an awkward situation made
worse by the language barrier. The chevalier's internment
here was probably the occasion for the first Catholic mass in
what has since become a predominantly Catholic city.

Follow School Street down from King's Chapel (away from Tremont, with the Parker House Hotel on your right) and pass the
**old City Hall,** with Richard S. Greenough's bronze statue of
**Benjamin Franklin** (1855), which was Boston's first portrait
sculpture. Franklin was born (1706) a few blocks from here on
Milk Street and attended the Boston Latin School, founded
near the City Hall site in 1635. (The school has long since moved
to the avenue Louis Pasteur, near the Fenway.) Franklin, as a
young man, went to Philadelphia, where he lived most of his
long life. Boston's municipal government moved to the new City
Hall in the 1960s, and the old Second Empire building now
houses a French restaurant.

At the Washington Street corner of School Street stands the
❷ **Globe Corner Bookstore** (*see* Shopping), until recently a museum of old editions and now once again a working bookstore,
thanks to the good offices of the *Boston Globe.* It was built in
1718, and throughout most of the 19th century it counted
among its clientele the leading lights of literary society—Emerson, Holmes, Longfellow, Lowell. The seminally important

# Downtown Boston

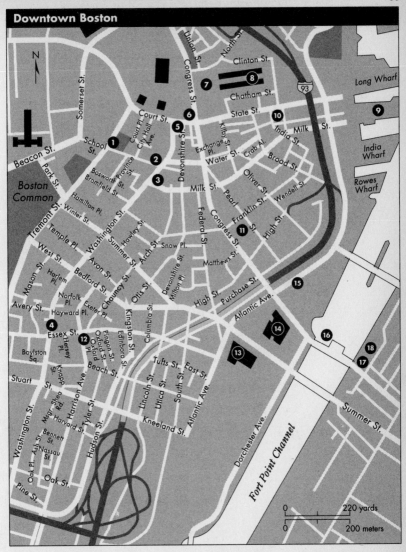

Boston publishers Ticknor and Fields also had offices here. Among the store's specialties are books about New England, books by New England authors, and travel titles.

**Time Out**  Rebecca's Café (56 High St.), with an array of fresh salads, sandwiches, and homemade pastries, is a comfortable place to stop for a casual lunch.

❸ The **Old South Meeting House** is a short block to the right down Washington Street, at the corner of Milk. Built in 1729, it is Boston's second oldest church. Unlike the older Old North, the Old South is no longer the seat of an active congregation. And its principal associations have always been more secular than religious. Some of the fieriest of the town meetings that led to the Revolution were held here, culminating in the tumultuous gathering of December 16, 1773, called by Samuel Adams to face the problem of three ships, laden with dutiable tea, anchored at Griffin's Wharf. The activists wanted the tea returned to England, the governor would not permit it—and the rest is history. To cries of "Boston harbor a tea-pot tonight" and John Hancock's "Let every man do what is right in his own eyes," the protestors poured out of the Old South, headed to the wharf with waiting comrades, and dumped £18,000 worth of tea into the water.

The Old South suffered no small amount of indignity in the ensuing Revolution. Its pews were ripped out by occupying British troops, and the interior was used as a riding school by Burgoyne's light dragoons. A century later it escaped destruction in the Great Fire of 1872, only to be threatened with demolition by developers. Aside from the windows and doors, the only original interior features surviving today are the tiered galleries above the main floor. The pulpit is a reproduction of the one used by colonial divines and secular firebrands. Public contributions saved the church, and it remains open to visitors today. *Tel. 617/482-6439. Admission: $2 adults, 75¢ children 6–18, $1.50 students and senior citizens. Open Apr. 1–Oct. 31, daily 9:30–5; Nov. 1–Mar. 31, weekdays 10–4, weekends 10–5. Lecture-concert series (free with admission) Oct.–Apr., Thurs. 12:15.*

Washington Street is the main commercial street of downtown Boston. Turning left on leaving the Old South, you follow a pedestrian mall and pass many of the area's major retail establishments (don't overlook the side streets). Soon you reach the two venerable anchors of Boston's mercantile district, Filene's and Jordan Marsh (*see* Shopping). William Filene founded his Boston store in 1881 near the site of the present eight-story building (1912). The famous automatic bargain basement was an innovation of his son, Edward Filene. Jordan Marsh was the creation of Eben Jordan, who arrived in Boston from Maine around 1840 with $1.25 in his pocket and opened Jordan Marsh (Marsh was a partner) in 1851. The huge store has been expanding on its Washington Street site since 1871, most recently with a spacious addition in the late 1970s.

Just beyond Jordan Marsh is Lafayette Place, a development opened in 1985. The indoor complex incorporates shops, 23 restaurants, and a 500-room hotel. This development is part of the ❹ pressure being brought to bear on the **Combat Zone** of lower Washington Street, a two-block area of nude-dancing bars, peep shows, "adult" bookstores, and "adult" movie houses. The Combat Zone was an early 1970s experiment that concentrated these establishments and their clientele in a small, easily circumscribed area following the demolition of Scollay Square. The Combat Zone occasionally lives up to its name; while it is not particularly dangerous during the daytime, it is not to be recommended to the casual stroller at night. Any advice we might offer on visiting or not visiting the Combat Zone may soon be irrelevant: Given downtown Boston's real estate climate, it's bound to be obliterated within the next few years.

Pressing on the Combat Zone from the other direction (on and about Stuart Street) are the Tufts New England Medical Center, Chinatown (which also perceives a threat from Tufts' expansion), and Boston's theater district. The theater district is small: The Wilbur, Shubert, and Colonial theaters and the Wang Center for the Performing Arts all cluster near the intersection of Tremont and Stuart streets. Yet the area does an increasingly lively business booking Broadway tryouts, road shows, and big-name recitals.

A right turn onto Washington Street from the doorstep of the Old South will take you past the Globe Corner Bookstore once again, past Pi Alley (named after the loose type, or "pi," spilled from the pockets of printers when upper Washington Street was Boston's newspaper row—or after colonial pie shops, depending on the story you believe), and to the rear of the Old State House near the intersection of Court Street.

**❺** The **Old State House** was the seat of the Colonial government from 1713 until the Revolution, and after the evacuation of the British from Boston in 1776 it served the independent Commonwealth until the new State House on Beacon Hill was completed. John Hancock was inaugurated here as the first governor under the new state constitution. Like many Colonial-era landmarks, it fared poorly in the years that followed. Mid-19th century photos show the old building clumsily chimnied and mansarded, with signs in the windows advertising a variety of businesses. In the 1830s the Old State House served as Boston City Hall. When demolition was threatened in the name of improving the traffic flow, the Bostonian Society organized a restoration, completed in 1882. Today its focus is upon the Colonial and early republican history of Boston; collections include the clothing John Hancock wore at his inauguration as governor, Revolutionary War artifacts, and historical paintings. The museum incorporates the holdings of the Marine Museum, until recently a separate entity on the same premises. This collection is made up of ship models, nautical paintings, and memorabilia of the days of sail. *206 Washington St., tel. 617/720–3290. Admission: $1.25 adults, 50¢ children 6–16, 75¢ senior citizens and college students, free to Massachusetts schoolchildren. Open Apr. 1–Nov. 1, daily 9:30–5; Nov. 1–Mar. 31, daily 10–4. The Old State House reopens in the spring of 1992, following more than a year's worth of structural renovations. Call for current ticket prices and hours.*

A brightly colored lion and unicorn, symbols of British imperial power, appear at the gable ends of the State Street facade of the Old State House. The originals were pulled down in 1776. For proof that bygones are bygones, we may look not only to the restoration of the sculptures but to the fact that Queen Elizabeth II stood on the Old State House balcony and addressed a cheering crowd during the U.S. bicentennial celebration in 1976.

Directly in front of the Old State House is a circle of cobblestones marking a far more sober juncture in the relations between Great Britain and its erstwhile colonies. The stones ❻ mark the site of the **Boston Massacre,** which occurred on the snowy evening of March 5, 1770, when a small contingent of British regulars fired in panic upon a taunting mob of Bostonians. Five townsmen died. In the legal action that followed, the defense of the accused soldiers was undertaken by John Adams and Josiah Quincy, both of whom vehemently opposed British oppression but who were devoted to the principle of fair trial. All but two of the nine regulars charged were acquitted; the others were branded on the hand for manslaughter.

We head down State Street, known before the Revolution as King Street and even then a nascent center of finance. In the 19th century State Street was headquarters for banks, brokerages, and insurance firms; while these businesses have now spread throughout the downtown district, "State Street" retains much the same connotation in Boston that "Wall Street" has elsewhere. The early commercial hegemony of State Street was symbolized by Long Wharf, built originally in 1710 and extending some 1,700 feet into the harbor. If today's Long Wharf does not appear to be that long, it is not because it has been shortened but because the land has expanded around it. State Street once met the water at Kilby Street on the south and Merchants Row on the north. Landfill operations were pursued relentlessly through the years, and the old coastline is now as much a memory as such Colonial State Street landmarks as Governor Winthrop's 1630 house and the revolutionary-era Bunch of Grapes Tavern, where Bostonians met to drink and wax indignant at their treatment by the British.

Turning left off State Street onto Merchants Row, we leave the old financial marketplace and encounter, first, an historic marketplace of ideas and, second, an old provisions market reborn as the emblem of downtown revitalization. Faneuil Hall ("the Cradle of Liberty") and the Quincy Market (also known as Faneuil Hall Marketplace) face each other across a small square thronged with people at all but the smallest hours.

❼ Like so many Boston landmarks, **Faneuil Hall** (pronounced "Fan'l") has evolved over the years. The original structure was erected in 1742, the gift of Peter Faneuil, whose intention was that the hall serve as both a place for town meetings and a public market. It burned in 1761 and was immediately rebuilt according to the original plan of its designer, the Scottish portrait painter John Smibert.

In 1772, Samuel Adams stood here and first suggested that Massachusetts and the other colonies organize a Committee of Correspondence to maintain semiclandestine lines of communication in the face of hardening British repression. Nine years earlier, James Otis had helped inaugurate the era that culminated in American independence when he dedicated the rebuilt hall to the "cause of liberty." In later years the hall lived up to Otis's dedication when Wendell Phillips and Charles Sumner pleaded the abolitionist cause from its podium.

Faneuil Hall was substantially enlarged and remodeled in 1805 according to the design of Charles Bulfinch, and this is the building we see today. Its purpose remains the same; the great balconied hall is made available to citizens' groups on presentation of a request signed by a required number of responsible parties. In national election years the hall is usually host to debates featuring contenders in the Massachusetts presidential primary.

At ground level the mercantile purposes Faneuil had in mind are still served. But instead of the meats and produce available in timeworn stalls until a dozen years ago, today's visitor finds shops more in keeping with the tone of the nearby Quincy Market restoration.

Inside Faneuil Hall is the great mural *Webster's Reply to Hayne,* Stuart's portrait of Washington at Dorchester Heights, and dozens of other paintings of famous Americans. On the top floors are the headquarters and museum of the **Ancient and Honorable Artillery Company of Massachusetts,** the oldest militia in the nation (1638). Its status is now ceremonial, but it is justly proud of the arms, uniforms, and other artifacts on display.

Why is there a weathervane in the shape of a grasshopper atop Faneuil Hall? One story has it that Sir Thomas Gresham, founder of the Royal Exchange in London, was found as an abandoned baby in a field in 1519 by children chasing grasshoppers. Gresham put a grasshopper weathervane atop the Exchange, of which Peter Faneuil became a member years later, and Faneuil liked the symbol and had one placed on Faneuil Hall. Today it is the symbol of the entire Quincy Market development. *Open Mon.–Sat. 9–5, Sun. 10–5. Closed Thanksgiving, Christmas, and New Year's Day. Faneuil Hall is scheduled to reopen in the spring of 1992, following more than a year's worth of structural renovations. Call for current hours.*

**8** **Quincy Market** consists of three structures, 535 feet in length, built to the design of Alexander Parris in 1826. The market is named after Boston mayor Josiah Quincy (not the Josiah Quincy who helped to defend the Boston Massacre soldiers), who promoted the project and the massive landfill operations that accompanied it to alleviate the cramped retailers' conditions in Faneuil Hall. The center building is of granite, with a Doric colonnade at either end and a classical dome and rotunda at the center; the north and south market buildings are predominantly brick.

Quincy Market served its purpose as a retail and wholesale distribution center for meat and produce for a century and a half. By the 1970s, though, the market area had become seedy. Some of the old tenants—the famous Durgin Park restaurant and a few butchers and grocers in the central building—had hung on through the years, but the old vitality had disappeared. Buildings were in disrepair and demolition was a distinct possibility. Fortunately, the old notions of urban renewal as something that had to be done with a bulldozer were beginning to yield to the idea of "recycling" buildings to new uses. With the participation of the Boston Redevelopment Authority, the architect Benjamin Thompson planned the renovation of all three Quincy Market buildings. The central structure has kept its traditional market-stall layout, but most of the new businesses on the first floor offer international and specialty foods (raw shellfish, cold pasta salads, sausages on sticks, cheesecake, baklava—you name it). Interspersed with these temptations are the updated stalls of provisioners who have been in the market since before you were born. Doe, Sullivan, the cheese seller, settled here in 1829.

Upstairs in the central building are sit-down restaurants, and along the arcades on either side are vendors selling photographs of Boston, silkscreened aprons, and boutique chocolate chip cookies. Nor is there a shortage of bars.

The north and south market buildings, separated from the central market by attractive pedestrian malls with trees and benches, house more substantial retail establishments, offices, and additional restaurants. There may be more restaurants in Quincy Market than existed in all of downtown Boston before World War II. Abundance and variety, albeit of an ephemeral sort, have been the watchwords of Quincy Market since its reopening in 1976. Some people consider it all hopelessly trendy; 50,000 visitors a day rather enjoy the extravaganza. You'll want to decide for yourself. *Open Mon.–Sat. 10–9, Sun. noon–6. Restaurants and bars generally open daily 11 AM–2 AM.*

At the end of Quincy Market opposite Faneuil Hall, the newly constructed **Marketplace Center,** between the market buildings and the expressway is filled with shops and boutiques. Beyond is Columbus Park, bordering on the harbor and on several of Boston's restored wharves. **Lewis Wharf** and **Commercial Wharf,** which long lay nearly derelict, had by the mid-1970s been transformed into condominiums, apartments, restaurants, and upscale shops. **Long Wharf** holds a new hotel designed to be compatible with the old seaside warehouses. Sailboats and power yachts ride here at anchor; Boston's workaday waterfront is now located along the docks of South Boston, in East Boston (directly opposite Columbus Park), and in the huge containerized shipping facilities at the mouth of the Mystic.

**Central Wharf,** immediately to the right of Long Wharf as you face the harbor, is the home of one of Boston's most popular attractions, the **New England Aquarium.** Here you'll find seals, penguins, a variety of sharks and other sea creatures—over 2,000 species in all, some of which make their home in the aquarium's four-story, 187,000-gallon observation tank, the largest of its kind in the world. Ramps wind around the tank, leading to the top and allowing visitors to view the inhabitants from many vantage points. Feeding time should not be missed; since it happens five times a day, you'll probably catch it at least once. The procedure lasts nearly an hour and takes divers 23 feet into the tank. There are also dolphin and sea lion shows aboard *Discovery,* a floating marine mammal pavilion, and whale watch cruises. The aquarium was for many years the winter home of the late André the Seal, made famous in a popular children's book. André summered in the Gulf of Maine and returned to the Aquarium each fall; having lived a full seal lifetime, André passed away in Maine in 1986, and all New England mourned him. *Tel. 617/973–5200 (whale watch information, 617/973–5277). Admission: $7 adults, $3.50 children 3–15, $6 senior citizens; free Thurs. after 4PM from Oct. to Apr. Open weekdays 9–5, Thurs. until 8, weekends 9–6. Closed Thanksgiving, Christmas, and New Year's Day.*

If you backtrack on Central Wharf and along Milk Street beneath the expressway, you will soon arrive at an open square dominated by a Greek Revival temple that appears to have sprouted a tower. That is just what it is. This is the **U.S. Custom House** (1847), the work of the architects Ammi Young and Isaiah Rogers. That is, the bottom part is their work. The tower (would skyscrapers have looked like this if they were built in the 1840s?) was added in 1915, making the Custom House the city's tallest building. Note the grafting job that was done on the great rotunda, surmounted by its handsome dome; the dome's outer surface was once the room of the building, and now it is imbedded in the base of the tower.

The U.S. Customs Service having moved into more modern quarters, the Custom House has been sold to the city of Boston, which is considering how the distinctive structure might best be used. We should hope that any renovation will include a reopening of the 25th-floor observatory, which offers a fine panorama of downtown Boston and the harbor. And they might fix the great four-sided clock, each side of which now gives a different time.

Virtually all tangible historical associations in the Government Center area were obliterated in the demolition of Scollay Square and the surrounding streets. It was in a garret on one of these streets that Alexander Graham Bell first transmitted a human voice—his own—by telephone. When the building where Bell had his workshop was torn down in the 1920s, the phone company had the room dismantled and reassembled in the headquarters lobby of the **New England Telephone Building.** There the room looks just as it did on June 3, 1875, when Bell first coaxed his voice across a wire. (His famous call to Thomas Watson, "Come here, I want you," was made nearly a year later in another part of town.) Telephone memorabilia and a 160-foot mural tell the story of the phone. *185 Franklin St. Admission free. Open weekdays 8:30–5.*

One corner of downtown that has been relatively untouched by high-rise development is the old **leather district,** which is nestled into the angle formed by Kneeland Street and Atlantic Avenue opposite South Station. This was the wholesale supply area for raw materials in the days when the shoe industry was a regional economic mainstay, and a few leather firms are still located here. The leather district is probably the best place in downtown Boston to get an idea of what the city's business blocks looked like in the late 19th century.

The leather district directly abuts **Chinatown,** which is also bordered by the Combat Zone and the buildings of the Tufts New England Medical Center. The Massachusetts Turnpike and its junction with the Southeast Expressway are another presence here, serving to isolate Chinatown from the South End in much the same way the Fitzgerald Expressway isolates the North End from downtown.

Chinatown's borders may be constrained, yet it remains one of the larger concentrations of Chinese-Americans in the United States, and it is a vibrant center for both the private and the public aspects of local Chinese culture. As in most American Chinatowns, it is the concentration of restaurants that attracts the visitors, and today the numerous Chinese establishments are interspersed with a handful of Vietnamese eateries—a reflection of the latest wave of immigration into Boston.

Most Chinese restaurants, food stores, and retail businesses are located along Beach and Tyler streets and Harrison Avenue. The area around the intersection of Kneeland Street and Harrison Avenue is the center of Boston's textile and garment industry, and a number of shops here specialize in discount yard goods (*see* Shopping).

**Time Out** It's a special treat to sample the Chinese baked goods in shops along Beach Street. Many visitors familiar with Cantonese and even Szechuan cookery will still be surprised and delighted with moon cakes, steamed cakes made with rice flour, and other sweets that seldom turn up on restaurant menus.

**⑬ South Station,** the colonnaded granite structure at the intersection of Atlantic Avenue and Summer Street, is the terminal for all Amtrak trains in and out of Boston. Behind the station's grand 1900s facade, a major renovation project has converted the terminal into a modern, intermodal transit center. As the Dewey Square area is one of Boston's most active renewal districts (witness the new Dewey Square Tower and the multistructure International Place, dominated by a cylindrical tower punctuated by hundreds of postmodern Palladian windows), it is appropriate that the old station was made over into an arrival-and-departure point worthy of a great city.

**⑭** Walk down Atlantic Avenue from South Station, past the strikingly designed **Federal Reserve Tower.** *600 Atlantic Ave., tel. 617/973–3451. Group tours by appointment.*

**⑮** Farther on along Atlantic Avenue, at the foot of Pearl Street, a plaque set into the wall of a commercial building marks the site of the **Boston Tea Party.** That this was the site of Griffin's Wharf is only further evidence of Boston's relentless expansion into its harbor: The narrow Fort Point Channel is now all that separates the old Shawmut Peninsula from the once-distant neck of land that became South Boston.

**⑯** When you cross Fort Point Channel on the Congress Street Bridge, you encounter—on a pier at the middle of the bridge—the *Beaver II,* a faithful replica of one of the Tea Party ships that was forcibly boarded and unloaded on the night Boston Harbor became a teapot. It anchored here as a part of the bicentennial festivities in 1976 and has stayed on. The interpretive center on the adjacent pier contains exhibits explaining what happened on that cold evening and what led up to it. Visitors receive a complimentary cup of tea. *Admission: $5 adults, $3 children 5–14, $4 senior citizens and students. Open daily 9–5; sometimes closed in Jan. for repairs.*

**⑰** At the opposite end of the bridge—you are now in South Boston, though not the residential part—is Museum Wharf, home of the popular **Boston Children's Museum.** The multitude of hands-on exhibits designed with kids in mind includes a petting zoo of small animals, computers, video cameras, and exhibits designed to help children understand cultural diversity, their bodies, and disabilities. Don't miss Grandmother's Attic, where kids can dress up in old clothing. The museum shops are a good source of children's books and gifts. Check local listings or call for a schedule of special exhibits, festivals, and performances. *300 Congress St., tel. 617/426–6500 (617/426–8855 for recorded information). Admission: $6 adults, $5 children 2–15 and senior citizens; $1 Fri. 5–9. Open Tues.–Sun. 10–5, Fri. until 9 (admission $1 after 5). Closed Mon. except during Boston school vacations and holidays.*

**18** Museum Wharf is also the home of the world's only **Computer Museum,** housing exhibits chronicling the spectacular development of machines that calculate and process information. There are more than 75 exhibits, including a two-story, walk-through model of a desktop computer. Computer-animated films are shown daily. Given the importance of high technology to the local economy, the establishment of this institution is an act akin to the hanging of the sacred cod in the State House. *300 Congress St., tel. 617/426–2800. Admission: $6 adults, $5 children, senior citizens, and students; ½ price Sat. until noon. Open Tues.–Sun. 10–5, Fri. until 9. Closed Mon. except during school vacations; closed Fri. evenings in winter.*

At the Northern Avenue crossing of Fort Point Channel, one block up from Congress Street where the channel meets the harbor, is a vast empty space currently used for parking. This is the Fan Pier, site of a hotly disputed and defeated proposal to develop a city within a city that would have been the largest Boston public works project since the filling of the Back Bay. Plans for the area are again in limbo.

## The Harbor Islands

Head back to Rowes or Long Wharf and, in summer, you can board a boat that will take you to one of the most scenic and historically interesting, yet perhaps most consistently overlooked of Boston attractions: the **Harbor Islands.** There are more than two dozen islands in the inner and outer harbors, most of them incorporated into **Harbor Islands State Park.** Some of the islands housed military installations during World War II; others were the sites of hospitals, prisons, even raffish resort hotels. Most have now reverted to a seminatural state. The focal point of the park is 30-acre Georges Island, on which the pre–Civil War **Fort Warren** stands, partially restored and partially in ruins. Confederate prisoners were once housed here. Until the advent of modern long-range electronic defenses, coastal installations such as this were vital to the nation's security. Georges Island is reached in summer by pedestrian-only ferries from Long and Rowes wharves. *Boston Harbor Cruises, tel. 617/227–4320. Fare: $5 round-trip, late May–early Oct.*

On Georges, visitors can take free water taxis to Gallups, Lovells, Peddocks, Grape, and Bumpkin islands. Bumpkin and Gallups are small islands, easily explored within an hour or so; Lovells and Grape each cover about 60 acres. Peddocks Island's 185 acres are dotted with the ruins of Fort Andrews; guided tours are recommended. All the harbor islands are accessible by private boat, with the exception of Thompson's Island, an education center. Activities on the islands include picnicking, hiking (there are plenty of ruins to explore and beautiful views), and fishing. Swimming is permitted on Lovells. Lovells, Great Brewster, Grape, Bumpkin, and Peddocks Calf islands have campsites. A camping permit is required. MDC headquarters, 98 Taylor St., Dorchester, MA 02122, tel. 617/727–5290, for Lovells and Peddocks islands. Harbor Islands

State Park, 349 Lincoln St., Bldg. 45, Hingham, MA 02043, tel.
617/740-1605.

**Time Out**  The sea air is bound to give you an appetite. **Bon Vivant of
Rowes Wharf** carries a full line of picnic supplies, including
cheeses, cold cuts, breads, wine, even the baskets.

## Tour 6. The Back Bay

*Numbers in the margin correspond with points of interest on
the Back Bay, the South End, and the Fens map.*

In the folklore of American neighborhoods, the Back Bay
stands with New York's Park Avenue and San Francisco's Nob
Hill as a symbol of propriety and high social standing. You will
still occasionally hear someone described as coming from "an
old Back Bay family," as though the Back Bay were hundreds of
years old and its stone mansions the feudal bastions of the Puritan settlers from the time they got off the boat.

Nothing could be further from the truth. The Back Bay is one of
Boston's new neighborhoods, scarcely 125 years old. Before the
1850s it *was* a bay, a tidal flat that formed the south bank of a
distended Charles River. Remember, Boston since time im-
memorial has been a pear-shaped peninsula joined to the mainland by an isthmus (the Neck) so narrow that in early Colonial
times a single gate and guardhouse were sufficient for its defenses. Today's Washington Street, as it leaves downtown and
heads toward the South End, follows the old Neck.

Filling along the Neck began in 1850 and resulted in the creation of the South End neighborhood we will look at later. To
the north, a narrow causeway called the Mill Dam (later Beacon
Street) was built in 1814 to separate the Back Bay from the
Charles. Bostonians began to fill in the shallows in 1858, using
gravel brought from West Needham by railroad at a rate of up
to 3,500 carloads per day. It took 30 years to complete the filling
as far as the Fens. When the work was finished, the old 783-acre
peninsula had been expanded by approximately 450 acres.

Thus the actual Back Bay became the neighborhood of Back
Bay. Almost immediately, fashionable families began to decamp from Beacon Hill and the recently developed South End
and to establish themselves in the brick and brownstone row
houses they built upon the made land. Churches and cultural
institutions followed, until by 1900 the streets between the
Public Garden and Massachusetts Avenue had become unquestionably the smartest, most desirable neighborhood in all Boston. An air of permanence and respectability drifted in as
surely as the tides once had; the Back Bay mystique was born.

**❶** A walk through the Back Bay properly begins with the **Public
Garden,** the oldest botanical garden in the United States. Its
establishment marked the first phase of the Back Bay reclama-
tion project. Although the Garden is often lumped together
with the Common, even in the minds of natives, the two are separate entities with different histories and purposes and a distinct boundary at Charles Street. The Common, as we have
seen, has been public land since Boston was founded in 1630.
The Public Garden belongs to a newer Boston; it occupies what
had been salt marshes on the edge of the Common's dry land.

The marshes supported rope-manufacturing enterprises in the early 1800s, and by 1837 the tract was covered with an abundance of ornamental plantings donated by a private citizen. The area was fully defined in 1856 by the building of Arlington Street, and in 1860 (after the final wrangling over the development of this choice acreage) the architect George Meacham was commissioned to plan the park that survives to this day. The central feature of the Public Garden is its irregularly designed pond, intended to appear, from any vantage point along its banks, much larger than its nearly four acres. The pond has been famous since 1877 for its **swan boats,** which make leisurely cruises during the warm months of the year. Like the Esplanade, the Public Garden pond is favored by ducks, and for the price of a few boat rides and a stale loaf of bread you can amuse children here for a good hour or more. The bridge over the pond has been described as the world's smallest suspension bridge.

The Public Garden boasts the finest formal plantings to be seen in central Boston. They line the beds along the main walkways and are changed with the seasons. The spring planting of tulips is especially colorful. And there is a good sampling of native and European tree species.

The dominant work among the park's statuary is Thomas Ball's equestrian George Washington (1869), which faces the head of Commonwealth Avenue at the Arlington Street gate. This is Washington in a triumphant pose as liberator, surveying a scene that, from where he stood with his cannons at Dorchester Heights, would have comprised an immense stretch of blue water. A few yards to the north of Washington (to the right if you're facing Commonwealth Avenue) is the granite and red marble Ether Monument, donated in 1866 by Thomas Lee to commemorate the first use of anesthesia 20 years earlier at Massachusetts General Hospital. Other Public Garden monuments include statues of the pioneer Unitarian preacher and transcendentalist William Ellery Channing, at the corner opposite his Arlington Street church; the author (*The Man Without a Country*) and philanthropist Edward Everett Hale, at the Charles Street Gate; and the abolitionist senator Charles Sumner and the Civil War hero Colonel Thomas Cass, along Boylston Street. *Open dawn–10 PM. Not recommended for strolling after dark, even if you find a gate open. Swan boats: $1 adults, 75¢ children, mid-Apr.–late Sept.*

The mall that extends down the middle of Commonwealth Avenue also has its share of statuary. The most interesting memorial here is the newest one, the portrayal of Samuel Eliot Morison seated on a rock as if he were peering out to sea. The statue is at the Exeter Street intersection.

**Time Out**     The **Cafe Florian** (85 Newbury St.) is a sidewalk cafe that provides homemade soups, sandwiches, wine by the glass, pastries and coffee, and a perfect vantage point to people watch.

If a walk in the Public Garden has left you in a mood more for verdure than for bricks and mortar, take the Fiedler Footbridge (corner of Beacon and Arlington) to the **Esplanade,** which continues along the Charles River for the entire length of the Back Bay. The best place to begin exploring the streets of the Back Bay is at the corner of Commonwealth Avenue and Arlington Street, with Washington and his horse looking over

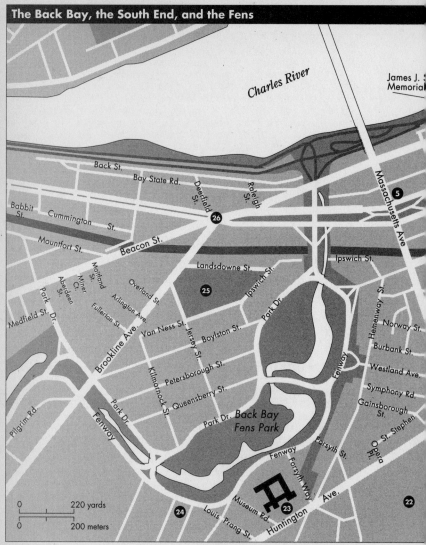

your shoulder. The grand design of the district is dramatically and immediately apparent here. The planners of the Back Bay were able to do something that had never before been possible in Boston: to lay out an entire neighborhood of arrow-straight streets. The planners were heavily influenced by the recent rebuilding of Paris according to the plans of Baron Haussmann. While other parts of Boston may be reminiscent of the mews and squares of London, the main thoroughfares of the Back Bay (especially Commonwealth Avenue) resemble nothing so much as they do Parisian boulevards.

Beginning at the Charles, the main east-west streets are Beacon Street, Marlborough Street, Commonwealth Avenue, Newbury Street, and Boylston Street. They are bisected by eight streets named in alphabetical order from Arlington to Hereford, with three-syllable street names alternating with two-syllable names. Service alleys run behind the main streets; though they are used now for garbage pickup and parking, they were built so that delivery wagons could be driven up to basement kitchens. That's how thorough the planning was.

Some aspects of the Back Bay, such as the way households were distributed, became matters more of change than of design. Old families with money congregated on Beacon Street, families with old Boston names but not much money gravitated to shady Marlborough. The nouveau riche tended to build on Commonwealth Avenue. Newbury and Boylston, originally residential rather than commercial streets, were the province of a mix of middle and upper middle class families, as were the side streets.

Back Bay is a living museum of urban Victorian residential architecture. The earliest specimens are nearest to the Public Garden (there are exceptions where showier turn-of-the-century mansions replaced 1860s town houses), and the newer examples are out around the Massachusetts Avenue and Fenway extremes of the district. The height of Back Bay residences and their distance from the street is essentially uniform, as are the interior layouts chosen according to lot width. Yet there is a distinct progression of facades, beginning with French academic and Italianate designs and moving through the various "revivals" of the 19th century. By the time of World War I, when development of the Back Bay was virtually complete, architects and their patrons had come full circle to a revival of the Federal period, which had been out of fashion for only 30 years when the filling began. If the Back Bay architects had not run out of land, they might have gotten around to a revival of Greek Revival.

An outstanding guide to the architecture and history of the Back Bay is Bainbridge Bunting's *Houses of Boston's Back Bay*, which is available in paperback in nearly all Boston bookstores. A reading of this thorough study can be expanded upon only by visits to Back Bay houses. A few are open to the public.

**❷** The **Gibson House** offers a representative look at how life was arranged in—and by—these tall, narrow, formal buildings. One of the first Back Bay residences (1859), the Gibson House is relatively modest in comparison with some of the grand mansions built during the decades that followed. Unlike other Back Bay houses, the Gibson family home has been preserved with all its Victorian fixtures and furniture intact—not restored, but preserved; a conservative family scion lived here until the 1950s and left things as they were. A stereopticon lies on a table in the study, a butler's pantry has a dumbwaiter and a copper-lined sink (so the dishes wouldn't scratch), the late 19th century basement kitchen is fully equipped, and a China Trade dinner service can be seen in the sumptuous second-floor dining room. Here you will understand why a squad of servants was a necessity in the old Back Bay. *137 Beacon St., tel. 617/ 267–6338. Admission: $3. Tours Wed.–Sun. at 1, 2, and 3.*

Among the grander Back Bay houses, two that now house public institutions can be entered for a view of at least their first-floor common areas. One is the **Baylies Mansion** (5 Commonwealth Ave.) of 1904, now the home of the Boston Center for Adult Education. Another is the **Burrage Mansion** (314 Commonwealth Ave.), built in 1899 in an extravagant French château style, complete with turrets and gargoyles, that reflects a cost-be-damned attitude uncommon even among the wealthiest Back Bay families. The Boston Evening Clinic is now housed in the Burrage house.

Two Back Bay mansions are the homes of organizations that promote foreign language and culture: the **French Library in Boston** (53 Marlborough St.) and the German-oriented **Goethe Institute** (170 Beacon St.) See the *Globe* Calendar section on Thursday for information on lectures, films, and other events in the handsome quarters of these respected institutions.

The largest Back Bay mansion is the **Oliver Ames Mansion** (355 Commonwealth Ave., corner of Massachusetts Ave.). Built in 1882 for a railroad baron and Massachusetts governor, this opulent château was recently renovated and now houses private offices and commercial shops.

The Great Depression brought an end to the old Back Bay style of living, and today only a few of the houses serve as single-family residences. Most have been cut up into apartments and, more recently, expensive condominiums. Interior details have experienced a mixed fate, suffering during the years when Victorian fashions were held in low regard and undergoing careful restoration now that the aesthetic pendulum has swung and moneyed condo buyers are demanding period authenticity. The blocks and blocks of original facades have survived on all but Newbury and Boylston streets, so the public face of the Back Bay remains much the same as it has always been. The greatest enemy of the brownstones is the weather; when water gets into cracks in the stones and freezes, it causes the spalling and defacement that is all too noticeable in buildings fronted with this porous material.

The Back Bay's residential streets are protected from incompatible development by strict zoning laws, yet the 20th century has hit hard along Newbury and Boylston streets. Newbury is Boston's Fifth Avenue, with Brooks Brothers, F. A. O. Schwarz, and dozens of specialty shops offering fashion clothing, china, antiques, paintings and prints, and expensive hardware. It is also a street of beauty salons and sidewalk cafes. Boylston Street, similarly busy but a little less posh, boasts elegant apparel shops. Here, too, is the severe pale gray stone mass of the **New England** (formerly New England Mutual Life Insurance) **Building,** within which are interesting murals and historical dioramas. Across from the New England's old headquarters (on the right between Berkeley and Clarendon as you face downtown) is the company annex, a huge postmodern structure at 500 Boylston Street.

**Time Out**  The **Harvard Book Store Cafe** (190 Newbury St.) serves meals or coffee and pastry—outdoors in nice weather. Since it's a real bookstore, you can browse to your heart's content.

Boylston Street, the southern commercial spine of the Back Bay, separates the sedate old district (some say not effectively enough) from the most ambitious developments this side of downtown. One block south of Boylston, on the corner of St. James Avenue and Clarendon Street, stands the tallest building in New England: the 62-story **John Hancock Tower,** built in the early 1970s and notorious in its early years as the building whose windows fell out. The stark and graceful reflective rhomboid tower, designed by I. M. Pei, had a problem with the loosening and dropping of its panes due to the seating of the glass in the sills and the wind torquing of the entire building. The problem was corrected: The building's 13 acres of glass were replaced to more rigorous standards, and the central core was stiffened. The 60th-floor observatory is one of the three best vantage points in the city, and the "Boston 1775" exhibit shows what the city looked like before the great hill-leveling and landfill operations commenced. *Observatory ticket office, Trinity Pl. and St. James Ave., tel. 617/247–1977. Admission: $2.75 adults, $2 children 5–15, and senior citizens. Open Mon.–Sat. 9 AM–10:15 PM, Sun. noon–10:15. Closed Thanksgiving and Christmas.*

The Hancock Tower stands at the edge of **Copley Square,** a civic space that is defined by three monumental older buildings. One is the stately, bowfronted **Copley Plaza Hotel,** which faces the square on St. James Avenue and serves as a dignified foil to two of the most important works of architecture in Boston, if not in the United States. At the left is **Trinity Church,** Henry Hobson Richardson's masterwork of 1877. In this church Richardson brought his Romanesque revival to maturity; all the elements for which Richardson was famous—bold polychromatic masonry, careful arrangement of masses, sumptuously carved interior woodwork—come together magnificently in Trinity.

A full appreciation of the architecture of Trinity Church requires an appreciation of the logistical problems of building it in this location. Remember, the Back Bay is a reclaimed wetland with a high water table; bedrock, or at least stable glacial till, lies far beneath the wet clay near the surface. Like all older Back Bay buildings, Trinity Church sits on submerged wooden pilings. But Trinity's central tower weighs 9,500 tons, and most of the 4,500 pilings beneath the church structure are under that tremendous central mass. The pilings are checked regularly, by means of a hatch in the subbasement, to make sure the water level is high enough to keep them from dry-rotting.

Don't miss the interior of Trinity Church. Richardson engaged some of the great artists of his day—John LaFarge, William Morris, and Edward Burne-Jones among them—to execute the paintings and stained glass that makes this a monument to everything that was right about the Pre-Raphaelite spirit and the nascent aesthetic of Morris's arts and crafts movement. LaFarge's brilliant paintings, including the intricate ornamentation of the vaulted ceilings, have been cleaned only once, in the late 1950s, and have never been substantially retouched. Today they look as though the paint were barely dry.

The Back Bay is a great neighborhood for ecclesiastical architecture. Many of the old downtown congregations relocated on the newly filled land and applied their considerable resources to building fine new churches. These experiments in the Gothic and Romanesque revivals have aged well and blend harmoniously with the residential blocks.

⑧ The **Arlington Street Church** (1861) is opposite the Park Square corner of the Public Garden. *Enter at 351 Boylston St. Open weekdays 10–5. Sun. service at 11.*

⑨ **Emmanuel Church** (1862), on Newbury Street between Arlington and Berkeley streets, offers free Bach cantatas each Sunday morning (*see* Off the Beaten Track). *Tel. 617/536–3355. Open Mon.–Thurs. 10–4 by appointment. Sun. service at 11.*

⑩ The **Church of the Covenant** (1867), at the corner of Newbury and Berkeley, has windows by Louis Tiffany. *Open Tues.–Fri. 9–noon. Sun. service at 10.*

⑪ The **First Baptist Church** (1872), at the corner of Clarendon Street and Commonwealth Avenue, is an earlier Richardson creation. *Open weekdays 10–4. Sun. service at 11.*

⑫ The **"New" Old South Church** (1875), successor to the Old South Meeting House of Tea Party fame, is on Copley Square at the corner of Boylston and Dartmouth streets. *Open weekdays 8:30–6, Sat. 9–4. Sun. service at 11.*

⑬ Opposite the New Old South and forming, with Trinity Church, a bulwark of Copley Square, stands the **Boston Public Library**. When this building was opened in 1895, it confirmed the status of McKim, Mead and White as apostles of the Renaissance Revival and reinforced a Boston commitment to the enlightenment of the citizenry that goes back 350 years to the founding of the Public Latin School.

Enter the older part of the library from the Dartmouth Street side, passing through the enormous bronze doors (they close at 5 PM) by Daniel Chester French, the sculptor of the Lincoln Memorial. Or walk around Boylston Street to Philip Johnson's addition of 1972, built in emulation of the mass and proportion of the original building, though not of its extraordinary detail. This airy, skylit structure houses the library's circulating collections. After passing the turnstiles, follow the hallway to your left to reach the old building, now the reference wing. At the desk near the door between the two buildings you can pick up information on the artwork you will presently see.

The corridor leading from the annex opens onto the courtyard around which the original library is built. A patio furnished with chairs rings a flower garden and fountain; from here the bustle of the city seems miles away. Beyond the courtyard is the main entrance hall of the building of 1895, with its vaulted ceiling, marble staircase, and immense stone lions commemorating Massachusetts regiments in the Civil War. The hall at the top of the stairs leads to Bates Hall, one of Boston's most sumptuous interior spaces. This is the main reference reading room, 218 feet long with a barrel-arch ceiling 50 feet high.

Charles McKim saw to it that the interior of his building was ornamented by several of the finest painters of the day. The murals at the head of the staircase, depicting the nine muses, are the work of the French artist Puvis de Chavannes; those in the book request processing room to the right are Edwin Abbey's interpretations of the Holy Grail legend. Upstairs, in the public areas leading to the fine arts, music, and rare books collections, are John Singer Sargent's mural series on the subject of Judaism and Christianity.

The old library building has been standing for almost 96 years now, and despite its structural soundness and architectural beauty it is showing the effects of age and deferred maintenance. Fortunately, a massive new renovation plan is in the works. Within the next few years McKim's palace of learning will sparkle, and we're promised that it will no longer be necessary to trek all the way to the new wing to visit the rest rooms. *Open Mon.–Thurs. 9–9, Fri. and Sat. 9–5.*

**⑭** If the John Hancock Tower is a bold intruder on the southeast corner of Copley Square, the southwest corner has to deal with an even more assertive modern presence. **Copley Place,** built between 1980 and 1984, comprises two major hotels (the highrise Westin, left, and the Marriott, right) and dozens of shops, restaurants, and offices attractively grouped on several levels around bright, open indoor spaces. The scale of the project bothers some people, as does the fact that so vast a complex of buildings effectively isolates the South End from the Back Bay. *Shopping galleries generally open weekdays 10–7, Sat. 10–7, Sun. noon–5.*

**⑮** The same complaint might have been made of the **Prudential Center,** which dominates the acreage between Boylston Street and Huntington Avenue two blocks west of the library. But the "Pru" was built almost 25 years ago, when monumental urban redevelopment projects had yet to be called into question; moreover, no love has been lost on the railroad yards the Pru displaced, which also blocked off the South End.

Yet the Pru has its problems. The elevation of its shopping mall from the street, and the ring road that surrounds it, make it less inviting to Boylston Street foot traffic. As for the **Prudential Tower** itself, Bainbridge Bunting made an acute observation when he called it "an apparition so vast in size that it appears to float about the surrounding district without being related to it." Ongoing modifications to the Boylston Street frontage of the Prudential Center will eliminate the ring road and better unite the complex with the urban space around it, but the tower will have to float on, vast as ever. More significant, the expansion of the adjacent Hynes Auditorium will enable Boston to attract larger conventions and help justify all the recent hotel building.

**⑯** Not long after Prudential staked its claim in the Boylston-Huntington blocks, it was followed by the headquarters complex of the **Christian Science Church.** The mother church of the Christian Science faith was established here by Mary Baker Eddy in 1879. Mrs. Eddy's original granite First Church of Christ, Scientist (1894) has since been enveloped by the domed Renaissance basilica added to the site in 1906, and both church buildings are now surrounded by the offices of the *Christian Science Monitor* and by I. M. Pei's complex of church administration

structures completed in 1973. The 670-foot reflecting pool,
maintained so that water constantly spills over its inner banks,
is a pleasant spot to stroll. *175 Huntington Ave., tel. 617/450–
3790. Open Mon.–Sat. 9:30–4, Sun. 11:15–2; Free tours on the
hour in the church and every ten minutes in the maparium.
Services Sun. 10 and 7, Wed. 7:30 PM.*

The best views of the pool and the precise, abstract geometry of
the entire complex are from the **Prudential Center Skywalk,** a
52nd-floor observatory that offers fine views of Boston, Cambridge, and the suburbs to the west and south. Tel. 617/236–
3318. *Admission: $2.75 adults, $1.75 children 5–15, students,
and senior citizens. Skywalk open Mon.–Sat. 10–10, Sun.
noon–10.*

With commerce and religion accounted for by the Prudential
Center and the Christian Science headquarters, the
neighborhood still has room for a temple to music. **Symphony
Hall,** since 1900 the home of the Boston Symphony Orchestra,
stands at the corner of Huntington and Massachusetts avenues, another contribution of McKim, Mead and White to the
Boston landscape. Acoustics, rather than exterior design,
make this a special place for performers and concertgoers.
Acoustical science was a brand new field of research when Professor Wallace Sabine planned Symphony Hall's interior, yet
his efforts were so successful that not one of the 2,500 seats is a
bad one from which to hear the Symphony, the Boston Pops, or
the frequent guest performers. *Tel. 617/266–1492. Tours by appointment with the volunteer office.*

## Tour 7. The South End

*Numbers in the margin correspond with points of interest on
The Back Bay, the South End, and the Fens map.*

Symphony Hall marks one corner of the Back Bay proper.
From here you can walk down Huntington Avenue to the Museum of Fine Arts and the Fens, returning to the Charles River
side of the Back Bay by way of Kenmore Square and Beacon
Street or Commonwealth Avenue. Or, keeping Symphony Hall
on your right, you can follow Massachusetts Avenue to Columbus Avenue, turn left on Columbus, and begin an exploration of
the South End. As Kenmore Square and the Fens district properly form a separate area, we'll walk instead toward the South
End, a neighborhood eclipsed by the Back Bay more than a century ago but now solidly back in fashion.

As we saw earlier, the filling of the shallows along Boston Neck
began nearly a decade before the main expanse of the Back Bay
was buried under Needham gravel. Streets were laid out and
building commenced immediately; most of the characteristic
bowfront houses of the South End (except those built around
1870 between Columbus and Huntington avenues) were constructed between 1851 and 1859. With the Back Bay still under
water, the spanking new rows of brick town houses in the South
End began to attract upwardly mobile residents of downtown
areas that were becoming more commercial, along with a few
adventurous residents of Beacon Hill.

The South End is an anomaly of planning and architecture in
Boston. It neither grew up haphazardly along cowpaths and
village lanes, like the old sections, nor followed a strict, uni-

form grid like that of the Back Bay. Bainbridge Bunting called its effect "cellular," and it is certainly more a sum of random blocks and park-centered squares than of bold boulevards and long, clear vistas. The observation is usually made that while the Back Bay is French-inspired, the South End is English. The houses, too, are different. In one sense they continue the pattern established on Beacon Hill (in a uniformly bowfronted style), yet they also aspire to a much more florid standard of decoration. Detailing can be a little extravagant in the Back Bay, but there it usually follows some established pattern; in the South End we find windows and entryway embellishments that seem to have been much more fancifully concocted, yet they are repeated so extensively that they must have been shipped by the carload as the new streets developed.

Even if the South End's beginnings were not glamorous, it is an intimate and nicely proportioned neighborhood that deserved a better reputation than it had at the outset. Consider the literary evidence: Howells's Silas Lapham abandoned the South End to build a house on the water side of Beacon as material proof of his arrival in Boston society. In *The Late George Apley*, John P. Marquand's Brahmin hero tells how his father decided, in the early 1870s, to move the family from his South End bowfront to the Back Bay—a consequence of his walking out on the front steps one morning and seeing a man in his shirtsleeves on the porch opposite. One gets the impression that this was a far worse offense than appearing stark naked on a condo balcony today. Regardless of whether Marquand exaggerated Victorian notions of propriety (if that were possible), the fact is that people like the Apleys did decamp for the Back Bay, the South End becoming what a 1913 guidebook called a "faded quarter."

A more practical reason for the relegation of the South End to the social backwaters was that it was literally out of the way. Railroad tracks separated it from the Back Bay, and disunity between state planners in the Back Bay and their city counterparts in the South End left the two districts with conflicting grid patterns that have never comfortably meshed. Ironically, the Prudential and Copley Place developments have only exacerbated the situation.

Whatever the reasons, the South End by 1900 was a neighborhood of lower middle class families and rooming houses. It had not lost its association with upward mobility, however, and blacks, many of them holders of the prestigious Pullman porter jobs on the railroads, began to buy the old bowfronts and establish themselves in the area.

There is still a substantial black presence in the South End, particularly along Columbus Avenue and Massachusetts Avenue, which marks the beginning of the predominantly black neighborhood of Roxbury. The early integration of the South End set the stage for its eventual transformation into a remarkable polyglot of ethnic groups. You are likely to hear Spanish spoken along Tremont Street, and there are Middle Eastern groceries along Shawmut Avenue. At the northeastern extreme of the South End, Harrison Avenue and Washington Street connect the area with Chinatown, and consequently there is a growing Asian influence. Still another minority presence among the neighborhood's ethnic groups, and sometimes belonging to one or more of them, is Boston's largest gay population.

Irish Roman Catholics are no longer well represented here, which is ironic, since they left behind the enormous Gothic **Cathedral of the Holy Cross** at the corner of Washington Street and Monsignor Reynolds Way. Although it is now used principally for such special occasions as the recent investiture of the new archbishop and the Pope's 1979 visit, it remains the premier church of the Archdiocese of Boston, New England's largest Catholic church. Incorporated in the front vestibule arch are bricks from a convent burned during anti-Catholic rioting in nearby Somerville in 1834. *Open weekdays 9–4, Sun. services at 8, 10.*

About 20 years ago, middle-class professionals, mostly white, began looking at the South End as though it had just been filled in and built over, and they didn't care who might be walking around in shirtsleeves. They bought old rooming houses—for as little as $40,000 just 10 years ago—and reconverted them to single-family occupancy, usually with one rental unit on the ground floor, below the high-stepped main entrance. Certain blocks thus became completely gentrified; elsewhere the house-by-house socioeconomic mix matches the area's ethnic diversity. That longtime low-income residents are also working to improve housing conditions can be seen in the sweat-equity residences of the Frankie O'Day Block on Columbus Avenue near Clarendon Street. And now that the prices of buildings have gone way up, condominium development has begun.

Although it would take years to understand the place fully, you can capture something of the flavor of the South End within a few hours' walk. To see elegant house restorations, go to **Rutland Square** (between Columbus Avenue and Tremont Street) or **Union Park** (between Tremont Street and Shawmut Avenue). These oases seem miles distant from the city around them. For upscale galleries and restaurants catering to young urban professionals, head to **Tremont Street.**

**Time Out**  **St. Botolph's on Tremont** (569 Tremont) serves gourmet Italian cuisine in light and airy yet striking surroundings. There's a bistro atmosphere, with the high-gloss black and red chairs, black tables, lush plants, and contemporary paintings hung high on the white walls. Open daily for lunch and dinner, dishes range from $6 to $12, and they can be eaten as leisurely or as quickly as your schedule permits.

You can return to the Back Bay from the South End via Dartmouth, Clarendon, or Berkeley streets. If you have more time, follow Columbus Avenue almost into Park Square, turn right on Arlington Street, then left onto one of the narrow streets of **Bay Village.** The neighborhood is a pocket of early 19th century brick row houses that appears to be almost a toylike replica of Beacon Hill. Edgar Allan Poe once lived here. It seems improbable that so fine and serene a neighborhood can exist in the shadow of busy Park Square—a 1950s developer might easily have leveled these blocks in an afternoon—yet here it is, another Boston surprise.

## Tour 8. The Fens

*Numbers in the margin correspond with points of interest on
The Back Bay, the South End, and the Fens map.*

Return now to the western end of the Back Bay and to Symphony Hall at the intersection of Massachusetts and Huntington avenues. With the front entrance of Symphony Hall on your right, walk down Huntington Avenue (note: this route is not recommended at night). On your left is the New England Conservatory of Music and, on Gainsborough Street, its recital Center, Jordan Hall. Just beyond, also on the left, is the

**㉒** sprawling campus of **Northeastern University** (360 Huntington Ave., tel. 617/437-2000).

Established in 1898, Northeastern has an enrollment of approximately 34,000, including part-time students. It is one of the world's largest cooperative education plan universities, where students in a wide variety of disciplines alternate periods of classroom study with terms of employment in related professions. Northeastern's engineering school is strong, and the university offers important programs in nursing, computers, business administration, pharmacy, criminal justice, marine sciences, and the human development professions. There is even a law school. Northeastern students are largely commuters who keep a low local profile.

**㉓** The **Museum of Fine Arts,** often called the MFA, opened in this building in 1909 after 33 years at a site (now demolished) in Copley Square. The location of the MFA here, between Huntington Avenue and the Fenway, helped to cap the half-century development of the Back Bay and its linkage with the brackish marshes that marked the old Brookline shore. Here the developers grew expansive; here public institutions such as the Harvard Medical School, long confined to cramped downtown quarters, were relocated in an atmosphere of grandeur previously denied Boston by her geographical and philosophical parameters.

The central topographical feature of this part of Boston is the marshland known as the **Back Bay Fens.** After all the work that had gone into filling in the bay, it would have been little extra trouble to obliterate the Fens with gravel and march row houses straight through to Brookline. But the planners, realizing that enough pavement had been laid between here and the Public Garden, hired none other than Frederick Law Olmsted to make the Fens into a park. Olmsted applied his genius for heightening natural effects while subtly manicuring their surroundings; today's Fens park consists of still, irregular reedbound pools surrounded by broad meadows, trees, and flower gardens.

The Fens mark the beginning of Boston's Emerald Necklace, a loosely connected chain of parks designed by Olmsted that extends along the Fenway, Riverway, and Jamaicaway to Jamaica Pond, the Arnold Arboretum, and Franklin Park. Farther off, at the Boston-Milton line, the vast Blue Hills Reservation offers some of the Boston area's best hiking, scenic views, even a ski lift. (We'll return to the Arboretum and Franklin Park later.)

The Museum of Fine Arts was founded in 1870, and for six years exhibitions of its relatively small collections were held on the upper floors of the Boston Athenaeum. In 1876 it moved to its own quarters in a Gothic structure where the Copley Plaza Hotel now stands in Copley Square. Just as the MFA was beginning to outgrow this space, the Fenway area was becoming fashionable, and in 1909 the move was made to Guy Lowell's somewhat severe BeauxArts building, to which the West Wing designed by I. M. Pei was added in 1981.

When you walk past Cyrus Dallin's *Appeal to the Great Spirit* and into the main entrance, count on staying for a while if you have any hope of even beginning to see what is here.

The connoisseurs who began the MFA collections were as enamored as any cultured Victorians with the great works of European civilizations; nevertheless, their initial acquisition was a work by an American, Washington Allston's *Elijah in the Desert*, and succeeding years have seen its holdings of American art grow to a size that surpasses those of all but two or three U.S. museums. The MFA has more than 50 works by John Singleton Copley alone; it has major paintings by Winslow Homer, John Singer Sargent (whose murals grace the building's grand staircase), Fitz Hugh Lane, Edward Hopper, and a galaxy of American painters ranging from the earliest phase of native New England folk art and colonial portraiture to the Hudson River School, turn-of-the-century realism, and the New York abstract expressionists of the 1950s and 1960s.

American decorative arts are amply represented here, particularly those of New England in the years before the Civil War. Rooms of period furniture, much of it from the matchless Karolik collection, show the progression of taste from the earliest Pilgrim pieces through the 18th-century triumphs of the Queen Anne style and the Hepplewhite, Sheraton, and Empire trends.

The MFA's displays of silver hollow ware and flatware from the Colonial and Federalist eras include pieces by John Coney, a Boston silversmith who flourished in the first decades of the 1700s. Coney took as apprentice a young French Huguenot named Apollos Rivoire, who anglicized his name and taught his craft to his son, Paul Revere. The holdings of the MFA will convince anyone who thinks of Revere simply as a sounder of alarms that the patriot was one of the greatest artists ever to turn his hand to silver.

The museum also boasts the most extensive collection of Asiatic art gathered under one roof anywhere in the world, with Chinese porcelains of the T'ang Dynasty especially well represented. The Egyptian rooms display statuary, mummies, furniture reproductions, and exquisite gold jewelry. The gathering of treasures at the MFA proceeds chronologically through the Hellenistic and Roman eras; the early Roman imperial period is recalled by marble busts, jewelry, and glassware.

European art is represented by works of the 11th through the 20th centuries; among the highlights are Donatello's marble relief *The Madonna of the Clouds* (in the second-floor Renaissance sculpture gallery) and paintings by Fiorentino and Van der Weyden. The French Impressionists are perhaps better represented here than at any New World museum other than the Chicago Art Institute; the 43 Monets, many of them recently cleaned, again vibrate with their original colors, and there are canvases by Renoir, Pissarro, Manet, and the Americans Mary Cassatt and Childe Hassam.

The museum has strong collections of textiles and costumes and prints dating from the 15th century, including a great deal of work by Dürer and Goya. (Many of the prints are kept away from light and may be seen only by appointment.) The museum's collection of antique musical instruments, expanded in 1979 by the acquisition of an important group of early keyboard instruments, is among the best in the world. (The hours for this collection differ from the regular museum hours; call for the schedule.) Frequent concert programs at the MFA use instruments closely modeled after those in the collection.

The museum's new West Wing, a handsome, airy, well-lit space, is used primarily for traveling exhibitions and special temporary shows drawn from the museum's holdings. The West Wing also houses the museum shop, where reproductions of Revere silver and other decorative items may be purchased. The recently renovated and reopened Evans Wing houses American paintings on the first floor and European paintings on the second. The museum has a good restaurant and a less formal cafeteria serving light snacks; both are in the West Wing. *465 Huntington Ave., tel. 617/267-9300 (617/267-9377 for recorded schedule and events information). Admission: $6 adults, $5 senior citizens, $3 children 6–17, free under 6; free to all Wed. 4–6. Open Tues.–Sun. 10–4:45, Wed. until 9:45. West Wing open Thurs. and Fri. until 9:45. 1-hr tours available.*

On the Fenway Park side of the Museum of Fine Arts, the newly constructed **Tenshin Garden**, the "garden at the heart of heaven," allows visitors to experience landscape as a work of art. A stone wall separates the formal garden from the nearby park, and a curved and graceful gate made of Japanese cypress opens onto a path of Mexican river stones that leads to a bench surrounded by white gravel. A combination of Japanese and American trees and shrubs fuse the concept of the Japanese garden with features of the New England landscape. Stone lanterns are placed at intervals, and a bridge at the center links longevity on the one side with prosperity on the other.

**㉔** Two blocks west of the MFA, on the Fenway, stands the **Isabella Stewart Gardner Museum,** an institution with as idiosyncratic a history as any in Boston. Isabella Stewart, a spirited young society woman, came from New York to Boston in 1860 to marry John Lowell Gardner. The Brahmin and his bride became enthusiastic art collectors, filling their Commonwealth Avenue mansion with treasures brought home from frequent trips to Europe. Gardner died in 1898, and "Mrs. Jack" set about building the Venetian palazzo of her dreams on the newly created Fenway. She called it Fenway Court and filled it with her acquisitions, opening it at a private party on New Year's Day 1903.

Mrs. Gardner lived on the top floor at Fenway Court until her death in 1924. Throughout the two decades of her residence she continued to build her collection under the tutelage of the young Bernard Berenson, who became one of the most respected art connoisseurs and critics of the 20th century. When she died, the terms of her will stipulated that everything in Fenway Court remain exactly as she left it, paintings, furniture, everything down to the last little object of *vertu* in a hall cabinet. (Out of a wish to protect the works from fading while respecting the stringent terms of the bequest, the museum's curators have had to install shades in some windows and on glass cabinet tops.)

Thus the Gardner Museum is a monument to one woman's taste—and a trove of spectacular paintings, sculpture, furniture, and textiles. There is much to see: *The Rape of Europa*, the most important of Titian's works in an American collection; paintings and drawings by Matisse, Whistler, Bellini, Van Dyck, Botticelli, and Rubens; John Singer Sargent's oil portrait of Mrs. Gardner herself, in the Gothic Room. On March 19, 1990, 13 works of art were stolen from Mrs. Jack's collection in one of the country's most talked-about art heists. Vermeer's "The Concert" was the most famous painting taken, and to date, none of the works have been recovered. Because the works of art were irreplaceable under the terms of Mrs. Jack's will, and because of the high cost of insurance, the Gardner Museum chose to go uncovered. Today, with over 2000 works in the collection and insurance rates dramatically lower because of a decrease in stolen art, the Gardner has re-evaluated its policy and carries insurance. At the center of the building is the magnificent courtyard, fully enclosed beneath a glass roof, in which there are always fresh flowers—poinsettias at Christmas, lilies at Easter, chrysanthemums in the fall—just as there were when Mrs. Jack lived here. The already-renowned Gardner Museum Café has become even more renowned lately with the addition of a new chef who has designed a creative menu with an Italian flair. The intimate restaurant overlooks the courtyard and in the spring and summer tables and chairs spill into the courtyard for even more relaxed dining. *280 The Fenway, tel. 617/566–1401 (617/734–1359 for recorded concert information). Admission: $5 adults, $2.50 children over 12, students, and senior citizens. Open Tues.–Sun. noon–5. Concerts Sept.–June. Café open Tues.–Fri. noon–3, weekends noon–4: tel. 617/566–1088. No reservations.*

㉕ Park Drive runs along the opposite side of the Fens from the MFA and the Gardner Museum. If you follow Jersey Street (now Yawkey Way) from Park Drive, you will reach the Boston shrine known as **Fenway Park.** This is one of the smallest and oldest baseball parks in the major leagues. It was built in 1912, when the grass on the field was real—and it still is today. Fenway has been a bittersweet place for the Red Sox, with a World Series victory in 1918; pennants in 1946, 1967, 1975, and 1986; and a divisional championship in 1988. Babe Ruth pitched here when the place was new; Ted Williams and Carl Yastrzemski slugged out their entire careers here. Yawkey Way is named for the late Tom Yawkey, who bought the team in 1933 as a 30th-birthday present for himself and spent the next 43 years pursuing his elusive grail. For Red Sox baseball fans, there is a great deal of myth associated with their support of the "Olde Towne Team." Fans are said to believe a "curse" hangs over the club due to their ill-fated trade of a young Babe Ruth to archrivals, the New York Yankees.

㉖ **Kenmore Square,** home to fast-food parlors, new wave rock clubs, an abundance of university students, and an enormous neon sign advertising gasoline, is two blocks north of Fenway Park. The neon sign is so thoroughly identified with the area that historic preservationists have fought successfully to save it—proof that Bostonians are an open-minded lot who do not require that their landmarks be identified with the American Revolution.

Kenmore Square is a block east of the Commonwealth Avenue campus of Boston University. You can board one of the Green Line trains at the Square for a surface-level ride through Brookline or out to Boston College, or you can head in the opposite direction for a quick (if it isn't rush hour) underground trip through the Back Bay to downtown.

## The "Streetcar Suburbs"

*Numbers in the margin correspond with points of interest on The "Streetcar Suburbs" map.*

The 19th-century expansion of Boston was not confined to the Back Bay and the South End. Toward the close of the century, as the working population of the downtown district swelled and public transportation (first horsecars, then electric trolleys) linked outlying suburbs with the core city, development of the "streetcar suburbs" began. These areas answered the housing needs of both the rising native middle class and the second-generation immigrant families who were outgrowing the narrow streets of the North and West Ends.

South Boston was a landfill project of the mid-1880s, and as such it is not a true streetcar suburb; its expansion predates the era of commuting. Some of the brick bowfront residences along East Broadway in City Point date from the 1840s and 1850s. But the neighborhood came into its own with the influx of Irish Americans around 1900, and the Irish still hold sway here. "Southie" is a Celtic enclave, as the annual St. Patrick's Day parade attests.

South Boston projects farther into the harbor than any part of Boston save Logan Airport, and the views of the Harbor Islands from along Day Boulevard or Castle Island are fine. At L Street and Day Boulevard is the L Street Beach, where an intrepid group called the L Street Brownies swims all year long and celebrates New Year's Day with a dip in the icy Atlantic. **❶** **Castle Island Park** is no longer on an island, but **Fort Independence,** when it was built here in 1801, was separated from the mainland by water. The circular walk from the fort around Pleasure Bay is delightful on a warm summer day. The statue near the fort is of Donald McKay, whose clipper ships once sped past this point on their way to California and the Orient.

Near the juncture of the South Boston peninsula with the Dorchester mainland, off Telegraph Street, stands the high **❷** ground of Thomas Park, where you will find the **Dorchester Heights Monument** (refurbished in 1983) and National Historic Site. In 1776 Dorchester Heights commanded a clear view of downtown Boston, where the British had been under siege since the preceding year. Here George Washington set up the cannons that Henry Knox, a Boston bookseller turned soldier and later secretary of war, had hauled through the wilderness following their capture at Fort Ticonderoga. The artillery did its job of intimidation, and the British troops left Boston, never to return. *Thomas Park (near G St.), tel. 617/242–5642. Admission free. Open daily; the monument is open July and Aug. Call to arrange tours at other times.*

# The "Streetcar Suburbs"

Logan International Airport

Boston Inner Harbor

Fort Independence **1**

Castle Island

Day Blvd.

City Point Beach

E. Broadway

Northern Ave.

Summer St.

**SOUTH BOSTON**

William St.

W. Broadway

Dorchester Heights Monument **2**

Boston Harbor

University of Massachusetts Boston Campus
John F. Kennedy Library **3**

Thompson Island

**DOWNTOWN**

Boston Common

**BACK BAY**

Charles River

Boylston St.

Albany St.

Tremont St.

Washington St.

93

Boston St.

Dorchester Ave.

Morrissey Blvd.

5 miles

5 km

0

Massachusetts Ave.

Huntington Ave.

Columbus Ave.

90

**THE FENS**

**ROXBURY**

Commonwealth Ave.

Beacon St.

Brookline Ave.

Warren St.

Blue Hill Ave.

Columbia Rd.

Franklin Park Zoo

1

28

**JAMAICA PLAIN**

Washington St.

Jamaicaway

28

**4**

9

Worcester Tnpk.

Arnold Arboretum

Arborway

203

**FOREST HILLS**

**5**

1

**BROOKLINE**

Harvard St. **6**

John F. Kennedy National Historic Site

30

N

South of the Dorchester Heights Monument, on the other side of Columbus Park, a stark, white, prowlike building at the tip of Columbia Point pays homage to one of Washington's successors as president, a native Irish Bostonian named John F.

**3** Kennedy. The **Kennedy Library** is the official repository of his presidential papers, his desk, and other personal belongings, and there are screenings of a film on his life. The new Steven M. Smith Wing, dedicated in February 1991, provides more exhibition space for the trove of Kennedy memorabilia. The harborfront site alone is worth a visit, even without the library's interpretive displays. *Columbia Point, tel. 617/929–4523. Admission: $3.50 adults, $2 senior citizens, free under 16. Open daily 9–5.*

Inland from Columbia Point are Dorchester, Roxbury, and Jamaica Plain, all rural retreats barely more than a century ago, now thick with tenements and the distinctive three-family or six-family triple-decker apartment houses of Boston's streetcar suburbs. Both Dorchester and Roxbury are almost exclusively residential, tricky to navigate by car, and accessible by elevated train (the Red or Orange Lines) only if you know exactly where you are going. The two contiguous neighborhoods border on **Franklin Park,** an Olmsted creation of more than 500 acres noted for its zoo.

**4** The 70-acre **Franklin Park Zoo,** near the Seaver Street-Blue Hill Avenue corner of the park, has been renovated during the past decade and has an especially fine walk-through aviary. The Waterfowl Pond and Children's Zoo are a three-acre facility designed especially for ages two to nine. The Tropical Forest Pavilion, scheduled to open this year, will have a gorilla exhibit and 32 other species of mammals, reptiles, birds, and fish. Franklin Park has a golf course and well deserves the daytime attention that offsets its nighttime reputation as a dangerous part of town. The park, 4 miles from downtown, is reached by the #16 bus from Forest Hills (Orange Line) or Andrew (Red Line). *Blue Hill Ave., tel. 617/442–2002 (617/442–0991 for recorded information). Admission $5 adults, $2.50 children 5–17, students, and senior citizens; free Tues. noon–closing. Park gates open Nov.–Feb., daily 9–3:30; Mar.–Oct., daily 9–5. Closed Christmas and New Year's Day.*

During the growing season, no one with an eye for natural beauty and more than a couple of days to spend in Boston

**5** should pass up the **Arnold Arboretum.** This 265-acre living laboratory, administered by Harvard University, is open to pedestrians during daylight hours all year long. It can be reached by taking the #39 bus from Copley Square or by taking the Orange Line to Forest Hills and the #16 bus to the Arboretum. The arboretum was established in 1872 according to the terms of a bequest from James Arnold, a New Bedford merchant. The arboretum contains more than 14,000 trees and shrubs native to the North Temperate Zone, and something is always in season from early April through September. The rhododendrons, azaleas, lilacs, magnolias, and fruit trees are spectacular in bloom. The Bonsai collection has individual specimens that are Japanese imports more than 300 years old. *Rtes. 1 & 203, Arborway, tel. 617/524–1717. Admission free. Grounds open daily dawn to dusk; visitor's center open 9–4. Hour-long guided tours Sun. at 2, May 1–Nov.*

If you have the time and stamina for a jaunt of approximately
3½ miles, it is possible to walk almost the entire distance from
the Arnold Arboretum to Kenmore Square within the Emerald
Necklace. Just follow the Jamaicaway north from its beginning
at the circle that marks the northern tip of the arboretum.
Within one long block you'll reach Jamaica Pond. Continue
along the Jamaicaway through Olmsted Park, past Leverett
Pond. From a point just north of here, either Brookline Avenue
or the Riverway will take you to the Fens and Kenmore Square.
Along the way you will pass many of the spacious freestanding
mansions built along the park borders of Jamaica Plain around
the turn of the century, when this was the choicest of the
streetcar suburbs. Not the least of your pleasures as you pass
along this stretch will be that you are walking, not driving. The
Jamaicaway was one of Boston's first attempts at moving traffic at a pace faster than a walk, and it worked well only for
horse-drawn carriages and the slower and narrower early auto-
mobiles. If you think that Boston still isn't very good at hurry-
ing cars around, remember that unlike most American cities, it
has been inhabited almost exclusively by pedestrians for two-
thirds of its history.

From Kenmore Square it's just a few minutes on the MBTA
Green Line to Coolidge Corner in Brookline, where a fourblock
walk north on Harvard Street takes you to the **John Fitzgerald
Kennedy National Historic Site.** This was the home of the 35th
president of the United States from his birth on May 29, 1917,
until 1920, when the family moved to nearby Naples and
Abbottsford streets. Mrs. Rose Kennedy provided the furnishings for the restored two-and-a-half-story, wood-frame structure. *83 Beals St., tel. 617/566-7937. Admission: $1 adults,
children under 16 and senior citizens free. Open daily 10–4:30
except Thanksgiving, Christmas, and New Year's Day; tours
on the ½ hour until 4.*

## Boston for Free

**Boston's Travel Planner** is available free (tel. 617/536–4100).

Thursday's *Boston Globe Calendar* and the *Boston Phoenix* are
excellent sources for listings of free events taking place in the
city that week. *Boston* magazine gives a monthly overview.

Church Concerts   Saturday's *Boston Globe* lists that Sunday's music programs,
most of which are free.

**King's Chapel** (School and Tremont Sts., tel. 617/227–2155)
hosts a half-hour recital Tuesday at 12:15.

Concerts   **City Hall Plaza Concerts** (Government Center, tel. 617/725–
4006 or 242–1775) take place every Wednesday in July and August, 7:30–10 PM, sponsored by the Boston Department of
Parks and Recreation.

The **Hatch Shell** on the bank of the Charles River is the site of
numerous concerts during the summer months, and the Boston
Pops and the Boston Ballet are among the performers. Bring a
blanket and a picnic basket and enjoy entertainment under the
stars.

**Longfellow Garden Concerts** (105 Brattle St., Cambridge, tel.
617/876–4491) feature the poet's favorite music in the garden of

the Longfellow House every other Sunday, June to early August, 3–4:30.

**Festivals**   **Boston's North End** comes alive during the summer months with a series of **Italian Fiestas** honoring various saints. The programs usually include a blessing, a procession, and lots of robust food and entertainment. For information, tel. 617/536–4100.

**Lectures**   In a city with so many schools and colleges, the most difficult task can be deciding which lecture to attend. Thursday's *Boston Globe* Calendar has a full listing.

The **Ford Hall Forum** (271 Huntington Ave., Suite 240, tel. 617/437–5800) offers a lecture series every spring and fall; the speakers may be political or literary figures. Thursday lectures at 7 in Faneuil Hall, Sunday lectures at 7 in Blackman Auditorium of Northeastern University (370 Huntington Ave.). Lectures are not held every week; call for the schedule. During the renovations at Faneuil Hall, lectures are held at the Old South Meeting House.

**Museums**   While most museums charge admission, several museums schedule a period when admission is free to all: **the Museum of Fine Arts,** Wednesday 4–6; the **Museum of Science,** Wednesday 1–5; the **Aquarium,** Thursday 4–8 in the off-season; **the Gardner Museum,** Wednesday noon–5; **the Children's Museum,** reduced to $1 Friday 5–9. In Cambridge, the **Harvard University Museums of Natural History, the Fogg Art Museum,** and the **Arthur M. Sackler Museum** are free on Saturday morning. **The Museum of Afro-American History** is free at all times.

**Television Show Tickets**   Shows that are produced locally for television networks often welcome live audiences. Call the stations for specific ticket information.

**WBZ** (Channel 4, NBC), 1170 Soldiers Field Road, Allston, tel. 617/787–7000.
**WCVB** (Channel 5, ABC), 5 TV Place, Needham, tel. 617/449–0400.
**WGBH** (Channel 2) and **WGBX** (Channel 44, PBS) 125 Western Avenue, Allston, tel. 617/492–2777.
**WHDH** (Channel 7, CBS), 7 Bulfinch Place, tel. 617/725–0777.
**WSBK** (Channel 38), 83 Leo M. Birmingham Parkway, Brighton, tel. 617/783–3838.
**WFXT** (Channel 25), 100 Second Avenue, Needham, tel. 617/326–8825.

## What to See and Do with Children

Kids who are interested in history will find much to enjoy in Boston. The city's historical legacy is vivid and accessible: Youngsters can see just where Paul Revere's lanterns were hung, and they can walk the decks of an undefeated man-of-war. Along with the history, Boston has museums, theaters, and parks to play in. Young readers visiting the Public Garden may recognize such sights as the Pepperpot Bridge from Robert McCloskey's *Make Way for Ducklings*.

**Boston Children's Museum** (Tour 5. Downtown Boston) *T stop, South Station.*
**Boston Children's Theatre** (New England Hall, 225 Clarendon St., tel. 617/277–3277). Students of the Boston Children's The-

atre School perform three plays between November and April. Stagemobile, a touring company, performs locally during the summer months.

The *Boston Parents Paper* (tel. 617/522–1515), published monthly and distributed free throughout the city, is an excellent resource for finding out what's happening.

**Historic Neighborhoods Foundation** (2 Boylston St., tel. 617/426–1885) offers tours geared to children, including "In Search of Grandmother's House," "Kids' Views of the North End," and "Kids' Views of the Waterfront."

**Make Way for Ducklings Tours, Boston By Little Feet,** and **Historic Neighborhoods Foundation Tours** (*see* Walking Tours)

**Museum of Fine Arts** prepares a free guide to help families get the most out of the museum; ask for it as you enter. Special workshops are held throughout the year for children of all ages. (Tour 8. The Fens) *T stop, Museum.*

**New England Aquarium** (Tour 5. Downtown Boston) *T stop, Aquarium.*

**Puppet Showplace** (32 Station St., Brookline, tel. 617/731–6400), the best small theater in the Boston area dedicated entirely to puppetry, draws on puppet performers from near and far.

**Swan Boats (Public Garden)** (Tour 6. The Back Bay) *T stop, Arlington.*

**USS *Constitution*** (Tour 4. Charlestown) *T stop, Haymarket; then MBTA bus 92 or 93 to Charlestown City Sq.*

## Off the Beaten Track

**The Boston Symphony Orchestra** holds 10 open rehearsals on Wednesday evenings at 7:30, usually during the winter months. Seats are unreserved and reasonably priced, and you will get to hear one of the world's great orchestras in practice session. *Symphony Hall, Massachusetts and Huntington Aves., tel. 617/266–1492.*

**Bova's Bakery** in the North End is the place for freshly baked rolls to take on a stroll along the waterfront. *76 Prince St., tel. 617/523–5601. Open 24 hours daily.*

**The Catalonian Chapel** at the Museum of Fine Arts is easy to overlook and well worth seeking out. The apse was moved from the Church of Santa Maria in Mur, Catalonia, complete with the only series of 12th-century Romanesque frescoes to be found outside Spain. It also houses an excellent collection of 15th-century Spanish altarpieces. *465 Huntington Ave., tel. 617/267–9300.*

**Emmanuel Church of Boston,** a Back Bay brownstone Gothic Episcopal church, is a popular spot for classical music lovers on Sunday morning at 11, mid-September through mid-May. The service includes a Bach cantata performed by a professional 16-piece orchestra and 16-member chorus. *15 Newbury St., tel. 617/536–3355. Admission free.*

**The Maparium** is a 30-foot stained-glass globe that gives you the experience of walking through the world on a glass bridge. *Christian Science Church, Massachusetts and Huntington Aves., tel. 617/450–3790. Admission free. Open Mon.–Sat. 9:30–4, Sun. 11–2.*

**Mt. Auburn Cemetery** was one of the country's first garden cemeteries, and it remains one of the loveliest. Since it opened in 1831, more than 80,000 persons have been buried here, among them Henry Wadsworth Longfellow, Mary Baker Eddy, Winslow Homer, and Edwin Booth. The warbler migrations in the fall and spring make this a popular spot with bird watchers. Two tour maps are available at the office: one for horticultural points of interest, the other for tombstones of note. *Mt. Auburn St., Cambridge, tel. 617/547–7105. Open daily 8–7 in summer, 8–4 in winter. T stop, Harvard; then the Watertown or Waverly bus to the cemetery.*

# Sightseeing Checklists

## Historical Buildings and Sites

This list of Boston's principal buildings and sites includes both attractions that were covered in the preceding tours and additional attractions that are described here for the first time.

**Oliver Ames Mansion** (Tour 6. The Back Bay) *T stop, Hynes Center.*

**Appleton Mansions** (Tour 1. Boston Common and Beacon Hill) *T stop, Park St.*

**Baylies Mansion** (Tour 6. The Back Bay) *T stop, Park St.*

**Blackstone Block.** At the Haymarket, Boston's oldest commercial block, named for the city's first settler, William Blaxton, is still home to the city's butchers after more than 100 years. In addition, it is the site for a thriving produce market every Friday and Saturday morning. *T stop, Haymarket.*

**Boston Athenaeum,** one of the oldest libraries in the country, was founded in 1807 and moved to its present imposing quarters, a national historic landmark building, in 1849. Its collection of more than 600,000 volumes is for the use of members (who pay an annual fee). Accredited researchers in need of materials not available elsewhere may be granted admission. The holdings are impressive: most of George Washington's private library; the King's Chapel Library sent from England in 1698; manuscripts and books associated with the Adams family; a collection of pre-1950 American art and photography. Occasional exhibitions of more recent works are open to the public. Free guided tours Tues. and Thurs. by appointment. *10 ½ Beacon St., tel. 617/227–0270. Admission free. Open weekdays 9–5:30, Sat. 9–4. Closed Sat. June–Sept., closed holidays and Bunker Hill Day. T stop, Park St.*

**Boston Common** (Tour 1. Boston Common and Beacon Hill) *T stop, Park St.*

**Boston Massacre Site** (Tour 5. Downtown Boston) *T stop, State.*

**Boston Public Library** (Tour 6. The Back Bay) *T stop, Copley.*

**Bulfinch Pavilion (Ether Dome).** (Tour 2. The Old West End) *T stop, Charles/MGH.*

**Bunker Hill Monument** (Tour 4. Charlestown) *T stop, Community College.*

**Burrage Mansion** (Tour 6. The Back Bay) *T stop, Hynes Center.*

**Capen House (Union Oyster House)** (Tour 3. Government Center and the North End) *T stop, Government Center.*

**Charlestown Navy Yard** (Tour 4. Charlestown) *T stop, Haymarket; then MBTA bus 92 or 93 to Charlestown City Sq.*

**Clough House** (Tour 3. Government Center and the North End) *T stop, Haymarket or North Station.*

**Club of Odd Volumes,** the second oldest book collectors' club in America, has its headquarters in an early 19th-century residence. *77 Mt. Vernon St. tel. 617/227-7003. Open to the public only for special exhibits. T stop, Park St.*

**Commercial Wharf's** condominiums and offices occupy the granite building that was part of Granite Wharf until 1868, when Atlantic Avenue was built. *East of Atlantic Ave. T stop, Aquarium.*

**Copley Plaza Hotel** (Tour 6. The Back Bay) *T stop, Copley.*

**Custom House** (Tour 5. Downtown Boston) *T stop, Haymarket.*

**Custom House Block,** once a storehouse for goods awaiting duty imposition, is now shops and offices. *Long Wharf. T stop, Aquarium.*

**Cyclorama (Boston Center for the Arts),** the second largest glass dome in the country (after the U.S. Capitol), was built by William Blackall in 1884 to house the painting *Battle of Gettysburg* by Paul Philippoteaux. Alfred Champion later used it as a garage and invented the first spark plug. Now it's used for exhibitions. *539 Tremont St. Admission by contribution. Open daily 9–5. T stop, Copley.*

**Dorchester Heights Monument** (The "Streetcar Suburbs") *T stop, Broadway; then City Point bus to G St.*

**Emerson College** (1929), designed by the architects who built the Ritz-Carlton Hotel, is one of the few Art Deco-style buildings in the Back Bay. *7 Arlington St. at Marlborough St. T stop, Arlington.*

**Exeter Theater.** Many still mourn the passing of Boston's oldest (1914) continually operating movie theater, now a home furnishings store and restaurant. *26 Exeter St. at Newbury St. T stop, Copley.*

**Faneuil Hall** (Tour 5. Downtown Boston) *T stop, Haymarket.*

**First Public School Site.** A plaque marks the site where Benjamin Franklin, John Hancock, and Samuel Adams attended the country's first school. *School St. at Old City Hall. T stop, Park St.*

**Fisher Junior College** occupies an elegant Victorian mansion (1903) that epitomizes old-world elegance. The marble hanging stairway with its 24K-gold plate balustrade, the Circassian walnut-paneled dining room, and the library with hand-carved rosewood doors and sterling silver knobs are among the gentle touches. *118 Beacon St., tel. 617/262-3240. Admission free. Open weekdays 8:30–4:30, and (Sept.–May) Sat. 9–3. T stop, Arlington.*

**Flour and Grain Exchange Building.** Built in 1889–1892 for the Chamber of Commerce. *177 Milk St. T stop, State.*

**Fort Warren** (The Harbor Islands).

**44 Hull Street,** Boston's narrowest house at 9 feet 6 inches wide, is 200 years old. *T stop, Haymarket or North Station.*

**Benjamin Franklin's Birthplace.** The Franklins' 15th child (of 17) was born here in 1706; a bronze bust commemorates the spot. *Boston Post Building, 17 Milk St. T stop, State.*

**French Library** (Tour 6. The Back Bay) *T stop, Arlington.*

**Frog Pond** (Tour 1. Boston Common and Beacon Hill) *T stop, Park St.*

**Gibson House** (Tour 6. The Back Bay) *T stop, Arlington.*

**Goethe Institute** (Tour 6. The Back Bay) *T stop, Arlington or Copley.*

**Chester Harding House.** A national historic landmark, the residence and studio of Chester Harding, a well-known painter, was built in 1808. The Boston Bar Association bought it in the early 1900s and restored it in 1962–1963. *16 Beacon St. Not open to the public. T stop, Park St.*

**Horticultural Hall.** The headquarters for the Massachusetts Horticultural Society, built in 1900, houses the country's oldest and most diverse horticultural library. *300 Massachusetts Ave., tel. 617/536–9280. Admission free. Open weekdays 8:30– 4:30, Wed. until 8, Sat. 10–2. T stop, Symphony.*

**Rose Fitzgerald Kennedy Birthplace.** Birthplace of John, Robert, and Teddy's mother. The Historic Neighborhoods Foundation's "Kennedy Roots Tour" includes this landmark. *4 Garden Court. Not open to the public. T stop, Haymarket.*

**Lewis Wharf,** now a complex housing condos, offices, and cafes, served originally as home port to the clipper ships of the 1850s. Its buildings were warehouses. *East of Atlantic Ave. near Commercial St. T stop, Aquarium.*

**Long Wharf,** Boston's oldest existing wharf, is now home port for tour boats. *East of Atlantic Ave. T stop, Aquarium.*

**Louisburg Square** (Tour 1. Boston Common and Beacon Hill) *T stop, Park St.*

**Massachusetts State House** (Tour 1. Boston Common and Beacon Hill) *T stop, Park St.*

**Mercantile Wharf Building,** constructed of Italian granite in 1857 to house the harbor's sailmakers and riggers, was renovated in 1976 for apartments and shops. *Atlantic Ave. between Cross and Richmond streets. T stop, Haymarket.*

**George Middleton House,** believed to be the oldest house on Beacon Hill, was built in 1797. The original owner was George Middleton, a black jockey and horsebreaker. *5–7 Pinckney St. Not open to the public. T stop, Park St.*

**Mt. Vernon Street** (Tour 1. Boston Common and Beacon Hill) *T stop, Park St.*

**New England Conservatory,** founded in 1867, is the oldest conservatory in the country. *290 Huntington Ave. T stop, Symphony.*

**New England Historic Genealogical Society.** New Englanders trace their family trees with the help of the society's collections, which date to the 17th century. The building itself dates from 1845. *101 Newbury St., tel. 617/536–5740. Admission free; fee to use the facility. Open Tues.–Sat. 9–5. Wed. and Thurs. until 9. On the first Wed. of each month at 7PM, an introductory lecture is given on how to perform your own genealogical study. T stop, Copley.*

**The New England.** The first chartered mutual life insurance company in the country houses dioramas of the development of the Back Bay (inside the Newbury Street entrance) and eight historic murals by Charles Hoffbauer (in the front lobby). *501 Boylston St. Admission free. Open daily 9–9. T stop, Arlington or Copley.*

**New England Telephone Building** (Tour 5. Downtown Boston) *T stop, Government Center.*

**Nichols House** (Tour 1. Boston Common and Beacon Hill) *T stop, Park St.*

**99 Salem Street** is the site of the country's oldest bakery; bread was baked here for the Continental Army. Now part of the open market. *T stop, Haymarket.*

**Northeastern University** (Tour 8. The Fens) *T stop, Northeastern.*

**Old Boston Art Club.** This Queen Anne Revival of 1881 was home to the Boston Art Club until 1948; it is now Copley High School. *152 Newbury St. Not open to the public. T stop, Copley.*

**Old City Hall** (Tour 5. Downtown Boston) *T stop, Park St.*

**Old Corner Bookstore (Globe Corner Bookstore)** (Tour 5. Downtown Boston) *T stop, State.*

**Harrison Gray Otis Houses (first, second, and third)** (Tour 1. Boston Common and Beacon Hill) *T stop, Charles/MGH or Bowdoin.*

**Park Street Station** (Tour 1. Boston Common and Beacon Hill) *T stop, Park St.*

**Phillips School,** built in 1824, became one of the city's first integrated schools in 1854. *Anderson and Pinckney Sts. T stop, Park St.*

**Piano Craft Guild.** When it was new in 1853, the Chickering piano factory was the second largest in the world. In 1972 it was renovated for artists' space. *791 Tremont St. T stop, Ruggles.*

**Pierce-Hichborn House** (Tour 3. Government Center and the North End) *T stop, Haymarket.*

**Quincy Market** (Tour 5. Downtown Boston) *T stop, Haymarket.*

**Paul Revere House** (Tour 3. Government Center and the North End) *T stop, Haymarket.*

**Rollins Place,** built in 1843 to house artisans and tradesmen who worked on Beacon Hill, has a *trompe l'oeil* Greek Revival villa at one end. *Revere St. T stop, Haymarket.*

**Sears Crescent** (Tour 3. Government Center and the North End) *T stop, Government Center.*

**17 Chestnut Street,** a Bulfinch building of 1808, was the home of Julia Ward Howe. *Not open to the public. T stop, Park St.*

**70–75 Beacon Street** are Greek Revival residences built by Asher Benjamin in 1828. *Not open to the public. T stop, Park St.*

**Somerset Club** (Tour 1. Boston Common and Beacon Hill) *T stop, Park St.*

**South Station** (Tour 5. Downtown Boston) *T stop, South Station.*

**Symphony Hall** (Tour 6. The Back Bay) *T stop, Symphony.*

**34 Beacon Street,** the former home of *the* Cabots of Boston, is now headquarters for Little, Brown and the New York Graphic Society. *T stop, Park St.*

**29A Chestnut Street** (Tour 1. Boston Common and Beacon Hill) *T stop, Park St.*

**Union Wharf** was constructed in 1846 and renovated in 1979 for condominiums. *North of Atlantic Ave. and Commercial St. T stop, Haymarket.*

**USS *Constitution*** (Tour 4. Charlestown) *T stop, Haymarket; then MBTA bus 92 or 93 to Charlestown City Sq.*

## Museums and Galleries

**Museums** This list of Boston's museums includes both museums that were covered in the preceding tours and museums that are described here for the first time.

**Boston Children's Museum** (Tour 5. Downtown Boston) *T stop, South Station.*

**Boston Tea Party Ship (*Beaver II*)** (Tour 5. Downtown Boston) *T stop, South Station.*

**Charlestown Navy Yard** (Tour 4. Charlestown) *T stop, Haymarket; then MBTA bus 92 or 93 to Charlestown City Sq.*

**Computer Museum** (Tour 5. Downtown Boston) *T stop, South Station.*

**First Corps of Cadets Museum,** established in 1726, has an example of almost every weapon in existence. *227 Commonwealth Ave., tel. 617/267–1726. Admission free. Open by appointment only. T stop, Prudential.*

**Isabella Stewart Gardner Museum** (Tour 8. The Fens) *T stop, Brigham Circle.*

**Institute of Contemporary Art.** Housed in a firehouse of 1884, renovated in the early 1970s by Graham Gund, the institute has no permanent collection but shows temporary exhibits by the famous and not-so-famous. *955 Boylston St., tel. 617/266–5152. Admission: $4 adults, $1.50 children under 14 and senior citizens, $3 students with ID; free Thurs. 5–8. Open Wed.–Sun. 11–5, Thurs.–Sat. until 8. T stop, Hynes Center.*

**Massachusetts Historical Society** has paintings, books, and manuscripts from 17th-century New England. *1154 Boylston St., tel. 617/536–1608. Admission free. Open weekdays 9–4:45. T stop, Hynes Center.*

**Museum of Afro-American History** (Tour 1. Boston Common and Beacon Hill) *T stop, Park St.*

**Museum at the John F. Kennedy Library** (The "Streetcar Suburbs") *T stop, Ashmont.*

**Museum of Fine Arts** (Tour 8. The Fens) *T stop, Museum.*

**Museum of Science** (Tour 2. The Old West End) *T stop, Science Park.*

**Museum of the Ancient and Honorable Artillery Company of Massachusetts** (Tour 5. Downtown Boston) *T stop, Haymarket.*

**Museum of the National Center of Afro-American Artists** represents Black artists in all media with regularly changing exhibits. *300 Walnut Ave., Roxbury/Jamaica Plain, tel. 617/442–8614. Admission: $1.25 adults, 50¢ children under 12 and senior citizens. Open Tues.–Sun. 1–5. T stop, Ruggles.*

**New England Sports Museum.** Exhibits encompass the spectrum of New England sporting interests, with lasers, video, and multi-image technology used to make the area's sports history come alive. *Christian A. Herter Park, 1175 Soldiers Field Rd., tel. 617/787–7678. Admission: $3.50 adults, $2.50 children 5–18, senior citizens free. Open Thurs. 11–8, Fri.–Sat. 11–5, Sun. noon–5. T stop, Central; then bus 12 to Western and Everett Sts.*

**Old State House** (Tour 5. Downtown Boston) *T stop, State.*

**Galleries** Art galleries display and sell works of art and antiques; admission to galleries is normally free. Except where noted, the T stop for all galleries is either Boylston or Arlington.

**Alpha Gallery.** Contemporary American and European painting, sculpture, and master prints. *121 Newbury St., tel. 617/536–4465. Open Tues.–Sat. 10–5:30.*

**Art Institute of Boston.** Monthly exhibits of student and faculty work, plus special exhibits. *700 Beacon St., tel. 617/262–1223. Open weekdays 9–5. T stop, Kenmore.*

**The Artful Hand.** Jewelry, glass, glass sculpture, wood, pottery, baskets, lamps, and furniture by more than 800 American artisans. *36 Copley Pl., 100 Huntington Ave., tel. 617/262–9601. Open Mon.–Sat. 10–7, Sun. noon–5. T stop, Copley.*

**Boston Visual Artists Union Gallery (BVAU).** Programs and services for visual artists in the areas of advocacy, creative stimulation, and professional development. *33 Harrison Ave., tel. 617/695–1266. Open Mon. and Thurs. noon–5, Sat. 10–5. T stop, Kenmore.*

**Bromfield Gallery.** Paintings, sculpture, and photography by gallery artists; the oldest artist-owned gallery in Boston. *90 South St., tel. 617/451-3605. Open Tues.-Sat.10-5:30.*

**Brodney Gallery.** Paintings, bronzes, jewelry, objects d'art, clocks, antiques. *811 Boylston St., tel. 617/536-0500. Open Mon.-Sat. 9:30-5. T stop, Prudential.*

**Childs Gallery.** American and European paintings, prints, drawings, watercolors, and sculpture from the 17th to the 20th centuries. *169 Newbury St., tel. 617/266-1108. Open Mon. 10-5, Tues.-Fri. 9-6, Sat. 10-5.*

**Copley Society of Boston.** The work of well-known and aspiring New England artists; a nonprofit membership organization founded in 1879. *158 Newbury St., tel. 617/536-5049. Open Tues.-Sat. 10:30-5:30.*

**Eugene Galleries.** Prints, etchings, old maps, city views, and books. *76 Charles St., tel. 617/227-3062. Open Mon.-Sat. 10:30-5:30, Sun. noon-4. T stop, Park St.*

**Gallery NAGA.** Contemporary works of photography and sculpture; furniture by local artists. *67 Newbury St., tel. 617/267-9060. Open Tues.-Sat. 10-5.*

**Guild of Boston Artists.** Representational watercolors, oils, graphics, and sculpture by guild members; a nonprofit gallery. *162 Newbury St., tel. 617/536-7660. Open Tues.-Sat. 10-5; closed July and Aug.*

**Haley and Steele.** Rare 18th- and 19th-century prints, including 19th-century sporting and bird prints. *91 Newbury St., tel. 617/536-6339. Open weekdays 10-6, Sat. 10-5.*

**Harcus Gallery.** Contemporary sculpture, paintings, graphics, and drawings; work by Nevelson, deKooning, Albers, Caro, and local artists. *210 South St., Leather District, tel. 617/262-4445. Open Tues.-Sat. 9:30-5:30. T stop, South Station.*

**Robert Klein Gallery.** Contemporary and vintage photographs by international and national photographers. *207 South St., tel. 617/482-8188. Open Tues.-Fri. 10-5:30, Sat. noon-5. T stop, South Station.*

**Barbara Krakow Gallery.** Contemporary American and European paintings, sculpture, drawings, and prints. *10 Newbury St., tel. 617/262-4490. Open Tues.-Sat. 10-5:30.*

**Ben Kupferman.** Unique jewelry and sculpture by the artist-owner. *115 Atlantic Ave. (across from Waterfront Park), tel. 617/742-1982. Tues.-Sat. 10-3. T stop, Aquarium.*

**Morgan Gallery.** Contemporary and pop art; works by Andy Warhol, Jasper Johns, Roy Lichtenstein, Jim Dine, and David Hockney. *222 Newbury St., tel. 617/536-2686. Open Tues.-Sat. 10-6.*

**New England School of Art and Design.** Student and faculty exhibits of graphics, sculpture, drawings, paintings, and photography in Gallery 28. *28 Newbury St., tel. 617/536-0383. Open weekdays 9-5, Sat. 10-4.*

**New England School of Photography.** The work of the students. *537 Commonwealth Ave., tel. 617/437-1868. Open weekdays 9-4. T stop, Kenmore.*

**Nielsen Gallery.** Paintings, sculpture, drawings, and prints; German expressionist and master prints from the 19th and 20th centuries. *179 Newbury St., tel. 617/266-4835. Open Tues.-Sat. 10-5:30.*

**Photographic Resource Center.** Major exhibits of established photographers and rising local talent. *602 Commonwealth Ave., tel. 617/353-0700. Open Tues.-Sun. noon-5. T stop, Blanford.*

**Pucker-Safari Gallery.** Contemporary paintings, sculpture, ceramics, and prints. *171 Newbury St., tel. 617/267–9416. Open Mon.–Sat. 10–5:30.*

**Rolly-Michaux.** Contemporary paintings, graphics, silk-screens, and sculpture; works by Calder, Picasso, Chagall, Miró, and Matisse. *290 Dartmouth St., tel. 617/536–9898. Open Tues.–Sat. 11–5.*

**Judi Rotenburg Gallery.** Principal gallery artists are the painters Zygmund Jankowski, Leon Kroll, and Joseph Solman and the sculptor Marianna Pineda. *130 Newbury St., tel. 617/437–1518. Open Mon.–Sat. 10–6.*

**Society of Arts and Crafts.** Contemporary artists and artisans working in all media. *175 Newbury St., tel. 617/266–1810. Open Mon.–Fri. 10–5:30, Sat. 10–5.*

**Stobart Gallery.** Marine prints and paintings. *113 Lewis Wharf, tel. 617/227–6868. Open Tues.–Fri. 10–5, Sat. noon–5. T stop, Aquarium.*

**Vose Galleries.** American paintings of the 18th, 19th, and early 20th centuries. *238 Newbury St., tel. 617/536–6176. Open weekdays 8–5:30, Sat. 9–4.*

---

## Parks and Gardens

**Arnold Arboretum** (The "Streetcar Suburbs") *T stop, Forest Hills or Arborway.*

**The Back Bay Fens** (Tour 8. The Fens) *T stop, Museum.*

**Belle Isle Park** is the last local vestige of the living salt-marsh environment that was once predominant in the lands around Boston Harbor. Parts of the developed park are high and dry; for a more interesting experience, bring watertight boots and explore the marsh itself. It's a prime area for birding. *T stop, Suffolk Downs.*

**Boston Public Garden** (Tour 6. The Back Bay) *T stop, Boylston.*

**Boston Harbor Islands State Park** (The Harbor Islands).

**Castle Island Park** (The "Streetcar Suburbs") *T stop, Broadway; then the City Point bus.*

**The Esplanade** (Tour 1. Boston Common and Beacon Hill) *T stop, Charles/MGH.*

**Franklin Park** (The "Streetcar Suburbs") *T stop, Ruggles; then the Franklin Park bus.*

**Marine Park.** At the eastern end of Broadway and Day Boulevard in South Boston, the park surrounds Pleasure Bay and includes Fort Independence. *T stop, Broadway; then Bus 9 or 11 to last stop.*

**Olmsted Park.** A link in Frederick Law Olmsted's Emerald Necklace, the park stretches alongside the Riverway and Jamaicaway to Jamaica Pond. There is sailing on the pond.

**Stony Brook Reservation.** More than 464 acres near Boston's southern boundaries, including a municipal golf course. Good for walking and cross-country skiing. *Best reached by car via Route 1 (Jamaicaway/VFW Parkway) and West Roxbury Parkway.*

**Waterfront Park.** A wonderful spot to look out at the harbor and enjoy a picnic of Quincy Market delicacies. *Atlantic Avenue between Mercantile St. and Long Wharf. T stop, Aquarium.*

---

## Beaches

Yes, Boston is on the ocean, and no, it is not renowned for its beaches. The harbor is a working harbor, one that has several million people living nearby, and consequently the water is not

Bahamas-pure. There are public beaches, however, and the Metropolitan District Commission (MDC) opens them only when certain standards of cleanliness are met. The best swimming is probably off the Harbor Islands. The mainland beaches, concentrated in Dorchester and South Boston, are largely neighborhood affairs, where occasional incidents have occurred when one group's sense of territory was violated by another. (These areas have been calm in recent years.)

The main beaches are Malibu Beach, Savin Hill Beach, and Tenean Beach, off Morrissey Boulevard, in Dorchester; Carson Beach, Castle Island Beach, City Point Beach, M Street Beach, and Pleasure Bay, off Day Boulevard, in South Boston.

These beaches are open from the end of June to the beginning of September. Lifeguards are on duty daily from 10 to 6 during this season. High temperatures and high tide may cause schedule changes. For further information, call the MDC Harbor District Office (tel. 617/727-5215).

Several excellent beaches a short distance from the city would make lovely day trips. Among the nicest are Nantasket Beach in Hull, Crane's Beach in Ipswich, Plum Island (*see* Excursions) in Newburyport, and Wingaersheek Beach in Gloucester.

## Churches

**African Meeting House** (Tour 1. Boston Common and Beacon Hill) *T stop, Park St.*
**Arlington Street Church** (Tour 6. The Back Bay) *T stop, Arlington.*
**Cathedral of the Holy Cross** (Tour 7. The South End) *T stop, Chinatown; then Bus 49 to Cathedral.*
**Charles Street Meetinghouse,** built in 1804 as a Baptist church, was bought in 1876 by the African Methodist Episcopal Church, which remained until 1939. It was used for community activities until recently, when it was converted into commercial stores. *Mt. Vernon and Charles Sts. Not open to the public. T stop, Charles/MGH.*
**Christian Science Church Headquarters** (Tour 6. The Back Bay) *T stop, Hynes Center.*
**Church of the Covenant** (Tour 6. The Back Bay) *T stop, Arlington.*
**Emmanuel Episcopal Church** (Tour 6. The Back Bay) *T stop, Arlington.*
**First Baptist Church** (Tour 6. The Back Bay) *T stop, Copley.*
**First and Second Church of Boston.** Built in 1867 as a new home for the city's oldest Puritan congregation, the church was destroyed by fire in 1968. The spire and frame of a rose window, all that were left standing, were incorporated into the design of the new church. *64-66 Marlborough St. at Berkeley St. Open weekdays 9-5, Sun. service at 11. T stop, Copley or Arlington.*
**King's Chapel** (Tour 5. Downtown Boston) *T stop, Park St. or Government Center.*
**"New" Old South Church** (Tour 6. The Back Bay) *T stop, Copley.*
**Old North Church (Christ Church)** (Tour 3. Government Center and the North End) *T stop, Haymarket or North Station.*
**Old South Meeting House** (Tour 5. Downtown Boston) *T stop, State.*

**Park Street Church** (Tour 1. Boston Common and Beacon Hill) *T stop, Park St.*
**St. Paul's Cathedral** (Tour 1. Boston Common and Beacon Hill) *T stop, Park St.*
**Trinity Church** (Tour 6. The Back Bay) *T stop, Copley.*
**Union United Methodist Church.** A country-style parish church designed by A. R. Estey, who also planned the Emmanuel Church. *485 Columbus Ave. Open weekdays 9:30–4:30, Sun. service at 10:45. T stop, Ruggles.*

## Statues and Monuments

**Colonel Thomas Cass** (Tour 6. The Back Bay) *T stop, Boylston.*
**William Ellery Channing** (Tour 6. The Back Bay) *T stop, Boylston.*
**James Michael Curley Memorial.** Designed by Lloyd Lillie and erected in 1980 as a memorial to Boston's flamboyant mayor. *Curley Memorial Park, Congress and North Sts. T stop, Government Center.*
**Ether Monument** (Tour 6. The Back Bay) *T stop, Boylston.*
**Benjamin Franklin** (Tour 5. Downtown Boston) *T stop, Park St.*
**Founders Memorial** commemorates the 300th anniversary of the founding of Boston; the first white settler, William Blaxton, greets John Winthrop. *Beacon and Spruce Sts., Boston Common. T stop, Park St.*
**William Lloyd Garrison,** the celebrated abolitionist, appears in a monument by Olin Warner (1885). *Commonwealth Ave. between Exeter and Dartmouth Sts. T stop, Copley.*
**Edward Everett Hale** (Tour 6. The Back Bay) *T stop, Boylston.*
**John Fitzgerald Kennedy** (Tour 6. The Back Bay) *T stop, Park St.*
**Thaddeus Kosciuszko,** the Polish general who fought with the Continental Army in the American Revolution, is depicted by Theo Alice Ruggles Kitson in a memorial of 1927. *Public Garden. T stop, Boylston.*
**Parkman Plaza** (Tour 1. Boston Common and Beacon Hill) *T stop, Park St.*
**Paul Revere Statue** (Tour 3. Government Center and the North End) *T stop, Haymarket or North Station.*
**Robert Gould Shaw Memorial** (Tour 1. Boston Common and Beacon Hill) *T stop, Park St.*
**Soldiers and Sailors Monument** (Tour 1. Boston Common and Beacon Hill) *T stop, Park St.*
**Charles Sumner** (Tour 6. The Back Bay) *T stop, Boylston.*
**George Washington** (Tour 6. The Back Bay) *T stop, Boylston.*

## Cemeteries

**Central Burying Ground** (Tour 1. Boston Common and Beacon Hill) *T stop, Boylston.*
**Copp's Hill Burying Ground** (Tour 3. Government Center and the North End) *T stop, North Station.*
**King's Chapel Burying Ground** (Tour 5. Downtown Boston) *T stop, Park St. or Government Center.*
**Mt. Auburn Cemetery** (*see* Off the Beaten Track).
**Old Granary Burial Ground** (Tour 1. Boston Common and Beacon Hill) *T stop, Park St.*
**Phipps Street Burying Ground** was laid out in 1631 and has tombstones dating from 1642. The obelisk memorializes John

Harvard, the location of whose remains is uncertain. *Phipps St., Charlestown. T stop, Community College.*

## Other Places of Interest

**Boston Architectural Center,** a school of architecture, was built in 1967 by Ashley, Myer & Associates, whose design won the school's competition. Note the Richard Haas trompe l'oeil. Exhibits and drawings. *320 Newbury St., tel. 617/536–3170. Admission free. Open weekdays 9–9, Sat. 9:30–5, Sun. noon–5. T stop, Hynes Center.*
**Chestnut and Mt. Vernon streets** (Tour 1. Boston Common and Beacon Hill) *T stop, Park St.*
**Chinatown** (Tour 5. Downtown Boston) *T stop, Chinatown.*
**City Hall** (Tour 3. Government Center and the North End) *T stop, Government Center.*
**Copley Place** (Tour 6. The Back Bay) *T stop, Copley.*
**Fenway Park** (Tour 8. The Fens) *T stop, Kenmore.*
**John Hancock Tower** (Tour 6. The Back Bay) *T stop, Boylston.*
**John F. Kennedy Federal Office Building** (Tour 3. Government Center and the North End) *T stop, Government Center.*
**Prudential Center** (Tour 6. The Back Bay) *T stop, Prudential.*
**Swan Boats (Public Garden)** (Tour 6. The Back Bay) *T stop, Arlington.*

# 4　Shopping

Boston's shops and stores are generally open Monday through Saturday from 9 or 9:30 until 6 or 7; many stay open until 8 late in the week. Some stores, particularly those in malls or tourist areas, are open Sunday from noon until 5. Most stores accept major credit cards—even the large department stores, like Filene's and Jordan Marsh, who have their own charge cards. Neiman Marcus accepts only its own card, but with the proper identification it's fairly easy to get one while you're there. Traveler's checks are welcome throughout the city (though it may be difficult for a small store to cash a check of large denomination). The state sales tax of 5% does not apply to clothing or food, except in restaurants. Boston's two daily newspapers, the *Globe* and the *Herald*, are the best places to learn about sales; Sunday's *Globe* often announces sales for later in the week.

## Major Shopping Districts

Most of Boston's stores and shops are located in an area bounded by Quincy Market, the Back Bay, downtown, and Copley Square. There are few outlet stores in the area, but there are plenty of bargains, particularly in the world-famous Filene's Basement and Chinatown's fabric district.

**Boylston Street,** in the heart of the Back Bay and parallel to Newbury Street, is home to more than 100 stores, among them Bonwit Teller and two quality menswear stores, Louis and Roots. At the west end of the Boylston Street shopping district is the Prudential Center complex.

**Charles Street** in Beacon Hill is a mecca for antique and boutique lovers. Many of the city's finest and prettiest shops are here.

**Copley Place,** an indoor shopping mall connecting the Westin and Marriott hotels, is a blend of the elegant, the unique, the glitzy, and the overpriced. The Neiman Marcus department store anchors 87 stores, restaurants, and cinemas. Prices in the shops on the second level tend to be a bit lower.

**Downtown Crossing,** Boston's traditional downtown shopping area, has been tarted up: It's now a pedestrian mall with outdoor food and merchandise kiosks, street performers, and benches for people watchers. Here are the city's two largest department stores, Jordan Marsh and Filene's (with its famous Basement), and Lafayette Place, a new indoor mall plagued by empty stores and little traffic.

**Faneuil Hall Marketplace** has small shops, kiosks of every description, street performers, and one of the great food experiences, Quincy Market. The intrepid shopper must cope with crowds of people, particularly on weekends. Nearby Dock Square is a great place to hunt for bargains in restaurant supply houses. Saturday is the best day to walk through Haymarket Square, a jumble of outdoor fruit and vegetable vendors, meat markets, and fish mongers. Fruit sold here is often very ripe, and you may have to discard some of it, but you will still end up with more for your money than if you go to a supermarket. Allow the vendors to choose your fruit.

**Marketplace Center,** one of the city's newest shopping attractions, is adjacent to Faneuil Hall Marketplace and smack in the middle of the "Walkway to the Sea" from Government Center to Boston's waterfront. Thirty-three stores on two levels ring a central plaza; they include Banana Republic, Sharper Image, Doubleday Books, numerous small shops, an outdoor gelato cafe, and a gourmet Japanese restaurant.

**Newbury Street** is Boston's version of New York's Fifth Avenue, where the trendy gives way to the chic and the expensive. Here are the most stylish clothing boutiques, the most up-to-date art galleries, and, in the Ritz Carlton Hotel, the most delicious blueberry muffins in town.

**Prudential Center's** specialty shops and department stores cluster in and around the center plaza, among them Lord & Taylor, Saks Fifth Avenue, the Brodney Gallery, and Au Bon Pain.

## Department Stores

**Filene's** (426 Washington St., tel. 617/357–2100). This full-service department store carries a complete line of men's and women's formal, casual, and career clothing bearing the major name brands and designer labels. Furs, jewelry, shoes, and cosmetics are found in the eight floors of merchandise. Yet the store's most outstanding feature is its two-level bargain basement, where items are automatically reduced in price according to the number of days they've been on the rack. The competition can be stiff for the great values on discontinued, overstocked, or slightly irregular items.

**Jordan Marsh Company** (450 Washington St., tel. 617/357–3000). For more than 130 years Jordan's has been New England's largest department store. It carries a full line of men's and women's clothing, including the products of many top designers, as well as housewares, furniture, and cosmetics. There is a bargain basement.

**Lord & Taylor** (760 Boylston St., at the Prudential Center, tel. 617/262–6000). Classic clothing, from casual to elegant, by such designers as Anne Klein and Ralph Lauren; accessories, home furnishings, housewares, and a beauty salon.

**Neiman Marcus** (5 Copley Pl., 100 Huntington Avenue, tel. 617/536–3660). The flashy Texas retailer's home in New England has three levels of high fashion and gadgetry.

**Saks Fifth Avenue** (Prudential Center, tel. 617/262–8500). From the more traditional styles to today's avant-garde apparel, Saks offers clothing to satisfy everyone's needs.

## Specialty Stores

Antiques   **Samuel L. Lowe, Jr. Antiques** (80 Charles St., tel. 617/742–0845). An excellent selection of Chinese export porcelain. Furniture and folk art. Marine art is a specialty; the collection includes scrimshaw, nautical instruments, whaling gear, and navigation books.
**Shreve, Crump & Low** (330 Boylston St., tel. 617/267–9100). The second floor has 18th- and 19th-century English and American furniture, silver, porcelain, and prints; and Oriental porcelain.

Baked Goods   **Montilio's** (549 Boylston St., tel. 617/267–4700, and Faneuil Hall Marketplace, tel. 617/367–2371). Fabulously rich rum cakes, strawberry short cake, ice-cream cakes, cookies, and pastries.

**Warburton's** (Washington and Bromfield Sts., tel. 617/426–7853). This British-based chain bakes meat-filled savories, nine varieties of muffin, danish, and croissants daily in each store. (Also at Government Center and across from the State House on Beacon St.)

**Books** **Barnes and Noble** (395 Washington St., tel. 617/426–5502, and 607 Boylston St., tel. 617/236–1308). Boston's biggest discount bookseller specializes in reduced prices on recent best-sellers and tables heaped with remainders (publisher's overstock of books printed in previous seasons) at bargain prices. Another department has classical records, tapes, and compact discs. Count on serendipity here; even the staff is hard-pressed to tell what they have and where it is.

**Boston University Bookstore** (660 Beacon St., tel. 617/267–8484). The largest bookstore in New England has three floors of current best-sellers, out-of-print collections, magazines, and maps.

**The Brattle Bookstore** (9 West St., tel. 617/542–0210). The late George Gloss built the Brattle into Boston's best used and rare bookshop, and his son Kenneth is carrying on. If the book you want is out of print, the Brattle either has it or can probably find it.

**Candy** **Godiva Chocolatier** (Copley Pl., 100 Huntington Ave., tel. 617/437–8490). The elaborately boxed chocolates are exquisite to look at, deliciously rich, and quite expensive.

**Sweet Stuff** (Faneuil Hall Marketplace, North Market Building, tel. 617/227–7560). Coconut chocolate-covered pretzels; candy pizza made of chocolate, marshmallow, and nuts; and jelly beans are among the house specialties.

**Clothing for Men and Women** **JoS. A. Bank Clothiers** (122 Newbury St., tel. 617/536–5050). For reasonably priced classic men's and women's apparel, Bostonians head to Bank's.

**John Barry, Ltd.** (75 Kneeland St., 10th floor, tel. 617/426–4291). New England's largest women's apparel wholesaler, known also as Flair of Boston, with dresses, suits, evening wear, sportswear, and accessories at 30% to 60% off.

**Bonwit Teller** (500 Boylston St., tel. 617/267–1200). Imported and American designer clothing and accessories, and an International Boutique and Designer Salon.

**Brooks Brothers** (46 Newbury St., tel. 617/267–2600, and 75 State St., tel. 617/261–9990). Traditional formal and casual clothing. The styling is somewhat more contemporary in the third-floor Brooksgate shop, but basically Brooks is Brooks: correct and durable down through the ages.

**Designers Clothing** (161 Devonshire St., tel. 617/482–3335). Designer and traditional clothing and the store's own label for both women and men.

**Louis** (234 Berkeley St., tel. 617/965–6100). Now located in the former Bonwit Teller building, Louis carries elegantly tailored designs and a wide selection of imported clothing and accessories, including many of the more daring Italian styles. They also have subtly updated classics in everything from linen to tweeds.

**Roots** (419 Boylston St., tel. 617/247–0700). A handsome men's shop specializing in tastefully updated traditional styles. A good place to find well-cut flannels and tweeds.

# Boston Shopping

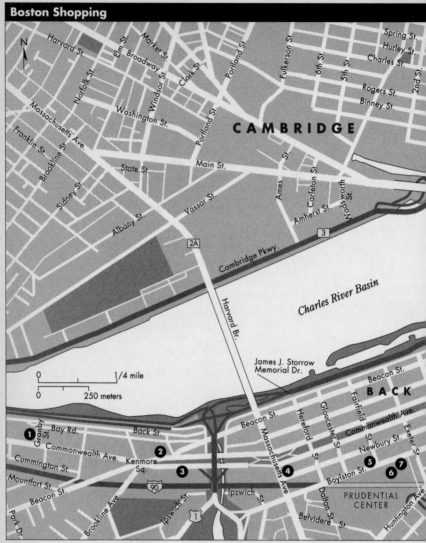

N

Harvard St.
Elm St.
Broadway St.
Market St.
Clark St.
Windsor St.
Norfolk St.
Washington St.
Massachusetts Ave.
Franklin St.
Brookline St.
Sidney St.
State St.
Albany St.
Vassar St.
Portland St.
Portland St.
Main St.
Fulkerson St.
6th St.
5th St.
Spring St.
Hurley St.
Charles St.
Rogers St.
Binney St.
2nd St.

**CAMBRIDGE**

Ames St.
Carleton St.
Amherst St.
Wadsworth St.

2A

3

Cambridge Pkwy.

*Charles River Basin*

Harvard Br.

James J. Storrow
Memorial Dr.

Beacon St.

**B A C K**

Fairfield St.
Gloucester St.
Hereford St.
Commonwealth Ave.
Newbury St.
Exeter St.
Boylston St.

0     1/4 mile
0   250 meters

Granby St.
Bay Rd.
Commonwealth Ave.
Cummington St.
Mountfort St.
Beacon St.
Park Dr.
Brookline Ave.
Back St.
Kenmore Sq.
Beacon St.
Massachusetts Ave.
Ipswich St.
Ipswich St.
Dalton St.
Belvidere St.
Huntington Ave.

PRUDENTIAL
CENTER

90

1

**1**
**2**
**3**
**4**
**5**
**6** **7**

Ann Taylor, **22**
Bally of
Switzerland, **12**
Barnes and Noble, **32**
Bonwit Teller, **15**
Boston University
Bookstore, **2**
Bova's Italian
Bakery, **41**

The Brattle
Bookstore, **28**
Brodney Gallery, **5**
Brooks Brothers, **17**
David P. Ehrlich
and Sons, **38**
Designers Clothing, **35**
Dorfman Jewels, **19**
Eastern Mountain
Sports, **1**

Eric Fuch's, **39**
Eric's of Boston, **26**
F.A.O. Schwarz, **18**
Filene's, **33**
Godiva Chocolatier, **9**
Helen's Leather
Shop, **25**
Hilton's Tent City, **42**
John Barry Ltd., **37**

Jordan Marsh, **29**
JoS. A. Bank
Clothiers, **16**
Lord & Taylor, **7**
Louis, **16**
Nautical Needs, **31**
Neiman Marcus, **8**
North End Fabrics, **36**
Nuggets, **3**
Pappagallo, **13**

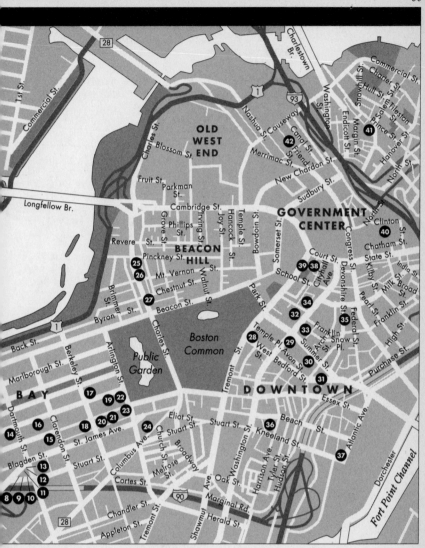

**Ann Taylor** (18 Newbury St., tel. 617/262-0763, and Faneuil Hall Marketplace, tel. 617/742-0031). High-quality fashions for both classic and trendy dressers. Shoes and accessories. When you want to know what's in style, this store's window is usually a reliable indication.

**Fabrics** **North End Fabrics** (31 Harrison Ave., tel. 617/426-2116). Almost everything in fabrics, including bridal, imported laces, designer fabrics, fun furs, theatricals, and woolens.
**Windsor Button Shop** (35 Temple Pl., tel. 617/482-4969). A large specialty store jammed with buttons, sequins, braids, trims, novelties, notions, muslin, felt, and other trimmings.

**Gifts** **Eric's of Boston** (38 Charles St., tel. 617/227-6567). Exquisite cards and gift wrappings from around the world; jewelry, European porcelains, dollhouse miniatures, and gifts fill every cranny of this delightful shop.
**The Society of Arts & Crafts** (175 Newbury St., tel. 617/266-1810). An excellent assortment of quality work by some of the country's finest craftspeople. Ceramics, jewelry, leather, batik, weaving, furniture.
**Women's Educational and Industrial Union** (356 Boylston St., tel. 617/536-5651). Cards, gifts, decorative items, children's clothing, and accessories are sold in the shop of this social and educational organization founded in 1877. There is an excellent needlework and collector's shop.

**Jewelry** **Dorfman Jewels** (24 Newbury St., tel. 617/536-2022). An elegant shop filled with the finest in watches, pearls, silver, and glass, as well as Mark Cross leather goods.
**Shreve, Crump & Low** (330 Boylston St., tel. 617/267-9100). A complete line of the finest jewelry, china, crystal, and silver. A beautiful collection of Steuben glass on the second floor. Also an extensive collection of clocks and watches. Shreve's, one of Boston's oldest and most respected stores, is where generations of Brahmin brides have registered their china selections.
**Tiffany & Co.** (Copley Pl., 100 Huntington Ave., tel. 617/353-0222). Fifth Avenue comes to Boston, with the finest in gems and precious metal jewelry.

**Records** **Nuggets** (482 Commonwealth Ave., tel. 617/536-0679). Used and out-of-print jazz and rock records, and a tremendous selection of new releases on disc, CD, and tape. The prices are excellent!
**Tower Records** (360 Newbury St., tel. 617/247-5900). One of the country's largest music chains has opened its largest store (so far) in the Back Bay. Three enormous floors stock every kind of music.

**Shoes** **Bally of Switzerland** (Copley Pl., 100 Huntington Ave., tel. 617/437-1910). Quality imported footwear and accessories for men and women.
**Helen's Leather Shop** (110 Charles St., tel. 617/742-2077). New England's biggest Western boot dealer for men and women carries boots of alligator, ostrich, buffalo, python, elephant, elk, and lizard. There are leather jackets, belts, luggage and accessories, briefcases, sandals, and leather backpacks. Boots from Lucchese, Larry Mahan, Dan Post, Tony Lama, Justin, and Frye.
**Pappagallo** (Copley Pl., 100 Huntington Ave., tel. 617/247-2532). Quality Italian footwear such as Eventura and Via Spiga.

**Sports Equipment** **Eastern Mountain Sports** (1041 Commonwealth Ave., Brighton, tel. 617/254–4250). New England's best selection of gear for the backpacker, camper, climber, skier, or all-round outdoors person. Everything from tents and sleeping bags to technical mountaineering equipment—and a wide selection of casual clothing. A good source for books and maps for those planning trips into the New England backcountry.

**Hilton's Tent City** (272 Friend St., tel. 617/227–9242). An excellent selection of hiking, backpacking, and camping equipment as well as boots and clothing. This is often the best place to locate hard-to-find items.

**Nautical Needs, Inc.** (99 Bedford St., tel. 617/426–9471). Nautical charts for the world, the largest selection of sea books on the East Coast, foul weather gear, navigational instruments, shoes, and videos.

**Tobacconists** **David P. Ehrlich and Sons** (32 Tremont St., Government Center, tel. 617/227–1720). A wide selection of finely blended tobaccos; cigars and pipes; and masculine gift items of the Dunhill variety. Fine beers and ales.

**L. J. Peretti Company** (2 ½ Park Square, tel. 617/482–0218). A Boston institution since 1870, this is one of the few places that still makes pipes. Peretti sells its own blends of tobacco, a large selection of others, and handmade imported cigars.

**Toys** **Eric Fuch's** (28 Tremont St., tel. 617/227–7935) offers great deals in toy replicas and miniatures, as well as fine model trains.

**F.A.O. Schwarz** (338 Boylston St., tel. 617/266–5101). This branch of the famed New York toy emporium offers the highest quality (and the highest priced) toys. A wide selection of trains, dolls, stuffed animals, games, and other intriguing playthings.

# 5 Sports and Fitness

### Participant Sports and Fitness

The mania for physical fitness is big in Boston. Lots of people play racquet sports on their lunch hours, and runners and roller skaters are to be seen constantly on the Storrow Embankment. Most public recreational facilities, including skating rinks and tennis courts, are operated by the Metropolitan District Commission (MDC) (tel. 617/727–5215).

**Bicycling**  The **Dr. Paul Dudley White Bikeway,** approximately 18 miles long, runs along both sides of the Charles River from Watertown Square to the Museum of Science. From spring through the end of summer, bikes may be rented ($15 per day, $35 per weekend, with identification) at Community Bike Shop (490 Tremont St., tel. 617/542–8623).

**Boating**  On the Charles River and Inner Harbor to North Washington Street, all types of pleasure boats (except inflatables) are allowed on the waters of Boston Harbor, Dorchester inner and outer bays, and the Neponset River from the Granite Avenue Bridge to Dorchester Bay.

Public landings and floats are located at **North End Waterfront Park,** Commercial Street, Boston Harbor; **Kelly's Landing,** Day Boulevard, South Boston; and at these locations along the Charles River:

**Clarendon Street,** Back Bay
**Hatch Shell,** Embankment Road, Back Bay
**Pinckney Street Landing,** Back Bay
**Brooks Street,** Nonantum Road, Brighton
**Richard T. Artesani Playground,** off Soldier's Field Road, Brighton

There is another launching area at the **Monsignor William J. Daly Recreation Center** on the Charles River, Brighton. Owners of trailerable boats planning to use this facility should make arrangements in advance (tel. 617/727–4708).

**Fishing**  There are just two locations for freshwater fishing in Greater Boston: along the shores of the Charles River; and at Turtle Pond, Stony Brook Reservation, Turtle Pond Parkway, Hyde Park.

For fishing from shore, try the John J. McCorkle Fishing Pier, Castle Island, and the pier at City Point, both located off Day Boulevard in South Boston.

**Golfing**  The Massachusetts Golf Association (190 Park Rd., Weston, tel. 617/891–4300) represents more than 220 clubs in the state and will provide information on courses that are open to the public and equipment rentals. The office is open Mon.–Fri. 9–4:30.

**Hiking**  There are excellent footpaths for hikers in the 450-acre Stony Brook Reservation in Boston's Hyde Park and West Roxbury sections.

**Jogging**  Both sides of the Charles River are popular with joggers. For the location of other paths in greater Boston, call or write the Metropolitan District Commission or the Department of Environmental Management, Division of Forests and Parks (*see* Bicycling). Another great source of information is the Bill Rodgers Running Center (Faneuil Hall Marketplace, tel. 617/723–5612). Many hotels provide jogging maps for guests.

**Physical Fitness**  The **Westin Hotel** (Copley Place, Back Bay, tel. 617/262–9600) has complete health club facilities. Nonguests are welcome to use the facilities for a $7 fee.

The extensive facilities of the **Greater Boston YMCA** (316 Huntington Ave., tel. 617/536–7800) are open for $2.50 per day to members of other YMCAs for up to two weeks, and to nonmembers for $90 for a three-month membership (you must present a photo ID).

Numerous hotels offer health club facilities for guests only (*see* Lodging): Back Bay Hilton, Boston Harbor Hotel at Rowes Wharf, Boston Marriott Copley Place, Boston Park Plaza Hotel & Towers, Copley Square Hotel (use of The Westin's Club and Back Bay Racquet Club for a small fee), 57 Hotel/Howard Johnson's (access to Boston Harbor Tennis Club), Four Seasons, Guest Quarters Suite Hotel, Hilton at Logan Airport, Lafayette Hotel, Marriott Long Wharf, Hotel Meridien, Midtown, Omni Parker House (use of nearby Fitcorp Health and Fitness Center), Ramada Inn, Ritz-Carlton, Sheraton Boston Hotel & Towers, The Westin.

**Skating**  The Metropolitan District Commission operates these public ice-skating rinks. For a complete schedule of hours of operation contact the Department of Parks and Recreation (tel. 617/727–9547).

**Charlestown Rink,** Rutherford Avenue near Prison Point Bridge
**Jamaica Plain Rink,** Jamaicaway, Willow Pond
**Brighton Rink,** Nonatum Road, Brighton
**Cleveland Circle Rink,** Cleveland Circle, Brighton
**North End Rink,** Commercial Street
**Melnea Cass Rink,** Washington Street at Martin Luther King Boulevard
**South Boston Rink,** Day Boulevard
**Neponset Rink,** Garvey Playground, Morrissey Boulevard, Dorchester
**Hyde Park Rink,** Turtle Pond Parkway

In winter skaters flock to the frozen waters of the Boston Public Garden's lagoon and the Frog Pond at Boston Common.

**Skiing**  **Blue Hills Ski Area,** Blue Hills Reservation, Washington Street, Canton, exit 2B from Route 128, is an MDC-managed downhill facility with a 1,400-foot double chairlift, 2 j-bars, and a rope tow. Its facilities include seven slopes, snowmaking, a ski school, and a restaurant. *Just south of Boston city limits off Route 128, tel. 617/828–5090 for ticket and ski school information, 617/828–5070 for recorded report on snow conditions.*

For those who are interested in serious skiing, Loon Mountain (tel. 603/745–8111) and Waterville Valley (tel. 603/236–8311) are both about 2½ hours north of Boston.

**Tennis**  **Charlesbank Park,** Charles Street (tel. 617/782–0090). A permit is required to use this facility, which is open from April to November and lighted until 11 PM. Permits are issued at Lee Pool next door (tel. 617/523–9746).

The Metropolitan District Commission (20 Somerset St., tel. 617/727–5215) maintains tennis courts throughout Boston. No permit is required to use these courts, which operate on a first-come, first-served basis:

**John J. Moynihan Playground,** Truman Highway, Hyde Park
**Francis D. Martini Music Shell,** Truman Highway, Hyde Park
**Monsignor Francis A. Ryan Memorial Playground,** River Street, Mattapan
**Charles Weider Park** (lighted), Sharon and Dale streets, Hyde Park
**Marine Park** (lighted), South Boston.

## Spectator Sports

Sports are as much a part of Boston as are codfish and Democrats. Everything you may have heard about the zeal of Boston fans is true, and out-of-towners wishing to avoid controversy would do well not to flaunt their partiality to the teams back home. (Visitors from New York, for example, should not bring their Yankees T-shirts.) College teams are followed with enthusiasm, especially Boston College and Harvard College football. College hockey fans look forward to the Beanpot Tournament in February.

**Baseball**  **Boston Red Sox,** American League (Fenway Park, tel. 617/267–8661 or 617/267–1700 for tickets). Baseball season begins early in April and finishes the first weekend in October.

**Basketball**  **Boston Celtics,** NBA (Boston Garden, tel. 617/523–3030 or 617/720–3434 for tickets). Basketball season runs from October to May, and they're running out of room for hanging the Celtics' championship flags among the rafters of the Garden.

**Football**  **New England Patriots,** NFL (Sullivan Stadium, Foxboro, tel. 800/543–1776). The Patriots would love to win a few games in a row. Sullivan Stadium is 45 minutes south of the city.
**Boston College Eagles** (Alumni Stadium and Shea Stadium, Chestnut Hill, tel. 617/552–3000).
**Boston University Terriers** (Nickerson Field, off Commonwealth Ave., tel. 617/353–3838).
**Harvard University Crimson** (Harvard University Stadium, North Harvard St. and Soldiers Field Road, Allston, tel. 617/495–2211).

**Greyhound Racing**  **Wonderland Racetrack** (190 VFW Pkwy., Revere, tel. 617/284–1300). General admission $1.75, clubhouse admission $2.75. Open daily at 6 PM, first race at 7:30. Matinee post time 1 PM Tuesday, Friday, and Saturday.

**Hockey**  **Boston Bruins,** NHL (Boston Garden, tel. 617/227–3223). The Bruins are on the ice, underneath the Celtics' parquet, from October until April, frequently on Thursday and Sunday evenings.

# 6 Dining

*The restaurants were selected by Mary H. Frakes, who writes the "Word of Mouth" restaurant column for the* Boston Phoenix.

The main ingredient in Boston restaurant fare is still the bounty of the North Atlantic, the daily catch of fish and shellfish that appears somewhere on virtually every menu, whether the cuisine be new French, traditional American, Middle Eastern, Oriental, or simply seafood. Every day, from Gloucester to New Bedford, the boats arrive with 30 to 40 varieties of fish to supply the area's restaurants, which may serve the harvest in chowders or bouillabaisse, baked, broiled, fried, or grilled, and even raw.

Seafood or no, the choice of dining experience in Boston is unusually wide. At one extreme, respected young chefs emphasize the freshest ingredients and the menu reflects the morning's shopping; at the other, the tradition of decades mandates recipes older than the nation and the menu seems forever unchanged. Between the extremes lies an extensive range of American, French, Italian, and other national and ethnic cuisines, their variety ample enough to create difficult decisions at mealtime.

Many restaurants offer a true dining experience, gourmet meals carefully presented in an artfully planned, often formal setting. Others rely on imaginative decor or spectacular city or harbor views to make up for a less imaginative menu. Still others enhance their plain or noisy quarters with hearty food at bargain prices.

Most bars offer meals—some even pride themselves on their food—but offerings are usually limited and lean toward whatever is microwavable. Outdoor vendors, chiefly around Boston Common, have pretzels, popcorn, and occasionally hot dogs. In the Quincy Market area it's a short stroll from the indoor food stands to a bench in the colorful outdoor marketplace.

Bostonians are not traditionally late diners. Many of the city's finest restaurants are busy by 7 PM, and those near the theater district begin filling up earlier. (Advise your waiter when you sit down if you plan to attend an after-dinner performance.) Some of the more popular restaurants will offer two seatings on weekends, generally at around 7 and 9; those who like to linger over coffee and cognac will probably find the second sitting more relaxing.

Many restaurants now offer "early bird" specials at greatly reduced prices. They are an excellent bargain, especially for those who like to eat early. The one drawback may be that some offer only a limited menu, and sampling a particular entree may mean going off the special. Restaurants often have luncheon specials whose quality equals that of dinner selections—at significantly lower prices.

While a more casual style has become evident in Boston restaurants, the formality that has always been an important aspect of the city still lingers. T-shirts and walking shorts may be acceptable in many places, but they are not appropriate in others. In most of Boston's better restaurants a man would feel comfortable wearing coat and tie, and woman wearing a dress. Some restaurants still require coats and ties for men.

As a general rule, you can expect to tip about 15% on a check of less than $60, about 20% on a check larger than $60.

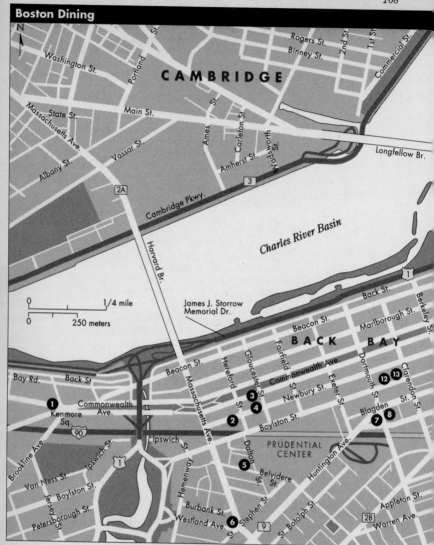

## Boston Dining

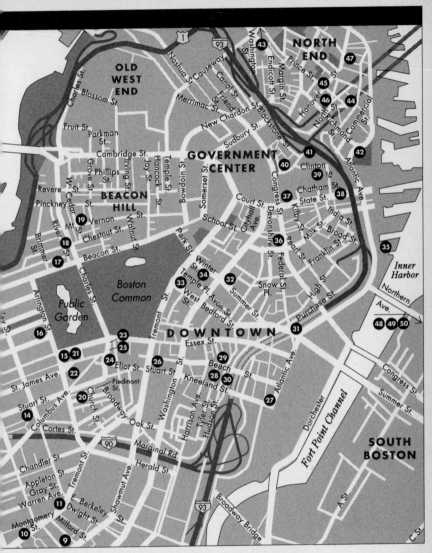

The following price categories are based on the average cost of a three-course dinner for one person, food alone, not including beverages, tax, and tip.

| Category | Cost* |
|---|---|
| Very Expensive | over $35 |
| Expensive | $20–$35 |
| Moderate | $10–$20 |
| Inexpensive | under $10 |

*per person; add 5% tax*

The following credit card abbreviations are used: AE, American Express; CB, Carte Blanche; D, Discover Card; DC, Diners Club; MC, MasterCard; V, Visa.

The most highly recommended restaurants are indicated by a star ★.

## French

**Back Bay**
★ **Aujourd'hui.** In less than a decade this formal dining room of the Four Seasons Hotel was one of the power rooms of the city. Its chairs are upholstered in tapestry, the china is antique, and the food reflects an inventive approach to regional ingredients and New American cuisine. Some entrees, such as rack of Colorado meadow lamb with layered potato and lasagna can be extremely rich, but the seasonal menu also offers low-calorie, low-cholesterol, "alternative cuisine" choices. Try for a window table overlooking the Public Garden. *200 Boylston St., tel. 617/ 451–1392. Reservations required. Jacket and tie advised. AE, DC, MC, V. Very Expensive.*

★ **L'Espalier.** In the spring of 1988 the chef's toque and the keys to the restored 19th-century town house passed from the acclaimed Moncef Meddeb, who had established this very special restaurant, to Frank McClelland, whom *Food and Wine* called one of America's top chefs. While the use of fresh native ingredients continues to be the starting point for the daily menu, the style of cooking has moved away from the nouvelle and esoteric toward the simpler, lighter preparations and larger portions that characterize contemporary French and American cuisine. The $56 fixed-price, three-course dinner might include roast native partridge with chanterelles, salmon steak with mint and wild onion butter and a salad of peas and radishes, and for dessert a luscious but low-calorie arrangement of figs and peaches with wild strawberry sauce and mascarpone cheese. A *menu dégustation*, which provides a sampling of many items, is available on request Monday through Friday. Under the influence of the youthful and energetic McClellands, the waiting staff and general atmosphere have become more relaxed; unchanged are the excellent wine list of 150 choices and the decor of the three intimate but elegant dining rooms, each with a marble fireplace and striking arrangements of fresh flowers. All have well-spaced tables. Large windows give the Salon and Parlor rooms a light, airy feeling, while the upstairs Library, with its dark peach walls and mahogany paneling, is somewhat more masculine and clubby. *30 Glouscester Street, tel. 617/262–3023.*

*Reservations essential. Jacket and tie suggested. AE, MC, V. No lunch. Closed Sun. Very Expensive.*

★ **Plaza Dining Room.** The romantic, Edwardian dining room at the Copley Plaza Hotel has always been elegant, its extensive menu sophisticated. The high-back, tapestry-covered chairs, the crystal chandeliers, a lavishly molded ceiling, mahogany Palladian-arched mirrors, and the baby grand playing discreetly in the background create an atmosphere suitable for haute cuisine. The extensive seasonal menu offers dishes that are classically French, with innovative touches and ingredients. For example, the steamed shrimp is served with an orange and curry dressing while medallions of Maine lobster are garnished with avocado and apple. The wine list is designed to impress, and the library at the entrance is perfect for an after-dinner brandy. *138 St. James Ave., tel. 617/267–5300. Reservations advised. Jacket and tie required. AE, CB, DC, MC, V. Very Expensive.*

**Downtown  Julien.** Vaulted ceilings take on a new perspective in the formal dining room of the Air France-affiliated hotel that occupies the historic Federal Reserve Bank building in the heart of the financial district. Limestone walls, massive chandeliers, and wing chairs surrounding discreetly placed tables combine to give diners a surpassing sense of privacy and well-being that is equally conducive to business deals or marriage proposals. The seasonal French menu emphasizes seafood and the devoted use of local fresh produce. Gone are the days of skimpy nouvelle cuisine dishes; the portions are ample, and calories are spared through the use of natural stock sauces rather than creams. Samples from a summer menu included crab and New England clams wrapped in cabbage leaves with pimiento and essence of coriander; fresh cod and smoked salmon with cabbage, gin, and juniper berries; pork tenderloin with spices, grilled almonds, and grapes. In addition to the standard pastry cart, desserts include passion fruit *gratin* (a warm minisoufflé) and bittersweet chocolate bits with grilled coffee sauce. The wine industry has acclaimed the excellence of the extensive, balanced list. *Hotel Meridien, 250 Federal St., tel. 617/451–1900. Reservations recommended. Jacket and tie required. AE, DC, MC, V. No lunch weekends. Very Expensive.*

**Le Marquis de Lafayette.** When Swissôtel located its Lafayette Hotel on the edge of the Combat Zone, it was determined to offset the tawdriness of the neighborhood with a dining room that would be one of the city's premier restaurants. Le Marquis achieved that goal quickly, its menu the creation of the French consulting chef Jacky Pluton. The ambience here is that of an English hunt club, with hunting prints and oils on the walls and crested china and a long-stemmed rose in a crystal vase on each table. The classically based, seasonal menu might include crab salad with baby greens and rose fish with cilantro and asparagas. The formal atmosphere and rigorous attention to culinary artistry call to mind the term "temple of gastronomy." *1 Ave. de Lafayette, tel. 617/451–2600. Reservations advised. Jacket and tie required. AE, CB, DC, MC, V. Very Expensive.*

## French/American

**Back Bay  Ritz-Carlton Dining Room.** The hotel and its formal dining room are traditional to such an extent that whenever the chef has tried to introduce changes in the age-old menu, the loyal patrons have stirred up an uncharacteristic fuss. Thus you shall ever find such tried-and-true dishes as New England clam chowder, lobster bisque, broiled scrod, chateaubriand béarnaise, Boston cream pie, dessert soufflés, and of course caviar. Each season a few extra dishes sneak onto the menu: Venison and wild mushroom paté and smoked pheasant breast with cabbage and Riesling sauce. The wine list offers rarities among its 200 labels. Impeccably trained and attentive waiters in tuxedos provide royal service—and have served royalty, the Prince of Wales for one. Doubtless royalty feels right at home in the regal but understated elegance of the room, with its color scheme of gold accented by cobalt blue. Ample windows provide a commanding view of the Public Garden, and an accomplished pianist adds the grace note. *Ritz-Carlton Hotel, 15 Arlington St., tel. 617/536–5700. Reservations required. Jacket and tie required. AE, DC, MC, V. Very Expensive.*

**South End**
★

**Hamersley's Bistro.** Fiona and Gordon Hamersley opened their French-American bistro in July 1987 and have gotten rave reviews. The black and white decor in both dining rooms is accented by a fire-engine-red bar and maître d' station. Specialties that have a permanent place on the daily menu include a garlic and mushroom sandwich served as an appetizer (the mushrooms change seasonally), and roast chicken with garlic, lemon, and parsley. The wine list, which changes to match the menu, includes French, Italian, Spanish, and Californian selections by the bottle and glass. *578 Tremont St., tel. 617/267–6068. Reservations accepted, recommended Fri. and Sat. nights. Dress: informal. MC, V. Moderate.*

## Classic American

**Back Bay**

**Grill 23.** Gray business suits are prominent at this steak house in the renovated Salada Tea building. Dark paneling, gigantic marble columns, and waiters in white jackets give it a men's-club feel, as do the brass plaques at the bar stools that identify regular patrons. The house salad, a melange of vegetables, is justly praised, and the kitchen concentrates on grilling meat and seafood with skill. If you want an $8 burger for lunch, come early; surprisingly for a steak house, they can run out. *161 Berkeley St., tel. 617/542–2255. Reservations suggested. Jacket and tie requested. AE, CB, D, DC, MC, V. No lunch Sat. and Sun. Expensive–Very Expensive.*

**Boodle's.** This London-style chophouse is one of the Back Bay's best kept restaurant secrets. Bible-thick steaks and fresh local fish, along with a variety of vegetables, are expertly grilled over hickory or mesquite. There are dozens of sauces to choose from, and guests are encouraged to share larger cuts of meat. The split-level dining room is furnished like a 19th-century club. *40 Dalton St. in the Back Bay Hilton, tel. 617/266–3537. Reservations suggested. Dress: informal. AE, CB, DC, MC, V. Expensive.*

**Morton's of Chicago.** The steaks are prime, the baked potatoes huge, the room packed and often noisy in one of Boston's classic steak houses. If you're particularly hungry, you might want to tackle the 24-ounce T-bone; if you haven't eaten for a week, try the 48-ounce super steak. The seafood selection includes swordfish. The Caesar and blue cheese dressings are homemade. Everything on the menu is à la carte. Your waiter will run down the menu and announce the day's specials. *1*

*Exeter Plaza, tel. 617/266–5858. Reservations recommended (be prepared to wait up to 1½ hours Sat.) Jacket and tie requested. AE, DC, MC, V. No lunch weekends. Expensive.*

**Charley's Eating and Drinking Saloon.** A 19th-century Victorian saloon serving American food: hamburgers, prime rib, sirloin steak, and London broil. *284 Newbury St., tel. 617/266–3000. Dress: informal. AE, MC, V. Moderate.*

**Beacon Hill**   **Hampshire House.** This restored 19th-century Federal town house holds several drinking and dining environments. Downstairs is the Bull and Finch Pub, model for the TV series *Cheers.* The first floor lounge, with its polished paneling and moose heads, has the feel of an elegant hunting lodge; overlooking the Public Garden, it is a fine place to have a drink and watch the world go by. (Enjoy the New Orleans jazz brunch with their in-house quartet on Sundays.) The Georgian Room on the first floor offers a smaller, more intimate dining space. The upstairs Baker Library looks out on the Public Garden. The cuisine is Continental. Scallop and shrimp Soltner, sauteed in butter with julienne carrots and leeks, is a house special, as are the broiled lamb chops with a three-mustard sauce. *84 Beacon St., tel. 617/227–9600. Reservations required. Jacket required. AE, DC, MC, V. Expensive.*

**Downtown**   **Locke-Ober Café.** This Boston landmark has changed little since it opened in 1875. It did, at last, admit women to the Men's Café in 1972, and several years ago it added a new bar, albeit with the authentic Victorian stained glass and hand-carved Dominican mahogany used elsewhere in the building. A bastion of Boston's Brahmins, Locke's has probably seen the consummation of more business deals and political agreements than any other place in Boston. Its mix of traditional Continental and New England food is immune to innovation: lobster Savannah, oysters Winter Place, hash, Dover sole, steak tartare, Indian pudding, and John F. Kennedy's favorite, lobster bisque, have been house specialties for decades. Some of the staff (who wear black ties and long white aprons) have been there almost as long. The Men's Café, with its square dark mahogany bar and huge silver tureens, is a rare reminder of an era long past. Upstairs are the pleasant but less interesting Ober Room and the private dining rooms. Virtually everything on the menu is à la carte. *3 Winter Place, tel. 617/542–1340. Reservations advised. Jacket and tie required. Valet parking after 6 PM. AE, DC, MC, V. No lunch Sat. or Sun. Very Expensive.*

**Blue Diner.** Don't let the fresh flowers, cloth napkins, and fancy wine list fool you; this is an original 1945 diner with genuine diner food (as well as more sophisticated offerings). It gets rave reviews for such original creations as grilled swordfish with melon chutney and down-home favorites like fresh roasted turkey with old-fashioned gravy, homemade cranberry sauce, and mashed potatoes. Save room for a slice of the homemade coconut pie. It's one of the few places in Boston open 24 hours—Thurs., Fri. and Sat. *178 Kneeland St., tel. 617/338–4639. No reservations. Dress: casual. AE, DC, MC, V. Inexpensive–Moderate.*

**Faneuil Hall**   **Durgin-Park.** Diners here will want to be hungry enough to cope with enormous portions and to tolerate a long wait. This bustling Quincy Market restaurant was serving hearty New England fare when the building was a working market instead of a tourist attraction, and it requires only a little imagination

to picture burly workingmen chowing down at the long commu-
nal tables where diners sit elbow to elbow with strangers.
Durgin-Park still serves such homey New England fare as Indian pudding and haunches of prime rib that would keep your dog
busy for hours. The atmosphere is uniquely Old Boston. *340
Faneuil Hall Marketplace, North Market Bldg., tel. 617/227–
2038. No reservations. Dress: casual. No credit cards. Moderate.*

**Houlihan's Old Place.** Roast duck, seafood, steaks, burgers,
omelets, and sandwiches are served amid art, antiques, and
greenery. Half-price hors d'oeuvres in the lounge during weekday Happy Hour, 4–6. *60 State St., State Street Bldg., tel. 617/
367–6377. Dress: no jeans, t-shirts, or athletic shoes after 7 PM.
Cover charge after 7 PM in the lounge. AE, DC, MC, V. Inexpensive–Moderate.*

## New American

**Back Bay** ★  **Biba.** The wildly inventive Biba was a place to see and be seen
from the day it opened in 1989. Its relaxed, eclectic decor combines bright colors and a cryptic mural of well-fed diners. The
menu format, which groups dishes as *meats, legumina,* and the
challenging *offal,* encourages inventive and inexpensive combinations, and the gutsy fare mixes flavors from five continents.
Dishes can be as simple as spaghetti with breadcrumbs or as
elaborate as spring baby lamb panzarotti with sheep's milk
cheese and wild leeks. The wine list emphasizes adventurous
selections from lesser-known areas. The downstairs bar, where
street-level windows permit people-watching, is good for an afternoon snack and late-night grazing. Allow plenty of time for
dining; service can be slow. *272 Boylston St., tel. 617/426–7878.
Reservations advised. Dress: casual but neat. MC, V. Moderate–Expensive.*

**Rocco's.** The emphasis at Rocco's is on a colorful dining experience. The atmosphere is lavish: Two enormous brass chandeliers hang from a 20-foot ceiling decorated with murals of
cherubs, maidens, and satyrs. Carved wooden fish and tropical
birds adorn the tabletops. Just as eclectic as the room are the
menu selections from Italy, Thailand, Cuba, Spain, Jamaica,
and elsewhere. Expect to find such treats as Tuscan-style
grilled rack of lamb, Oriental duck, and Irish lamb stew. The
menu changes frequently. Dessert selections might include
chocolate caramel macadamia nut tart and maple pecan torte. *5
Charles St. S, Transportation Bldg., tel. 617/723–6800. Reservations suggested. Dress: informal. AE, CB, DC, MC, V. Moderate–Expensive.*

**Back Bay Bistro.** Engagingly informal and not too expensive,
the Back Bay Bistro has a menu more exciting than your average neighborhood bar and grill: excellent soups, good country
pâté, nightly specials, and respectable sandwiches. Wine by
the glass and by the bottle enhance the bistro ambience. *565
Boylston St., tel. 617/536–4477. Reservations recommended
for parties of 5 or more. Dress: casual. AE, DC, MC, V. No
lunch Sun. and Mon. Moderate.*

**Beacon Hill**  **Another Season.** Here the Continental menu changes every
month, with nightly specials; the offerings are creative variations on classical European themes. Trout *moutarde,* chicken
Amsterdam, and homemade sorbets are representative selections. Because Another Season has only a beer and wine li-

cense, their excellent wine list is well suited to their menu. A $19 prix-fixe menu is served Monday–Thursday. *97 Mount Vernon St., tel. 617/367–0880. Reservations advised. Dress: neat attire requested. MC, V. Closed Sun. Expensive.*

**Downtown**    **Cornucopia.** It took courage to open a trendy restaurant here in a downtown neighborhood, and the gamble has paid off. The decor in this intimate, multilevel charmer is an updated art deco: Pyramidal stained-glass chandeliers float above oak tables painted with geometric pastel shapes. An imaginative New American menu, which changes seasonally, features combinations such as grilled mahi-mahi with rum-spiked fruit salsa. Other fare uses more traditional ingredients, for example, roast duck breast with vegetables in a plum sauce. A firm believer in the appropriate pairing of wine and food, the restaurant suggests a specific wine to accompany each dish. Moreover, the wine list is reasonably priced and innovative, and there's a large selection of wines by the glass. *15 West St., tel. 617/338–4600. Reservations suggested. Dress: casual but neat. AE, M, V. No dinner Mon. Closed Sun. Moderate–Expensive.*

**Faneuil Hall**    **Seasons.** Popular with businesspeople and politicians (City Hall ★   is just a block away), this solarium-like restaurant on the fourth floor of the Bostonian Hotel overlooks the bustling Faneuil Hall Marketplace and is a good place to entertain when you want to impress. The cuisine of chef Anthony Ambrose is American with international influences and changes seasonally. Selections from a summer menu included steamed halibut with oriental spices and apple paper, rack of lamb with lemon thyme sauvignon, and for dessert, macadamia nut and coconut flan with mango sorbet. The wine list is exclusively American. It is a private club at lunchtime. *Bostonian Hotel, North and Blackstone Sts., tel. 617/523–3600. Reservations suggested. Jacket requested. AE, DC, MC, V. Very Expensive.*

**North End**    **Restaurant Jasper.** Jasper White, who trained a number of ★   Boston's best chefs, has a national reputation as a creator of contemporary New England cuisine. The menu leans heavily on local seafood and seasonal produce. Dishes might be as nouvelle as a salad of grilled duck with cranberries and spiced nuts—or as traditional as a New England boiled dinner cooked to perfection. The exposed brick walls and red lacquer furniture create a contemporary atmosphere, and the luscious desserts are anything but Puritan. *240 Commercial St., tel. 617/523–1126. Reservations required. Dress: neat but casual. MC, V. No lunch. Closed Sun. and Mon. Very Expensive.*

**South End**    **St. Cloud.** The setting is swank, the clientele chic at this trendy bistro in a historic South End brownstone. The menu looks to the cuisine of a dozen lands: Thai noodle salads, Mexican salsas, Greek spinach cheese pastries, and good old American bluefish. The entrees lean to simply grilled meats and fish with interesting condiments. When available, the date pear tart is the dessert to have. *557 Tremont St., tel. 617/353–0202. Reservations recommended. Dress: informal. AE, DC, MC, V. Expensive–Very Expensive.*

**Waterfront**    **Rowes Wharf Restaurant.** The dining room of the Boston Harbor Hotel offers a waterfront view without the noise and mediocre food of the megarestaurants. Built in 1987, the restaurant nonetheless has such traditional touches as upholstered armchairs, gathered swag curtains, mahogany paneling, and shaded wall sconces. The food is a subdued New American cuisine, with entrees such as fresh tagliatelli with mushrooms and poached Maine lobster over chorizo paella. The outdoor waterside cafe is a winner in summer. *70 Rowes Wharf, tel. 617/439–3995. Reservations suggested. Jacket required. AE, CB, DC, MC, V. Moderate–Expensive.*

## Chinese

**Back Bay** **Mr. Leung.** If you've been to Sally Ling's—which has moved from Commercial Street to the Hyatt Regency Hotel in Cambridge (*see* Dining in the Cambridge chapter)—it will come as no surprise to you to learn that Mr. Leung helped to set up that successful restaurant. Here again, the ambience is deceiving. The black lacquered walls, exquisite flower arrangements, waiters in tuxedos, and a ceiling studded with tiny spotlights make an unusual setting for a Chinese restaurant. But one taste of the Peking duck (for two) or lobster sauteed with ginger and scallops and you'll know you're in the Chinese equivalent of nirvana. *545 Boylston St., tel. 617/236–4040. Reservations accepted. Jackets required. AE, MC, V. Expensive.*

**Downtown** **Carl's Pagoda.** No one would come to this small upstairs restaurant looking for atmosphere, but its devoted clientele raves about the outstanding Cantonese cuisine, particularly the tomato soup, clams in black bean sauce, ginger shrimp, and Chinese sausages with vegetables. The knowing or adventuresome diner will simply ask Carl to prepare a meal and expect to be surprised, for some of his special dishes are not on the menu. Dinner only. *23 Tyler St., tel. 617/357–9837. Reservations suggested. Dress: informal. No credit cards. No liquor. Moderate.*

**Weylu's Wharf.** On the waterfront, with a view of the Boston skyline, Weylu's specializes in Mandarin and Szechuan cuisine. To such traditional dishes as hot and sour soup and moo shu pork, the chef has added new specialties, among them *fu young three-treasure* (shrimp, chicken, scallops, and vegetables in white wine sauce) and General Tso's Chicken, a deep-fried chicken dish in a tangy, orange sauce. Try also the scallion pancakes and crispy aromatic beef. The decor is contemporary Chinese, set in peach and green. *254 Summer St., tel. 617/423–0243. Reservations accepted. Dress: informal. AE, MC, V. Moderate.*

★ **Ho Yuen Ting.** Every night a waiting line forms outside this Chinatown hole-in-the-wall. The reason is simple: Ho Yuen Ting serves some of the best seafood in town. The house specialty is a sole and vegetable stir-fry served in a spectacular whole, crisply fried fish. Come with friends so you can also enjoy the clams with black bean sauce, lobster with ginger and scallion, and whole steamed bass. *13A Hudson St., tel. 617/426–2316. Reservations accepted. Dress: informal. No credit cards. Inexpensive–Moderate.*

**Imperial Teahouse Restaurant.** On the first floor is a traditional Cantonese restaurant with a representative menu. The livelier second floor is a large, airy dining room with the most extensive dim sum selection in Chinatown. *Dim sum* denotes both the meal (a veritable Chinese brunch, served daily 9–3) and the variety of dumplings and buns, tiny spareribs, morsels of pork, chicken, clams, shrimp, and other foods that you select from roving carts and pay for by the item. *70 Beach St., tel. 617/426–8543. Reservations accepted weekdays only and for dinner for groups of more than 4; the line moves fast, but expect a 15-to-20-minute wait for dim sum. Dress: informal. AE, CB, DC, MC, V. Inexpensive–Moderate.*

## Italian

**Back Bay**  **Bnu.** Conveniently located in the heart of the theater district, this tiny cafe specializes in pizzas, pasta dishes, and salads. The linguini with tenderloin tips and light cream sauce, veal scallopini sauteed with wild mushrooms and thyme, and grilled vegetable and polenta salad are enthusiastically recommended. The decorator borrowed design elements from 2,000 years of Mediterranean architecture: faux marble columns, art deco chairs, neon, and Regency fabrics. *123 Stuart St., Transportation Bldg., tel. 617/367–8405. Reservations accepted only for 5:45 and 6 PM pretheater sittings. Dress: informal. MC, V. Inexpensive–Moderate.*

**Beacon Hill**  **Ristorante Toscano.** Here is the food mama would make—if
★  mama were an expert cook in a tiny village in Tuscany. Homemade pasta and *foccaccia* (pizzalike bread), fork-tender veal, succulent game birds, and a rich *tiramisou* (chocolate, cream, and sponge cake dessert) are among the dishes that attract a blue-blooded Beacon Hill clientele. The exposed brick walls of the dining room are tastefully decorated with Italian scenes. *41 Charles St., tel. 617/723–4090. Reservations recommended. Dress: informal. AE. No lunch Sun. Expensive–Very Expensive.*

**North End**  **Felicia's.** Since the 1950s, Felicia Solimine has been providing the solid Italian home cooking that has earned her the devotion not only of Bostonians but of out-of-town luminaries as well. (Luciano Pavarotti is said to go off his diet here when he's in town.) Those who in the past have stood in line waiting for a table in this second-floor restaurant will be pleased to know that there is now a lounge on the third floor, complete with a 60-foot mural of Venice. In recent years Felicia's has been riding on its reputation, and the quality of its fare has slipped. Favorite specialties are the chicken *verdicchio*, angel-hair pasta, and cannelloni. Only beer and wine are served. *145A Richmond St., tel. 617/523–9885. Reservations accepted except Fri. and Sat. Dress: casual. AE, CB, DC, MC, V. Moderate.*

**Ristorante Lucia.** Some aficionados consider Lucia's the best Italian restaurant in the North End. Its specialties from the Abruzzi region include batter-fried artichoke hearts or mozzarella in carrozza as appetizer and the chicken alla Lucia or *pollo arrabiatta* (chicken breast sauteed with a spicy tomato sauce). Check out the upstairs bar, with its pink marble and its takeoff on the Sistine Chapel ceiling. *415 Hanover St., tel. 617/523–9148. Reservations recommended. Dress: informal. AE, MC, V. No lunch Mon.–Thurs. Moderate.*

## Japanese

**Back Bay**  **Restaurant Genji.** Genji is a traditional Japanese restaurant with characteristically soothing atmosphere and gracious service. Upstairs, diners sit around a table grill as chefs make fancy moves with their knives and serve up Japanese steak dishes. Downstairs, with a choice of Oriental or Western seating, more traditional dishes are offered: tempura, teriyaki, excellent sushi. *327 Newbury St., tel. 617/267–5656. Reservations suggested on weekends. Dress: informal. AE, CB, DC, MC, V. Moderate–Expensive.*

**Faneuil Hall**  **Tatsukichi-Boston.** Sushi and sashimi are specialties, as are pot-cooked dinners and *kushiagi* (deep-fried kebobs). Meals are served in a modern Japanese setting with Western or Oriental seating. The downstairs Foreign Affairs Lounge has live entertainment. *189 State St., tel. 617/720–2468. Reservations recommended. Dress: informal. AE, DC, MC, V. No lunch Sat., closed Sun. Moderate.*

**Kenmore Square**  **Miyako.** Small in size, large in ambition, this restaurant in a
★  basement serves some of the most exotic sushi in town. Among its estimable hot dishes are *age-shumai* (shrimp fritters), *hamachi teriyaki* (yellowtail teriyaki), and *agedashi* (fried bean curd). The waitresses are uncommonly personable, too. *468 Commonwealth Ave., tel. 617/236–0222. Reservations accepted. Dress: informal. MC, V. No lunch Sun. Moderate.*

## Mediterranean

**Charlestown**  **Olives.** This sunny version of a contemporary trattoria is well
★  worth the short trip over the Charles to Charlestown. Occupying an intimate, relaxed storefront space, Olives is a new bistro that provides imaginative cooking at a reasonable price. The restaurant is named for Olivia English, who runs the front of the house while her husband, Todd English, tends the wood-fired brick oven and the spit-roasting in the kitchen. The name also connotes the Mediterranean-style cuisine, which is oriented to those countries where olives are grown. The open-face roast lamb sandwich has become a signature dish. But be prepared to be sent down the street to a neighborhood bar while you wait for a table; this is one of the area's most popular restaurants. *67 Main St., Charlestown, tel. 617/242–1999. No reservations. Dress: casual but neat. MC, V. No lunch. Closed Mon. Moderate–Expensive.*

## Middle Eastern

**South End**  **Nadia's Eastern Star.** Nadia's is not the place to come for elegant, leisurely dining. But if you like vast portions of *hoomis* (chick pea dip), *baba ganooj* (roasted eggplant pâté), *kufta* (ground lamb meatloaf), and expertly grilled shish kebabs served without pretense or fuss, this lively Middle Eastern restaurant is for you. The dining room will make you see red: red tablecloths and red curtains. A popular haunt of night owls, Nadia's hops to Arabian music. *280 Shawmut Ave., tel. 617/ 338–8091. Dress: informal. No credit cards. No lunch. Moderate.*

## Seafood

**Back Bay**  **Turner Fisheries.** The restrained Puritan gray, blue, and white decor, subdued contemporary jazz, green-shaded accountants' lamps, and mahogany sideboards all hint that this is a tasteful fish house. A wide selection of seafood may be ordered broiled, grilled, fried, baked, or blackened, but any meal should begin with the chowder—which has been inducted to the Chowderfest Hall of Fame, having won the yearly Chowderfest competition too many times to contend. Be judicious in ordering; that chowder packs a mighty rich punch. *10 Huntington Ave., tel. 617/424-7425. Dress: casual. Reservations strongly suggested. AE, CB, D, DC, MC, V. Moderate–Expensive.*

**Legal Sea Foods.** What began as a tiny adjunct to a fish market has grown to important status, with additional locations in Cambridge, Chestnut Hill, the Copley Place Mall, and Kendall Square. Always busy, Legal still does things its own way. Each dish is served when it is ready, and not necessarily by the person who took the order. Dishes are not allowed to stand until the orders for a table are completed but are brought individually to insure freshness. The style of food preparation is, as always, simple: Seafood is raw, broiled, fried, steamed, or baked; fancy sauces and elaborate presentations are eschewed. You can have a baked stuffed lobster or mussels au gratin, but otherwise your choice lies among the range of sea creatures available that day, cooked in their simplest forms. The smoked bluefish pâté is among the finest appetizers anywhere. Homemade ice creams are welcome desserts. The wine list is carefully selected, the house wine equally so. *64 Arlington St., Park Sq., in the Boston Park Plaza Hotel, tel. 617/426-4444. No reservations; expect to wait. Dress: informal. AE, DC, MC, V. Moderate.*

**Faneuil Hall**  **Union Oyster House.** Established in 1826, the Union Oyster House is Boston's oldest restaurant. For nearly two decades its best feature has been a first-floor shellfish bar where the oysters and clams are fresh and well chilled—a handy place to stop for a dozen oysters or cherrystone clams on the halfshell. The upstairs rooms at the top of the narrow staircase are dark with low ceilings—very Ye Olde New England. A recent bar addition has a lighter feel. *41 Union St., tel. 617/227-2750. Reservations accepted. Dress: informal. AE, DC, MC, V. Moderate.*

**North End**  **Joseph's Aquarium.** Joseph's is a small restaurant with a small bar and, in good weather, a view past bobbing pleasure craft and granite or brick condominiums to the inner harbor. The fare is straightforward seafood in a simple setting, the clientele generally businessmen at lunch, a young crowd at dinner. *101 Atlantic Ave. (Mercantile Building), at the northern end of Waterfront Park, tel. 617/523-4000. Dress: casual. AE, CB, DC, MC, V. Moderate–Expensive.*

**The Daily Catch.** Shoulder-crowding small, with an informal oyster bar, this storefront restaurant in the North End (Little Italy) specializes in calamari dishes, lobster *fra diavolo*, linguini with clam sauce—and extremely low prices. A second restaurant has opened at 261 Northern Avenue, across from Jimmy's Harborside, and a third is at 385 Summer St. in Somerville. Hours of operation vary greatly; call for times. *323 Hanover St., tel. 617/523-8567. No reservations. Dress: casual. No credit cards. Inexpensive.*

**Waterfront**  **Anthony's Pier 4.** This is perhaps the most famous of Boston restaurants, and diners pay a price for its popularity in waiting time, assembly-line service, and often mediocre food. If you can bear the tourist trap atmosphere, you will find a terrific view of the harbor and a menu that offers a wide variety of seafood (as well as dishes for carnivores). New England specialties include finnan haddie, clam chowder, and Indian pudding for dessert. Excellent lobsters are ordered by size. The wine list is of award-winning stature, and the house wine is first rate. In good weather the outdoor patio is a great place to wait, and there's an indoor lounge. *140 Northern Ave., tel. 617/423–6363. Reservations suggested. Jacket required, tie preferred. AE, CB, DC, MC, V. Moderate–Expensive.*

**Jimmy's Harborside.** Rivaling Anthony's—and preferred by many—Jimmy's is an exceedingly popular seafood establishment with a solid reputation. The bright, three-tiered main dining room was designed to ensure that every table has an unobstructed view of the harbor, and the Early American decor is enhanced by magnificent tapestries made in Appalachia. Upstairs, the Merchants Club dining room, with its China trade theme, is more formal and intimate. In addition to the many fresh seafood preparations that have long been standard fare, the menu now offers such specials as pasta primavera with a medley of sautéed shrimp, veal, and pork tenderloin. As a change from chowder or traditional bouillabaisse, try the scampi Luciano, a bouillabaisse made with white wine, cream, and a variety of fresh fish and shrimp. The wine list has been expanded and revised to showcase American wines. The Boat Bar, the scene of high-spirited camaraderie, is a favorite watering hole of politicians, among them Tip O'Neill. *242 Northern Ave., tel. 617/423–1000. Limited reservations. Jacket preferred after 6 PM. AE, CB, DC, MC, V. Moderate–Expensive.*

**No-Name Restaurant.** From its humble beginning as a nameless hole-in-the-wall for Fish Pier workers, the No-Name has grown into one of Boston's favorite seafood restaurants. It still attracts the workers, but now they share the usually crowded quarters with businesspeople, tourists, and families in town from the suburbs. An added dining room upstairs has reduced the waiting time, yet diners still sit elbow to elbow, feasting on the No-Name staples: fried seafood, boiled lobster, broiled scallops, and the fish of the day—always in generous servings. *15½ Fish Pier, off Northern Ave., tel. 617/338–7539. Reservations only for large groups. Dress: informal. No credit cards. Inexpensive–Moderate.*

## Thai

**Back Bay**  **Star of Siam.** Here you'll find the cooking of Thailand, with many highly seasoned dishes. Among the selections are sauteed beef in curry sauce, sauteed shrimp with cashews, dancing squid, and *pad Thai* (pan fried noodles). *93 Church St., behind Boston Park Plaza Hotel, tel. 617/451–5236. Reservations accepted for more than 3 persons. Dress: informal. AE, MC, V. No lunch weekends. Inexpensive–Moderate.*

**Thai Cuisine.** Those who have business at Northeastern University, tickets for a Symphony Hall event, or simply an adventurous palate will welcome the Thai Cuisine. Dishes can be very highly spiced, but an asterisk signals that the kitchen will make adjustments. The food is not merely exotica for the uninitiated; it is well cooked, and the kitchen uses first-rate ingredients. A main course of half a duck is the only sizable entree on the menu; the rest are the kind you order and share, Oriental fashion, with two or three. *14A Westland Ave., tel. 617/262–1485. No reservations. Dress: informal. AE, DC, MC, V. No lunch Sun. Inexpensive.*

**Downtown** **Montien.** A favorite with theatergoers, the pretty Montien restaurant features dishes seldom seen on Thai menus, like *kat thuong-tong* (chicken tartlets with corn and coriander) and stuffed boneless chicken wings, called cupid wings, in addition to such Southeast Asian classics as *pla sarm ros* (spicy whole fish) and *pad Thai* (pan-fried noodles). Decorated with canopied booths, chandeliers, and silk flowers, the dining room has a romantic atmosphere seldom found at ethnic restaurants. *63 Stuart St., tel. 617/338–5600. Reservations suggested. Dress: casual. AE, DC, MC, V. No lunch weekends. Moderate.*

# 7 Lodging

Boston can be an expensive city to stay in. A significant number of hotels have been built in recent years, and most of them fall in the *Expensive* to *Very Expensive* price range. Even some of the old, moderately priced standbys such as the Lenox Hotel have remodeled and raised their tariffs.

The good news is that many of the city's most costly lodging places offer very attractively priced weekend packages. These weekend rates (and their availability) will vary; for a free copy of the *Boston Travel Planner*, contact the Greater Boston Convention and Visitors Bureau (Box 490, Boston, MA 02199, tel. 617/536–4100).

Travelers who seek alternatives to hotel accommodations will find a variety of options in Boston's bed-and-breakfast establishments, hostels, YMCA and YWCA facilities, and rental apartments.

## Hotels

The hotel reviews here are grouped first according to the price categories described below. While each category is defined only by specific dollar amounts, the hotels we have selected within a given category nevertheless share certain characteristics.

*Very Expensive* hotels tend to be either Boston traditions that deserve their continued reputations or new hotels that have set their sights high and are living up to their ambitions. Impeccable service is a hallmark; nearly all provide 24-hour room service and knowledgeable concierges, and fine dining is to be expected.

*Expensive* hotels offer much the same quality in room appointments, but they are often larger and their service less personal. Here are the better hotels catering to business travelers, usually of good value, with less of the grand manner.

*Moderate* hotels generally cost less because they emphasize comfortable accommodations rather than exceptional service, because their location is peripheral, or perhaps because they have been eclipsed by pretentious neighbors and have settled into a more modest niche.

*Inexpensive* hotels and motels are those that provide the clean basics without concern for replacing every cracked tile.

Within each price category, the hotel reviews are grouped by location. One happy result of the hotel-building boom of recent years is that visitors have an extensive choice of hotel location. There are hotels throughout the Back Bay, the Fens, Downtown Boston, in the Old West End, and at Logan Airport.

The major hotel chains represented in Boston are Hilton, Holiday Inn, Howard Johnson, Hyatt, Marriott, Omni, Sheraton, Sonesta, and Westin. Most of their properties offer clean, predictable accommodations at competitive (if often high) prices.

With Boston's many colleges, conventions, and tourist attractions, the city's hotels generally maintain a very high rate of occupancy, particularly in spring, summer, and fall. To avoid inconvenience and frustration, do not arrive without a confirmed reservation.

# Boston Lodging

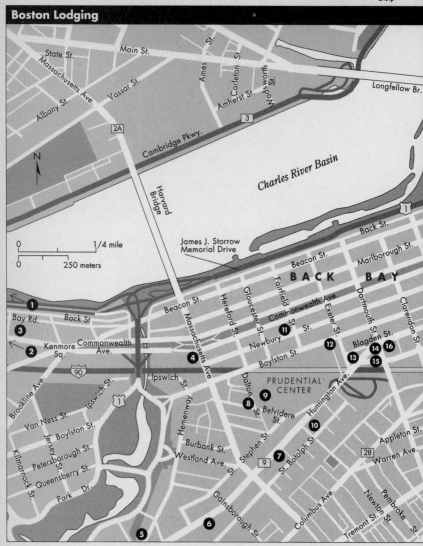

Back Bay Hilton, **8**

Beacon Inns, **11**

Berkeley Residence Club (YWCA), **17**

Boston Harbor Hotel at Rowes Wharf, **26**

Bostonian, **27**

Boston International Hostel, **5**

Boston Marriott Copley Place, **15**

Boston Park Plaza Hotel & Towers, **19**

The Colonnade, **10**

Copley Plaza, **16**

Copley Square Hotel, **13**

Eliot Hotel, **4**

57 Hotel/Howard Johnson's, **21**

Four Seasons, **20**

Greater Boston YMCA, **6**

Guest Quarters Suite Hotel, **1**

Hilton Airport, **30**

Holiday Inn, **29**

Hotel Meridien, **25**

Howard Johnson's Fenway, **3**

Lafayette Hotel, **23**

Lenox Hotel, **12**

Marriott Long Wharf, **28**

Midtown, **7**

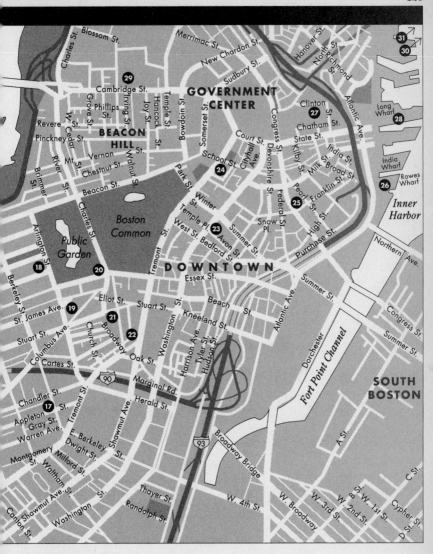

Omni Parker
House, **24**

Ramada Hotel, **31**

Ritz-Carlton, **18**

Sheraton Boston Hotel
& Towers, **9**

Terrace Motor
Lodge, **2**

Tremont House, **22**

The Westin, **14**

Keep in mind that the prices of hotel rooms do not generally include parking, an expense that can run $10–$15 or more a night. A Massachusetts occupancy tax of 9.7% is added to all hotel bills.

The following rate categories apply to regular weekday rates for a double room for two, excluding tax and service charges. They do not reflect special weekend or package rates or seasonal promotions.

| Category | Cost* |
| --- | --- |
| Very Expensive | over $195 |
| Expensive | $150–$195 |
| Moderate | $95–$150 |
| Inexpensive | under $95 |

**double room; add 9.7% state tax*

The following credit card abbreviations are used: AE, American Express; CB, Carte Blanche; D, Discover Card; DC, Diners Club; MC, MasterCard; V, Visa.

The most highly recommended properties are indicated by a star ★.

**Very Expensive**
*Back Bay*

**The Colonnade.** Facing the Prudential Center from across Huntington Avenue, this small modern hotel has always seemed a little out of the way, not quite Back Bay, not quite the South End. Yet it is certainly convenient to Symphony Hall and the Christian Science Church complex, and it has two good restaurants. Children under 12 stay free in their parents' room. *120 Huntington Ave., 02116, tel. 617/424–7000 or 800/962–3030. 288 rooms. Facilities: seasonal rooftop swimming pool, fitness room, snack bar in season; valet and concierge service, barber and beauty salons, multilingual staff, baby-sitting service. AE, CB, DC, MC, V.*

★ **Four Seasons.** The only hotel (other than the Ritz) to overlook the Public Garden, the newer 15-story Four Seasons specializes in luxurious personal service, old-world elegance, and comfort. The rooms have king-size beds, individual climate control, minibars, fresh flowers daily, cable movies, and 24-hour room service. A room overlooking the Garden is worth the extra money. The antique-filled public rooms include a relaxed piano lounge, and Aujourd'hui, a fine restaurant serving American cuisine. Small pets are welcome. *200 Boylston St., 02116, tel. 617/338–4400 or 800/332–3442. 288 rooms and suites. Facilities: lounge, concierge, heated indoor pool, sauna, exercise machines, whirlpool, valet parking. AE, CB, DC, MC, V.*

★ **Ritz-Carlton.** Since 1927 this hotel overlooking the Public Garden has been one of the most luxurious and elegant places to stay in Boston, and many people consider it the only place to stay in town. Its reputation for quality and service (there are two staff members for every guest) continues. All the rooms are traditionally furnished and equipped with bathroom phones, and some rooms have refrigerators. The most coveted rooms remain the suites in the older section, which have working fireplaces and the best views of the Public Garden. For an extra charge, guests can enjoy accommodations on the top three floors, with their own private club. Public rooms include the elegant cafe, with a window on chic Newbury Street; the sumptuous second-floor main dining room; the sedate Street Bar; and The Lounge. Small pets are welcome. *Arlington and Newbury Sts., tel. 617/536–5700 or 800/241–3333. 278 rooms, 48 suites. Facilities: exercise room, affiliation with nearby spa, valet parking, concierge, 24-hour room service, laundry service, beauty and barber salons, multilingual staff, baby-sitting. AE, CB, DC, MC, V.*

**Sheraton Boston Hotel & Towers.** The twin towers of the Sheraton Boston stand, like the Prudential tower, somewhat aloof from the city around them. But Boston's (and New England's) largest hotel and convention center is bustling and well equipped to provide all the amenities. The lobby is brightly lit, cavernous, and somewhat sterile; the guest rooms are cozy, if not large, and comfortably furnished in traditional mahogany with mauve and gray accents. All rooms have color TV (with in-room movies) and wide windows. The higher floors facing the Charles River or the Christian Science Church complex provide the best views. Travelers wanting to escape the convention atmosphere should consider the Towers, which offers more luxurious and less hectic surroundings for approximately 20% more money. Small pets are allowed. Children under 17 stay free in their parents' room. There are special rates for students, faculty, and retirees. Parking, with unlimited in and out, is $15 a day. *Prudential Center, 39 Dalton St., 02199, tel. 617/236–2000 or 800/325–3535. 1,250 rooms. Facilities: indoor/outdoor swimming pool with lifeguard and poolside service, fitness room, Jacuzzi, 3 restaurants, 4 lounges, business center, retail stores, car rental area, concierge, sightseeing office, beauty and barber salons. AE, CB, DC, MC, V.*

**The Westin.** The second of the two anchor hotels of Copley Place, The Westin is the tallest of Boston's hotels (36 floors). A skybridge connects it to the shopping galleries. The rooms are big and handsomely furnished in an updated Queen Anne style; those on the Charles River side offer wonderful views. The restaurants include the Brasserie, the Ten Huntington Bar and Grill, and Turner Fisheries, with an oyster bar. Small pets are welcome. *Copley Pl., tel. 617/262–9600 or 800/228–3000. 800 rooms, 48 suites. Facilities: an excellent health club with an indoor pool, Jacuzzi, sauna, exercise room, valet parking (very expensive). AE, CB, DC, MC, V.*

*Downtown* ★ **Boston Harbor Hotel at Rowes Wharf.** Boston's newest and one of its most elegant luxury hotels has opened right on the water, providing a dramatic new entryway to the city for travelers arriving from Logan Airport via the water shuttle that docks at the hotel. The Boston Harbor Hotel is part of a $193 million, 15-story development recently completed at Rowes Wharf; it includes Foster's Rotunda, a copper-domed observatory that provides striking views of the harbor and city. The hotel is within walking distance of Faneuil Hall, downtown, the New England Aquarium, and the North End. The guest rooms begin at the eighth floor, and each has either a city view or a water view; the decor has hints of mauve or green and cream, and the traditional furnishings include a king-size bed, sitting area, minibar, and remote control TV. The bathrooms have phones, guest bathrobes, hair driers, and amenity kits. Some rooms have balconies. The hotel is proud of its collection of more than 100 works of art celebrating the historical and artistic traditions of the city, all on display in the public spaces on the first and second floors. The elegant and comfortable Rowes Wharf Restaurant offers seafood and American regional cuisine as well as sweeping harbor views. The spectacular Sunday buffet is expensive at $32 per person but worthwhile for those with healthy appetites. There are also an outdoor cafe and a bar. Small pets are welcome. *70 Rowes Wharf, 02110, tel. 617/439–7000 or 800/752–7077. 230 rooms, including 26 suites. Facilities: health club and spa with 60-foot lap pool, whirlpool, sauna, steam and massage rooms; concierge, hair salons, gift shop, marina, commuter boat to the South Shore, water shuttle, valet parking. AE, CB, DC, MC, V.*

**Bostonian.** One of the city's smallest hotels and one of its most charming, the Bostonian epitomizes European-style elegance in the fresh flowers in its rooms, the private balconies, and the French windows. The Harkness Wing, constructed originally in 1824, has rooms with working fireplaces, exposed beamed ceilings, and brick walls. The rooms tend to be a bit small but are extremely comfortable. All bathrooms have telephones and oversize bathtubs. The service is attentive, and the highly regarded Seasons Restaurant has a glass-enclosed rooftop overlooking the marketplace. Children under 12 stay free in their parents' room. *Faneuil Hall Marketplace, 02109, tel. 617/523–3600 or 800/343–0922. 153 rooms. Facilities: Jacuzzi in some suites, 24-hour room service, valet parking. AE, CB, DC, MC, V.*

★ **Lafayette Hotel.** Rising 22 stories above Washington Street and the new Lafayette Place, this Swissôtel borders the Combat Zone, the financial district, and the city's main shopping area. The designers have invested the hotel with an atmosphere of calm and elegant restraint, very much in the early 19th-century Federalist style. The mahogany lobby with its Waterford crystal chandeliers and Chippendale reproduction room furnishings enhance the genteel environment. All rooms have an in-house movie channel and bathroom phones. The ballroom may be Boston's most elegant. Le Marquis de Lafayette Restaurant offers some of the city's finest dining, and there are the less formal Cafe Suisse and the Lobby Bar. Pets are welcome. *1 Ave. de Lafayette, 02111, tel. 617/451–2600, 800/992–0124, or (in MA) 800/325–2531. 500 rooms, including 43 suites. Facilities: health club, a large indoor heated pool, concierge, 24-hr room service, multilingual staff. AE, CB, DC, MC, V.*

★ **Hotel Meridien.** The respected French chain refurbished the old downtown Federal Reserve Building, a landmark Renaissance-Revival building erected in 1922. The rooms, including some cleverly designed loft suites, are airy and naturally lighted, and all have been redecorated recently. Most rooms have queen-size or king-size beds; all rooms have a small sitting area with a writing desk, a minibar, modern furnishings, in-room movies, and two phones, one of them in the bathroom. Julien, one of the city's finest restaurants, is here, as is the Cafe Fleuri, which serves an elegant award-winning Sunday brunch. There are two lounges. Teddy bears and crayons are given to children on arrival. Some pets are permitted. *250 Franklin St., 02110, tel. 617/451–1900 or 800/543–4300. 326 rooms, including several bilevel suites. Facilities: health club with whirlpool, dry sauna, and exercise equipment; indoor pool, concierge, 24-hr room service, nonsmoking floor, valet parking. AE, CB, DC, MC, V.*

**Marriott Long Wharf.** One of the newer Boston hotels, the Long Wharf fits in nicely with the restored waterfront buildings in the vicinity of the New England Aquarium, Waterfront Park, and the North End. The rooms are not balconied, though they appear to be from the outside. Most rooms offer views of the harbor, and all rooms open onto the five-story atrium. The rooms, all renovated in 1990, have king-size or double beds, individual climate control, color TV with in-room movies, and direct-dial phones. A small surcharge will put you in the concierge class on the top floor, with free Continental breakfast, cocktail hour, and the best views. Children under 18 stay free in their parents' room. *296 State St., 02109, tel. 617/227–0800 or 800/228–9290. 400 rooms. Facilities: 2 restaurants, lounge, indoor pool with poolside service, outdoor sundeck, health facilities, whirlpool, tanning salon, sauna, game room. AE, CB, DC, MC, V.*

**Expensive**
*Back Bay*

**Back Bay Hilton.** The 26-story Hilton occupies a corner pocket between the Prudential Center and the Christian Science complex. No hotel (except the Sheraton) is closer to Hynes Convention Center. The Back Bay Hilton is a perfect spot for those who like quiet: all rooms are soundproofed, and there are only 16 on each floor. New owners plan a renovation; the present rooms are of standard size, with small bathrooms and no outside sinks, and they are tastefully decorated in blues and browns, with oriental hints. Many rooms have balconies. The spacious and comfortable lobby carries through on the oriental guest room decor. Boodle's, a British-style grill, and Club Nicole, a jazz night club, are popular with locals as well as visitors. Fit-Corp, a state-of-the-art health facility, is headquartered here, and guests use the facilities at reduced rates. Children of all ages stay free in their parents' room. *40 Dalton St., 02115, tel. 617/236–1100 or 800/874–0663. 340 rooms. Facilities: health club, sauna, indoor swimming pool, sundeck, nonsmoking floors, lobby newsstand and gift shop, 24-hr garage. AE, CB, DC, MC, V.*

★ **Copley Plaza.** The stately, bow-fronted classic among Boston hotels, built in 1912, acquired a new owner at the start of 1989 and has since been completely renovated. Guest rooms have carpeting from England, customized furniture from Italy, and new bathroom fixtures surrounded by marble tile. The Plaza Bar has seating to accommodate a piano bar; Copley's Bar has been redone. A separate concierge area has been created. The hotel staff is multilingual, children under 18 stay free in their parents' room, and pets are welcome. *138 St. James Ave., 02116, tel. 617/267–5300 or 800/826–7539. 396 rooms, 49 suites. Facilities: 2 restaurants, 2 bars, beauty and barber salons. AE, CB, DC, MC, V.*

**Boston Marriott Copley Place.** This is one of Boston's biggest and most ornate hotels, connected to the Copley Place shopping galleries and, by an enclosed footbridge, to the Prudential Center and Hynes Auditorium complex. The Marriott's 38 floors rise over an expansive four-story atrium that has lots of greenery and a waterfall. The rooms, tastefully decorated with Queen Anne furnishings, all have color cable TV with free HBO, AM/FM radio, and individual climate control. Four floors are designated nonsmoking. *110 Huntington Ave., 02116, tel. 617/236–5800 or 800/228–9290. 1,147 rooms including 70 Concierge Level. Facilities: 3 restaurants, 2 lounges, indoor pool, complete health club, 24-hour room service, valet parking, game room, gift shop. AE, CB, DC, MC, V.*

*Downtown* **Omni Parker House.** Said to be the oldest continuously operating hotel in America, though its present building dates only
from 1927 (and has had extensive renovations), the Parker
House is centrally located, one block from the Common and
practically in the central business district. All rooms have color
TV, some have refrigerators; some rooms have showers only.
Parker House rolls, invented here, are still a feature in the
main dining room, where Sunday brunch is an extravaganza.
Children under 16 stay free in their parents' room. There are
special rates for students. *60 School St., 02108, tel. 617/227–
8600 or 800/843–6664. 546 rooms. Facilities: 2 restaurants, 2
bars, complimentary use of nearby Fitcorp Health and Fitness
Center, valet and room service, barber and beauty salons, multilingual staff, baby-sitting service. AE, CB, DC, MC, V.*

*West of the Fens* **Guest Quarters Suite Hotel.** This relatively new 15-story hotel
★ (formerly the Embassy Suites) overlooking the Charles River is
just off major highways, out of the city, and on the Boston-
Cambridge line. Every unit is a suite containing a living room
(with a sofa bed), a bedroom, and a bath. All suites have a refrigerator and entertainment bar, speaker phones, king-size
bed, two remote-control TVs (with a movie channel) concealed
in a custom-designed armoire, bedside desk, and armchair.
One of the three telephones is in the bathroom, which is furnished with a large marble vanity and well-lit mirrors. There's
a complimentary Continental breakfast every morning and a
private manager's reception every evening. Parking is $12 a
day. *400 Soliders Field Rd., 02134, tel. 617/783–0090 or 800/
424–2900. 310 suites, including 5 bilevel penthouses. Facilities: indoor swimming pool, whirlpool and sauna, game room,
restaurant, lounge, downtown shuttle. AE, CB, DC, MC, V.*

**Moderate** **Boston Park Plaza Hotel & Towers.** Built in 1927 as flagship for
*Back Bay* the Statler hotels, the Plaza has had extensive renovations and
is an excellent choice for those who want to be at the heart of
the action. The hotel is just a block away from the Public Garden (of which some rooms on the top floor have a fine view), a
stone's throw from the new Transportation Building, and a
short walk from Newbury and Boylston streets, Copley
Square, and downtown. The rooms vary in size, but all are
equipped with direct-dial phones, air-conditioning, and in-
room movies. Some of the rooms that were enlarged have two
bathrooms. Unless you want to look out on a brick courtyard,
ask for an outside room. Plaza Towers, at the top of the hotel, is
an intimate 82-room hotel-within-a-hotel that offers larger and
more luxuriously appointed rooms, express check-in and
check-out and more personalized service—at an increased
rate. The lobby is spacious, elegant, and welcoming, with
plants, crystal chandeliers, and comfortable couches. The popular Legal Sea Foods is one of three restaurants; there are two
lounges, and the Terrace Room has live shows and entertainment. Children stay free in their parents' room. *1 Park Plaza
at Arlington St., 02117, tel. 617/426–2000 or 800/225–2008. 966
rooms. Facilities: Health club, 24-hr room service, overnight
laundry and dry cleaning, foreign currency exchange, specialty shops, garage parking available, travel agency,
hairstylist, all major airline ticket offices. AE, CB, DC, MC,
V.*

**Copley Square Hotel.** One of Boston's oldest hotels (1891), the
Copley Square is still one of the best values in the city. It has
recently undergone extensive renovations. The hotel is popular

with Europeans and is European in flavor. The lobby is small, decorated in browns and subtle mauves, with oriental touches. The rooms, which are set off long, circuitous hallways, vary tremendously in size from very small to spacious. Some of the furnishings have been replaced; others will be refurbished. Yet all rooms have direct-dial phones, air conditioners, windows you can open, color TV, and automatic coffee makers with the necessary materials. If you want a quiet room, ask for one on the courtyard. The popular Cafe Budapest is downstairs. Children under 12 stay free in their parents' room. *47 Huntington Ave., 02116, tel. 617/536–9000 or 800/225–7062. 150 rooms. Facilities: use of Westin Hotel's Health Club for a small fee, family suites, airport limousine service, coffee shop, overnight parking across the street. AE, CB, DC, MC, V.*

**Eliot Hotel.** An ambitious renovation has brought a new elegance and lots of marble to a formerly modest nine-floor, European-style, family-run hotel. The Eliot now offers marble baths, new period furnishings, and a marble-clad lobby. One-bedroom and two-bedroom suites are available. The quietest rooms are those that do not face Commonwealth Avenue and those on the higher floors. All rooms have air-conditioning and color cable TV. There is no restaurant; the popular bar next door is not owned by the hotel; parking is at a nearby garage. *370 Commonwealth Ave., 02215, tel. 617/267–1607. 12 rooms, 81 suites. Facilities: laundry room. AE, CB, DC, MC, V. Rates include Continental breakfast.*

**57 Hotel/Howard Johnson's.** The location is part Park Square, part theater district, which makes this hotel a serviceable, centrally located property popular with commercial travelers. All rooms have color TV with free HBO, air-conditioning, and private balconies. Children under 18 stay free in their parents' room. *200 Stuart St., 02116, tel. 617/482–1800 or 800/654–2000. 354 rooms. Facilities: heated indoor pool with lifeguard and poolside service, sun deck, sauna, free indoor parking, baby-sitting service. AE, CB, DC, MC, V.*

**Lenox Hotel.** Constructed in 1900, the Lenox has long been a comfortable—if unexciting—hotel popular with those on a budget. Extensive renovations have transformed it into affordable elegance, however, and soon it may be necessary to promote the Lenox to the *Expensive* category toward which it has been inching. Originally the Waldorf-Astoria, the Lenox has extremely wide corridors that are now freshly carpeted and papered. The soundproofed guest rooms have spacious walk-in closets, color TV, AM/FM radio, and air-conditioning. Bathrooms come equipped with hair driers, shaving mirrors, and amenities. The decor is Early American or Chinese on the lower floors, French Provincial on the top floor. Structural renovations have uncovered a number of handsome archways and elaborate moldings, particularly in the airy and spacious corner rooms, where there are even some working fireplaces. The lobby is ornate and handsome, trimmed in blues and golds and set off by a large, welcoming fireplace that evokes the ambience of a country inn. Diamond Jim's Piano Bar, with its loyal local clientele, is recently remodeled, and a popular spot for joining in on sing-alongs. Children under 18 stay free in their parents' room. *710 Boylston St., 02116, tel. 617/536–5300 or 800/225–7676. 220 rooms. Facilities: 2 restaurants, valet service, valet pay parking, baby-sitting service, shuttle service to airport. AE, CB, DC, MC, V.*

**Midtown Hotel.** Side by side with several much more expensive hotels, the older, low-rise Midtown Hotel remains popular with tour groups and keeps a low profile. It's near Symphony Hall and the Christian Science Church complex and not far from the Museum of Fine Arts. The entire place has been recently renovated. All rooms have color TV and air-conditioning. Children under 18 stay free in their parents' room. *220 Huntington Ave., 02115, tel. 617/262–1000 or 800/343–1177. 160 rooms. Facilities: outdoor pool with lifeguard in season, health facilities with steam room (men only), valet service, barber and beauty salons, free parking. AE, DC, MC, V.*

*Kenmore Square*  **Howard Johnson's Kenmore Square.** This is the best bet for those who want to be near the Boston University campus or Fenway Park. All rooms have modern furnishings, with color TV and air-conditioning. Howard Johnson's has a restaurant and a lounge. Pets are allowed. Children under 18 stay free in their parents' room. *575 Commonwealth Ave., 02215, tel. 617/267–3100 or 800/654–2000. 179 rooms. Facilities: indoor pool with lifeguard, free parking, multilingual staff, baby-sitting service, nonsmoking rooms. AE, CB, DC, MC, V.*

*Logan Airport*  **Hilton.** The airport's proximity to downtown means that the Hilton is close to the action, too. The recently renovated rooms are modern, soundproofed, air-conditioned; each has color TV with in-room movies. There's a restaurant and lounge, and pets are allowed. Children stay free in their parents' room. *75 Service Rd., Logan International Airport, East Boston 02128, tel. 617/569–9300 or 800/445–8667. 542 rooms. Facilities: outdoor pool, free parking, valet, baby-sitting service, free 24-hr shuttle service to airlines. AE, CB, DC, MC, V.*

**Ramada Hotel.** The Ramada is in East Boston, 1½ miles from the airport and near the Suffolk Downs racetrack. All rooms have color TV and air-conditioning. Children under 18 stay free in their parents' room. *225 McClellan Hwy., East Boston, 02128, tel. 617/569–5250 or 800/228–2828. 350 rooms. Facilities: restaurant and bar, outdoor swimming pool, sauna, free 24-hr shuttle to airport, free parking, room service until 10 PM. AE, CB, DC, MC, V.*

*Old West End*  **Holiday Inn.** This is the nearest hotel to Massachusetts General Hospital; it is also convenient to state and city offices and to Beacon Hill. The rates here may seem high compared with those of suburban Holiday Inns, but you're paying for that location. The building's 15 floors include two restaurants and a rooftop bar with pianist and dancing. All rooms are air-conditioned and equipped with TV. Small pets are allowed. Children under 18 stay free in their parents' room. *5 Blossom St., 02114, tel. 617/742–7630 or 800/465–4329. 300 rooms, some efficiencies. Facilities: outdoor pool with lifeguard and poolside service; laundry facilities, parking, baby-sitting service. AE, CB, DC, MC, V.*

*Theater District*  **Tremont House.** The once popular 12-story Bradford Hotel, closed for three years, then bought and completely renovated by the Quality International chain, is again a welcome constituent of the Boston hotel scene. Because the Bradford was built as national headquarters for the Elks Club in 1925, when things were done on a grand scale, its spacious lobby has high ceilings, marble columns, a marble stairway, and lots of gold leaf. The 16-foot, four-tiered crystal chandelier is a replica of the original, which was made in West Germany (five similar chandeliers hang in the ballroom). The guest rooms tend to be small; they are furnished in 18th-century Thomasville reproductions and decorated with prints from the Museum of Fine Arts. (Note the authentic Elks Club brass doorknobs.) The double rooms have queen-size beds, but two double beds are available. The bathrooms also tend to be small; all have tub-and-shower combinations. All rooms have color cable TV. Good news for deli lovers: One of New York's most popular spots for corned beef and blintzes, the Stage Delicatessen, has opened a deli here with a promise to truck in authentic Kosher pickles from the Big Apple. The Roxy, a dance club, and the Juke Box, a nightclub, are popular. *275 Tremont St., 02116, tel. 617/426–1400 or 800/331–9998. 281 rooms. Facilities: room and laundry service, concierge, nonsmoking floor, handicap accessible, valet parking. AE, CB, DC, MC, V.*

**Inexpensive** **Beacon Inns and Guesthouses.** These furnished studio apart-
*Back Bay* ments in converted town houses, similar to European *pensions*, offer simple, basic accommodations. All have private baths and kitchenettes. They house both transient and permanent guests; visitors are screened. Weekly rates are available. *248 Newbury St., 02116, tel. 617/266–7276. 20 rooms in summer, 10 rooms in winter. MC, V.*

*Brighton* **Terrace Motor Lodge Best Western.** Out beyond Boston University, almost in Brookline, the Terrace has a somewhat incongruous appearance as a highway motel on a city street. Yet it's economical, all rooms have color TV and air-conditioning, and downtown is just a trolley ride away. Kitchenettes are available. All rooms were completely renovated in 1989. Children under 16 stay free in their parents' room. *1650 Commonwealth Ave., 02135, tel. 617/566–6260. 73 rooms. Facilities: free parking, free Continental breakfast. AE, CB, DC, MC, V.*

## Bed-and-Breakfasts

A bed-and-breakfast is overnight lodging and breakfast in a private residence. While Boston does not have a large number of bed-and-breakfasts, there are several, and they are usually very reasonable, with daily rates in the $55–$120 per room range. Reservations may be made through these central information and booking organizations:

**Bed & Breakfast Agency of Boston** (47 Commercial Wharf, Boston 02110, tel. 617/720–3540 or 800/248–9262) lists 100 homes in the most visited areas of the city.
**Bed & Breakfast Associates Bay Colony Ltd.** (Box 57166, Boston 02157, tel. 617/449–5302). This service has 130 Boston and Cambridge listings; a directory costs $5.
**New England Bed and Breakfast, Inc.** (1753 Massachusetts Ave., Cambridge 02138, tel. 617/498–9819)
**Host Homes of Boston** (Box 117, Boston 02168, tel. 617/244–1308)

## Hostels

**Greater Boston Council of American Youth Hostels** (1020B Commonwealth Ave., Boston 02215, tel. 617/731–5430) will provide information on low-cost hostels throughout the Boston area.
**Boston International Hostel** is an inexpensive, youth-oriented hostel near the Museum of Fine Arts and Symphony Hall.

Guests sleep in dormitories accommodating four to six persons and must provide their own linens or sleep sacks (sleeping bags are not permitted). The maximum stay is three nights in summer, six nights off-season. Reservations are highly recommended. Doors close at midnight. *12 Hemenway St., 02115, tel. 617/536–9455. Capacity 220 in summer, 100 in winter. Cash or traveler's check with proper ID. Preference is given to members of the American Youth Hostel network during high season. To become a member write to The Greater Boston Council of American Youth Hostels, 1020 Commonwealth Ave., Boston 02215, tel. 617/731–5430.*

## YMCAs and YWCAs

**Berkeley Residence Club,** run by the YWCA, provides single and some double rooms for women only. Meals are available at additional charge. There is no curfew, and the desk is staffed around the clock. No children or pets. *40 Berkeley St., 02116, tel. 617/482–8850. 200 rooms. Shared bath. TV, lounge, laundry facilities. MC, V.*

**Greater Boston YMCA,** near the Museum of Fine Arts and Symphony Hall, is a coed facility with single and double rooms. No children or pets. You can write in advance for accommodations. *316 Huntington Ave., 02115, tel. 617/536–7800. 60 rooms in winter, more in summer. Almost all rooms have shared baths; all rooms have TV. Access to pool and sports facilities, laundry, cafeteria. Free breakfast.*

## Apartment Rentals

**American Accommodations** (91 Charles St., tel. 617/523–2757) provides short-term luxury furnished apartments throughout the city.

# 8 The Arts and Nightlife

# The Arts

Boston is a paradise for patrons of all the arts, from the symphony orchestra to experimental theater and dance to Orson Welles film festivals. One source of information and schedules is the daily newspaper. Thursday's *Boston Globe* Calendar and the weekly *Boston Phoenix* provide comprehensive listings of events for the coming week. *Boston* magazine's On the Town section gives a somewhat less detailed but useful monthly overview.

Boston's supporters of the arts are avid, and tickets often sell out well in advance of an event. If you want to attend a specific performance, it will be wise to buy tickets when you make your hotel reservations. Some theaters will take telephone orders and charge them to a major credit card. Ticket brokers will usually have tickets for a variety of events. Most of them take major credit cards, and all charge a service fee of $1.50–$5 per ticket, depending on the event. If you order far enough in advance, your tickets will be mailed to you; otherwise they will be held at the box office.

**Bostix** is Boston's official entertainment information center and the largest ticket agency in the city. Half-price tickets are sold here for the same day's performances; the "menu board" in front of the booth announces the available events. Cash and checks are accepted for tickets bought in advance, cash only for same-day tickets. People often begin queuing well before the agency opens. *Faneuil Hall Marketplace, tel. 617/723–5181. Open Tues.–Sat. 11–6, Sun. 11–4. Closed major holidays.*
**Concert Charge** (tel. 617/497–1118) is open Monday–Saturday 9–6.
**Ticketron** (tel. 800/382–8080) allows phone charges to major credit cards, Monday–Friday 9 AM–10 PM, Saturday 9–8. Sunday 10–6. No refunds, exchanges, or cancellations.

## Theater

Boston has long played the role of tryout town, a place where producers shape their productions before taking them on to Broadway. While many shows come to Boston in this way, there is an equally strong tradition of local theater that dates from the first cracks in the wall of the Puritan disapproval of play-acting. The Boston theater scene today is a lively one that embraces the traditional and the avant-garde, performed by a vigorous mix of student groups and professionals.

**Commercial Theaters** **American Repertory Theatre** (Loeb Drama Center, Harvard University, 64 Brattle St., Cambridge, tel. 617/547–8300). This is the long-established resident professional repertory company founded by Robert Brustein, who is artistic director. Now associated with Harvard University, the highly respected ART produces both classic and experimental works in the flexible theater at Harvard.
**Charles Playhouse** (76 Warrenton St., tel. 617/426–5225). *Shear Madness*, in its 11th season on the playhouse's Stage II, has become a local institution; it's an "audience participation" whodunit set in a hair salon. Stage I features *Nunsense* (tel. 617/426–6912), a satirical revue about five dancing and singing nuns.

**Colonial Theatre** (106 Boylston St., tel. 617/426–9366). The Colonial is one of Boston's most lavish proscenium theaters even though it is situated within an office building. Designed by Charlence H. Blackhall and opened in 1900, the Colonial remains the home of major productions, often on the way to or from Broadway. The period decor has been richly restored and preserved.

**Emerson Majestic Theatre** (539 or 219 Tremont St., tel. 617/578–8727). Emerson College, the nation's only private institution devoted exclusively to communications and performing arts, has undertaken the extensive multimillion-dollar job of restoring this 1903 Beaux-Arts building. The Majestic hosts professional productions from all walks of Boston's cultural scene, from avant-guard dance to drama to classical concerts.

**The Huntington Theatre Company** (264 Huntington Ave., tel. 617/266–3913). Occupying a theater opened in 1925 by Henry Jewett's repertory company, the Huntington is Boston's largest professional resident theater company. Under the auspices of Boston University, with Peter Altman as producing director, the company performs five plays annually, a mix of established 20th-century plays and classics.

**New Ehrlich Theater** (529 Tremont St., tel. 617/482–6316). In the Cyclorama Building (the Boston Center for the Arts), and under the artistic direction of Richard Freeman, this theater originates its own productions—classic and modern plays and new works.

**Shubert Theatre** (265 Tremont St., tel. 617/426–4520). Owned and managed by the Shubert Organization since it opened in 1910, the theater primarily accommodates major productions en route to or voyaging from Broadway.

**Wang Center** (270 Tremont St., tel. 617/482–9393). Originally the Metropolitan, this huge theater designed by Blackhall opened in 1925 as a movie palace. Restructured today for opera, dance, and drama, the theater houses large-scale productions, notably the Boston Ballet seasons. The overhaul of the center was made possible through the philanthropy of the late Dr. An Wang.

**Wilbur Theatre** (246 Tremont St., tel. 617/423–4008). Another of Blackhall's handsome theaters, the Wilbur ranks as the great Boston favorite. An intimate house that features quality productions, the theater has been impeccably restored to its 1914 elegance; its portals are modeled after the Thomas Bailey Aldrich home on Beacon Hill.

**Small Theaters and Companies**

**Back Alley Theater** (1253 Cambridge St., Inman Sq., Cambridge, tel. 617/491–8166). The regular seasons of newer and experimental plays have included premieres. ImprovBoston, the area's longest running improvisational comedy troupe, is based here.

**Charlestown Working Theater** (442 Bunker Hill Ave., Charlestown, tel. 617/242–3534). Experimental works are the regimen of this theater.

**Le Grand David and His Own Spectacular Magic Company (Cabot Street Theater),** (286 Cabot St., Beverly, tel. 508/927–3677). The world-famous performance incorporates magic, music, and comedy in the lavish style of the turn of the century.

**Lyric Stage** (54 Charles St., tel. 617/742–8703). In the old theater over the markets on Beacon Hill, where the Charles Playhouse company began, the Lyric now presents New England and American premieres.

**Nickerson Theatre** (30 Accord Park Dr., Norwell, tel. 617/871–2400). The professional regional theater offers a season of drama, comedy, music, and mystery. A new play is produced every six weeks; subscription tickets are available.

**Public Theater** (1175 Soldiers Field Rd., Brighton, tel. 617/782–5425). Plays are performed during the summer at the theater in Herter Park.

**Puppet Showplace** (32 Station St., Brookline, tel. 617/731–6400). Dedicated entirely to puppetry, the Puppet Showcase draws on puppeteers from far and near.

**Theatre Lobby** (216 Hanover St., tel. 617/227–9872) consists of a cabaret dinner theater and a more intimate theater in the round that seats 175; performances are Tuesday through Sunday.

**Wheelock Family Theatre** (180 The Riverway (Rte. 1), tel. 617/734–5200). Associated with Wheelock College, the theater encourages plays and musicals with broad appeal. The producer is Susan Kosoff.

## Music

For its size, Boston is the most musical city in America. (New York City may have twice as many events, but it has more than 10 times Boston's population.) Boston is unsurpassed in the variety and caliber of its musical life. Whether the offerings are classical, contemporary, experimental, ethnic, traditional, or popular, whether locally produced or imported, Boston audiences expect to and get first quality. Boston has been synonymous with culture for so long that the association is now a stereotype, but it is no less true. Of the many contributing factors, perhaps the most significant is the abundance of universities and other institutions of learning, which are a rich source of performers, music series, performing spaces, and audiences.

Concert Halls **Berklee Performance Center** (136 Massachusetts Ave., tel. 617/266–1400 or 617/266–7455 for recorded information). Associated with Berklee College of Music, the center is best known for its jazz programs.

**Boston Conservatory of Music** (31 Hemenway St., tel. 617/536–6340). Many of the musical events here are free.

**Boston University Concert Hall** (School for the Arts Bldg., 855 Commonwealth Ave., tel. 617/353–3345). Associated with Boston University, many of the concerts here are free.

**Gardner Museum** (280 The Fenway, tel. 617/353–3831 for schedule information). Concerts in the Tapestry Room at 1:30 PM Sunday, 12:15 PM Thursday, and 6 PM Tuesday are included in the museum admission: $6 adults, $3 students and senior citizens.

**Hatch Memorial Shell.** The bank of the Charles River reverberates to the sounds of the Boston Pops at a series of free outdoor summer concerts.

**Jordan Hall at the New England Conservatory** (30 Gainsborough St., tel. 617/536–2412). One of the world's acoustic treasures, ideal for chamber music yet large enough to accommodate a full orchestra, the hall is home to the Boston Philharmonic.

**Kresge Auditorium** (77 Massachusetts Ave., Cambridge, tel. 617/253–2826). Concerts hosted by the Massachusetts Institute of Technology are given here.

**Longy School of Music Pickman Recital Hall** (27 Garden St.,

Cambridge, tel. 617/876–0956). Pickman Hall is an excellent acoustical setting for smaller ensembles and recitals.

**Museum of Fine Arts** (465 Huntington Ave., tel. 617/267–9300). Jazz and folk concerts take place in the courtyard every Thursday evening at 7:30 from late June through mid-August (bring a blanket and a picnic basket). The resident Boston Museum Trio and numerous guest artists appear in **Remis Auditorium** from September to May.

**Symphony Hall** (301 Massachusetts Ave., tel. 617/266–1492). One of the world's most perfect acoustical settings, Symphony Hall is home to conductor Seiji Ozawa, the Boston Symphony Orchestra and the Boston Pops and is used by visiting orchestras, chamber groups, and soloists and for presentations by many Boston performing groups. The Pops concerts take place in May and June. The Boston Symphony Chamber Players programs and the Youth Concert Series (led by Assistant Conductor Carl St. Clair and Harry Ellis Dickson, conductor laureate and father of Kitty Dukakis) are also given here.

**Wang Center for the Performing Arts** (268 Tremont St., tel. 617/482–2595 or 617/482–9393 for ticket information). The Wang Center is ideal for big productions where acoustical considerations are less critical.

**Church Concerts** Boston's churches offer outstanding music programs. The Saturday *Boston Globe* provides a current listing. Among the most impressive forums are:

**Emmanuel Church** (15 Newbury St., tel. 617/536–3355)
**King's Chapel** (58 Tremont St., tel. 617/227–2155)
**All Saint's Church** (1773 Beacon St., Brookline, tel. 617/738–1810)
**First Church in Cambridge Congregational** (11 Garden St., Cambridge, tel. 617/547–2724)

**Concert Performers** Boston's reputation as the Early Music Capital of America is unchallenged. Much of the credit goes to such organizations as the **Cambridge Society for Early Music** (Box 336, Cambridge 02238, tel. 617/489–3613), which since 1951 has prompted the performance and appreciation of early music and administers the annual Erwin Bodky competition for excellence in the performance of early music.

**Alea III** (855 Commonwealth Ave., tel. 617/353–3340). This group, associated with Boston University, presents a season of performances at Boston University.

**Boston Camerata** (140 Clarendon St., tel. 617/262–2092). Formed in 1954, the Camerata offers a series of medieval, Renaissance, and baroque vocal and instrumental concerts.

**Boston Museum Trio** (465 Huntington Ave., tel. 617/267–9300). This group, in residence at the Museum of Fine Arts, garners high praise for highly skilled performances of baroque chamber music.

**Boston Early Music Festival and Exhibition** (Box 2632, Cambridge 02238, tel. 617/661–1812). A series of concerts on period instruments take place at many locations in the area throughout the year.

**Boston Musica Viva** (Longy School of Music, 295 Huntington Ave., tel. 617/353–0556). Contemporary masterpieces and newly commissioned works are performed.

**Choral Groups** It is hard to imagine another city's having more active choral groups. Many outstanding choruses are associated with Boston schools and churches.

**Boston Cecilia** (1773 Beacon St., Brookline, tel. 617/232–4540). This chorus, led by Donald Teeters and dating back to 1875, holds regular concerts at Jordan Hall.
**Chorus Pro Musica** (645 Boylston St., tel. 617/267–7442). Under the direction of Jeffrey Rink, the chorus appears with various symphony orchestras.
**Cantata Singers** (Box 375, Cambridge 02238, tel. 617/267–6502). The Cantata Singers, directed by David Hoose, perform music dating from the Renaissance to the present.
**Handel & Haydn Society** (295 Huntington Ave., tel. 617/266–3605). America's oldest musical organization, with a history of performances dating to 1815, the society presents instrumental and choral programs. Performances are at Symphony Hall.
**Wintersauce Chorale** (Box 8008, Boston 02114, tel. 617/523–4634). The brainchild of George Guilbault, this group delights audiences with a concert series of lighter fare at John Hancock Hall.

**Chamber Music** Boston is blessed with an impressive array of highly talented chamber groups, some of them the product of successful undergraduate alliances. Many colleges have their own resident string quartets and other chamber ensembles, and concerts of chamber music, often free to the public, are given almost every night of the week.

**Boston Chamber Music Society** (529 Main St., Suite 201, Charlestown, tel. 617/241–5577). Under the artistic direction of Ronald Thomas, the society gives a 12-concert series each year, appearing at Sanders Theater, Jordan Hall, and on Martha's Vineyard in the summer.
**Boston Symphony Chamber Players** (301 Massachusetts Ave., tel. 617/266–1492). Members of the Boston Symphony Orchestra are the personnel of this outstanding ensemble.
**Longy School of Music** (27 Garden St., Cambridge, tel. 617/876–0956). A continuing chamber music series presents free performances every week at the school.

**Concert Series** *Boston Globe* Jazz Festival (tel. 617/929–2000 for Public Affairs). An annual event sponsored by the city's leading newspaper, the festival features prominent jazz musicians and attracts thousands of fans from across the country. Performances take place over a week in mid-June, at several locations throughout the city.
**Charles River Concerts** (729 Boylston St., Boston, tel. 617/262–0650). The programs feature young and lesser known artists whose careers merit greater exposure; concerts are given at halls throughout the city.
**International Artists Series** (2 Chatham St., Worcester, tel. 508/752–4796). A variety of musicians and such groups as the Vienna Boy's Choir and the Preservation Hall Band perform at Worcester's Mechanics Hall.
**Bank of Boston Celebrity Series** (Statler Bldg., Suite 832, 20 Park Plaza, Boston 02116, tel. 617/482–2595) presents 50 events annually—renowned orchestras, chamber groups, recitalists, vocalists, dance companies.
**Water Music, Inc.** (12 Arrow St., Cambridge, tel. 617/876–7777). Classical, jazz, reggae, and blues—and other music—

are performed on a boat that cruises Boston Harbor on Friday evenings, mid-June through September.

## Opera

**Boston Concert Opera** (Box 459, Boston 02123, tel. 617/262–6682). The Concert Opera has been performing four operas a year with a 50-piece orchestra, without sets or costumes, but their recent success with the staged and costumed *Merry Widow* may prompt more performances in this manner. They have presented such works as *Aida*, *Iolanthe*, and *Showboat* at various concert halls.

**Boston Lyric Opera Company** (811 Boylston St., tel. 617/267–1512). The Lyric Opera, a professional company, presents three fully staged productions each season. They have performed operas of Massenet, Mozart, Strauss, and others, and they always include a 20th-century work in their repertory. A composer-librettist workshop is held in February.

**Opera Company of Boston** (539 Washington St., tel. 617/426–5300). The celebrated Opera Company of Boston, under the brilliant direction of Sarah Caldwell, has established itself as a world force in opera. The company presents international and local artists in a season of four productions that are often innovative and include perennial favorites, infrequently performed standards, and world premieres of contemporary works.

## Dance

**Dance Umbrella** (tel. 617/492–7578) is one of New England's largest presenters of contemporary dance performances. It provides services and advocacy for the area's dance companies and presents national and international touring companies. Performances are scheduled in theaters throughout Boston. The Umbrella also offers information on all dance performances in the Boston area.

**Art of Black Dance and Music** (tel. 617/666–1859). The group performs the music and dance of Africa, Latin America, and the Caribbean.

**Beth Soll and Company** (tel. 617/547–8771). The choreographer Beth Soll, who teaches at MIT, draws on everyday life for dance themes; her style has been linked to European expressionism. The company performs at theaters all over Boston.

**Boston Ballet** (42 Vernon St., Newton, tel. 617/964–4070). The city's premier dance company performs at the Wang Center for the Performing Arts. In addition to a fine repertory of classical and modern works, it presents annual performances of the popular *Nutcracker* around Christmas.

**Concert Dance Company** (tel. 617/661–0237). One of the oldest contemporary dance companies in New England, Concert Dance presents the works of such masters and innovators as Merce Cunningham, Mark Morris, and Laura Dean. The company performs in halls throughout the city.

**Copley Square Ballet** (667 Boylston St., Boston, tel. 617/437–9401). A small, relatively new company based at the Ana Roje School of Ballet in Copley Square, the troupe has a style rooted in the Russian technique introduced by Nicholas Legat.

**Dance Collective** (tel. 617/576–2737). Themes from contemporary life are explored in the collaborative efforts of four local choreographers: Judith Chaffee, Ruth Wheeler, Martha Armstrong Gray, and Dawn Kramer.

**Mandala** (tel. 617/868-3641). A popular group of dancers and musicians, Mandala performs lively international folk dances in full costume.

**National Center of Afro-American Artists Dance Company** (300 Walnut Ave., Roxbury, tel. 617/442-8014). Associated with the Elma Lewis School of Fine Arts, the company emphasizes the work of black composers, choreographers, and performers of folk and modern dance.

## Film

With its large population of academics and intellectuals, Boston has its share of discerning moviegoers. However, while there's no shortage of first-run cinemas scattered throughout downtown, Park Square, and the Prudential Center area, it has become difficult to find cinemas that specialize in revivals and foreign films. Many former art houses have closed or converted to first-run, and aficionados must content themselves with waiting for a library or college film festival or renting a film and watching it on a VCR. The local newspapers have current listings of film showings.

**Boston Film & Video Foundation** (1126 Boylston St., tel. 617/536-1540) features the work of local and national independent filmmakers.

**Coolidge Corner Cinema** (290 Harvard St., Brookline, tel. 617/734-2500) programs first-run movies, retrospectives, foreign films, and documentaries.

**The French Library** (53 Marlborough St., tel. 617/266-4351) shows a different French film every weekend, with screenings Friday, Saturday, and Sunday at 8.

**Harvard Film Archive** (Carpenter Center for the Visual Arts, 24 Quincy St., Cambridge, tel. 617/495-4700) programs the work of directors not usually shown at commercial cinemas; two screenings daily.

**Loews Harvard Square Theater** (10 Church St., Cambridge, tel. 617/864-4580) shows foreign films and revivals.

**Loews Janus Cinema** (Galleria, 57 John F. Kennedy St., Cambridge, tel. 617/661-3737) programs revivals and foreign films.

**Museum of Fine Arts** (465 Huntington Ave., tel. 617/267-9300). International and avant-garde films, early cinema, and the work of local filmmakers are shown Thursday and Friday nights in the Remis Auditorium.

**The Classic Film Series** (270 Tremont St., tel. 617/482-9393) at the Wang Center for the Performing Arts takes place from January–April. Films are shown on Mondays at 7:30 PM, but from 6–7:30 PM the Jazz Pops Ensemble plays music from the era or the movie, sometimes both. Tickets are $6, and season subscriptions are available.

**Loews Nickelodeon Cinema** (606 Commonwealth Ave., tel. 617/424-1500) is one of the few theaters in the city that shows first-run independent and foreign films as well as revivals.

# Nightlife

Boston restaurants, clubs, and bars, often clustered in distinctive areas in various parts of the city, offer a broad spectrum of evening and late-night entertainment. Live music possibilities range from new wave efforts to punk rock to sophisticated jazz piano stylings, and there are comedy clubs and discos—and bars where socializing holds all one's attention.

The Quincy Market area may be the center of the city's nightlife; it has been thronged with visitors from the day the restoration opened in 1976. Here in the shadow of historic Faneuil Hall you'll find international cuisine and singles bars among the specialty shops and boutiques.

Copley Square is the hub of another major entertainment area, and Kenmore Square, near the Boston University campus, has clubs and discos devoted to rock and new wave groups.

The breathtaking views of the city at night are from the Top of the Hub Restaurant, 60 stories up atop the Prudential Center, and the Bay Tower Room at 60 State Street. Both have convivial bars and live music.

Thursday's *Boston Globe* Calendar, a schedule of events for the upcoming week, includes an extensive listing of live entertainment under *Nightlife*. The weekly *Boston Phoenix* has another excellent listing. The monthly *Boston* magazine, while a bit less current, is a good source of information. A list of phone numbers for recorded information on events throughout the city is given at the very beginning of this chapter (*see* The Arts).

## Bars and Nightclubs

**Bay Tower Room.** By day a private club, by night this is an enchanted spot where you sip a drink, look out over the panorama of Boston Harbor, and enjoy the music of a fine jazz trio. *60 State St., tel. 617/723–1666. Open Mon.–Sat. 4:30 PM–1 AM. Call 9–5 for reservations. No cover. Jacket and tie required. AE, CB, DC, MC, V.*

**Bull and Finch Pub.** The original Bull and Finch was dismantled in England, shipped to Boston, and reassembled here, an obvious success. This was the inspiration for the TV series *Cheers;* you might not find Normie or Woody, but you'll be able to hoist a few with the Beacon Hill locals who congregate here. Try the Bloody Mary! *84 Beacon St., tel. 617/227–9605. Open daily 11 AM–1:30 AM. No cover. Dancing Thurs., Fri., Sat. AE, DC, MC, V.*

**The Cafe** is a pleasant spot for late-night drinks or a light after-theater dinner. A jazz harpist provides the perfect background. *Ritz Carlton Hotel, 15 Arlington St., tel. 617/536–5700. Daily 5:30–midnight. AE, CB, DC, MC, V.*

**Claddagh.** One of Boston's newest Irish pubs, with all the Irish coat-of-arms hanging by the bar, the Claddagh has an informal atmosphere and lots of sing-alongs. *Dartmouth St. and Columbus Ave., tel. 617/262–9874. Open daily 11:30 AM–midnight. Live entertainment Thurs.–Sat. evenings. AE, MC, V.*

**Copley's.** With its old-world elegance, high ceiling, and spacious bar, Copley's is a place for the proper Bostonian. A recent face-lift has made it cozier. Located in the Copley Plaza Hotel.

*Copley Sq., tel. 617/267–5300. Open daily 11 AM–1:30 AM. No cover charge. AE, DC, MC, V.*

**Daisy Buchanan's** is a favorite hangout of athletes; you might run into Larry Bird or Mike Greenwell at the bar. The jukebox is loud. *240a Newbury St., tel. 617/247–8516. Open daily 11 AM–2 AM. No cover charge. No credit cards. Free hot dogs Sat., Sun.*

**Frogg Lane.** This is a popular spot in the heart of the swinging Quincy Market. The jukebox is very loud. *Faneuil Hall Marketplace, tel. 617/720–0610. Open Mon.–Thurs. 11:30 AM–midnight, Fri.–Sat. 11 AM–1 AM, Sun. noon–11 PM. No cover charge. AE, MC, V.*

**Hampshire House Lounge.** Located above The Bull and Finch Pub, the Hampshire House has the atmosphere of an old Back Bay drawing room with paneled walls, moose heads, and paintings. Piano entertainment Wednesday–Saturday evenings and during Sunday Brunch. *84 Beacon St., tel. 617/227–9600. Open Sun.–Thurs. 11:45 AM–11:30 PM, Fri.–Sat. 11:45 AM–12:30 AM. No cover charge. AE, DC, MC, V.*

**Jacob Wirth's.** The founder's portrait hangs on the wall above the large, ornately carved back bar of the establishment he opened more than 115 years ago. It's a turn-of-the-century American tavern, the kind of place where your grandfather might have stopped for a cold one on his way home from work; but also the place that was recently named one of the best bars in Boston. Be sure to wash down your bratwurst or pigs knuckles with a mug of Wirth's own special dark beer. There is an excellent selection of other beers and liquors. *33 Stuart St., tel. 617/338–8586. Open Mon.–Sat. 11:30 AM–10 PM. AE, DC, MC, V.*

**St. Cloud Restaurant and Bar.** One of the newest "in" spots, this cozy, friendly bar in the heart of the fashionable South End is pleasant for a late-evening rendezvous. *Tremont and Clarendon Sts., tel. 617/353–0202. Open Mon.–Sat. 11:30 AM–11:30 PM, Sun. 11:30 AM–11 PM. No cover charge. AE, DC, MC, V.*

## Jazz Clubs

Clubs often alternate jazz with other kinds of music; always call ahead for program information and times. The *Boston Jazz Line* (tel. 617/262–1300) reports jazz happenings.

**The Bar at Zachary's.** Laid-back but swinging jazz sounds allow listening or dancing in an intimate, comfortable atmosphere. *Colonnade Hotel, 120 Huntington Ave., tel. 617/424–7000. Open Tues.–Sat. 5–11. AE, CB, DC, MC, V.*

**Cabaret Jazzboat.** Cruise Boston Harbor on board the *Bay State* while listening or dancing to live jazz. Cash bar, light supper, and snacks are available. Cruises last two hours. Purchase tickets in advance. *Water Music, Inc., tel. 617/876–8742. Departs Fri. 7:30 PM and 9:30 PM, mid-June–Sept. AE, MC, V.*

**Marriott Hotel Terrace Bar** is an airy, comfortable bar with a swinging jazz trio performing Friday and Saturday nights. *110 Huntington Ave., tel. 617/236–5800. Daily 3 PM–1 AM. No cover charge. AE, CB, DC, MC, V.*

**The Plaza Bar.** Boston's answer to New York's Oak Room in the Plaza Hotel, the elegant Plaza is one of Boston's very special places. *Copley Plaza Hotel, Copley Sq., tel. 617/267–6495. Mon.–Sat. 5 PM–1 AM. Live entertainment Mon.–Sat. nights. AE, MC, V.*

**New Orleans North.** Cajun and Dixieland Jazz is performed here by a four-piece ensemble. It's a great hangout for those who enjoy jazz in the tradition of Louis Armstrong, and it's a popular restaurant. *835 Beacon St., tel. 617/424–6995. Open Wed.–Sun. 9 PM–1 AM. No cover charge. AE, DC, MC, V.*

**Westin Hotel.** Art Matthews and his Trio entertain on Sunday and Monday evenings in the warm and comfortable Turner Fisheries Bar in one of Boston's newer hotels. *10 Huntington Ave., Copley Sq., tel. 617/262–9600, ext. 7425. Mon.–Sat. 3 PM–1 AM. No cover charge. AE, DC, MC, V.*

## Rock Clubs

**Axis.** One of three dance places stacked on top of each other in this building in Kenmore Square, Axis attracts a "funkier" mixed crowd with its selection of urban underground music. Strobe lights pulsate off of black walls and ceiling. Sunday is gay night when Axis and Citi, below it, combine forces and permit dancers to circulate between the two clubs. *15 Landsdowne St., tel. 617/262–2424. Open Wed.–Sun. 10 PM–2 AM. Cover charge. AE, MC, V.*

**Bunratty's.** Here's a popular, often crowded spot to listen to local hard rock groups perform every day of the year. Large-screen TV and game room. *186 Harvard Ave., Allston, tel. 617/254–9820. Open Mon.–Sat. noon–2 AM, Sun. 2 PM–2 AM. Cover charge after 8 PM. No credit cards.*

**The Channel.** A huge, noisy club featuring rock, reggae, and new wave music performed by local as well as national and international bands, The Channel has two dance floors, four bars, and a game room. The crowd is mostly in their early 20s (you must be 21 to get in). Tickets from Ticketron or at the box office *25 Necco St. (near South Station), tel. 617/451–1050 or 617/451–1905. Open daily 8 PM–1 AM. No credit cards.*

**The Jukebox VHF.** The decor of one of Boston's "in" spots includes old jukeboxes and a 1954 Ford plunging into the room from over the bar. The music runs to 50s nostalgia. It's packed nightly, and there's usually a wait on weekends. *Quality Inn, 275 Tremont St., tel. 617/542–1123. Open Thurs.–Sat. 8 PM–2 AM. Cover charge. No credit cards.*

**Kenmore Club.** One cover charge admits you to this three-club complex. There's recorded rock and roll, occasional live bands, disco, light shows, lots of mirrors and video, and, in Narcissus, a place for serious dancers. *533 Commonwealth Ave., tel. 617/536–1950. Open daily 8 PM–2 AM. Cover charge. AE, MC, V.*

**The Paradise.** This small, basic club is known for big-name talent such as Sinead O'Connor and Robin Trower. New wave, rock, jazz, folk, blues, alternative pop/rock, and country all take turns on stage here, and the audience mix varies with the entertainment. This is the best venue for live shows; artists play here for the more intimate setting. Tickets must be purchased in advance at Ticketmaster (tel. 617/931–2000) or at the box office. *967 Commonwealth Ave., tel. 617/254–2052 or 254–2053.*

**The Rat (The Rathskeller).** The Cars, the Police, Talking Heads, and many other groups got their start at this popular Kenmore Square punk rock club. It has cheap drinks, pinball, video, primarily students from nearby Boston University, and an incredible noise level. *528 Commonwealth Ave., tel. 617/536–2750. Open daily 7 PM–2 AM. Cover charge. No credit cards.*

## Comedy Clubs

**Comedy Connection.** Boston's top comedians perform in this popular cabaret-style club in the heart of the theater district. *Charles Playhouse, 76 Warrenton St., tel. 617/426–6339. Shows Sun.–Thurs. at 8:30, Fri.–Sat. at 8:30 and 10:30.*

**Duck Soup Comedy Club.** Boston's newest comedy club is also its most upscale, located in the basement of the Wilbur Theater in the heart of the theater district. National headliners perform here for an over-25 crowd. *246 Tremont St., tel. 617/542–8511. Shows Thurs.–Sun. Cover charge. AE, MC, V.*

**Nick's Restaurant & Comedy Shop.** Local comics perform every night at this club and bar in the heart of the theater district, and occasionally a well-known comedian pops in. Reservations suggested. *100 Warrenton St., tel. 617/482–0930. Open daily until 2 AM. Cover charge and minimum. AE, MC, V.*

**Stitches.** "Where stars are born," according to *Boston* magazine, and a favorite for lovers of comedy since 1982, Stitches has shows Tuesday through Sunday. Sunday is open mike night. *835 Beacon St., tel. 617/424–6995. Cover charge. AE, MC, V.*

## Discos

**Citi.** This fast-paced club is also one of Boston's largest. In Kenmore Square, it features high-energy disco and a giant dance floor that can accommodate more than 1000 people. Thursday is international night. A local DJ spins discs on weekend nights. *15 Landsdowne St., tel. 617/262–2424. Open Wed.–Sun. 10 PM–2 AM. Cover charge. AE, MC, V.*

**Rachel's.** Dance nightly to the disco sound or enjoy wide-screen video in the Boston Marriott on the waterfront; Rachel's is popular for late-night revelry and for its 95¢ appetizers, weekdays 5–7. *Long Wharf, 296 State St., tel. 617/227–0800. Open daily 11:30 AM–1:30 AM. Cover charge on weekends. AE, CB, DC, MC, V.*

## Singles

**Cityside Bar.** A well-known singles haven, Cityside offers live entertainment nightly by local rock groups. It's a good spot, but it can be crowded and noisy. *262 Faneuil Hall Marketplace, tel. 617/742–7390. Open daily 9:30 PM–2 AM. Cover charge Thurs.–Sat. AE, DC, MC, V.*

**Houlihan's.** This dance place and restaurant in the marketplace area is a favorite of professional singles. The DJ provides the music for dancing. Jeans, T-shirts, and athletic shoes are not allowed after 5 PM. *60 State St., tel. 617/367–6377. Dance nightly 9 PM–2 AM. Cover charge after 7 PM. Thurs.–Sun. AE, DC, MC, V.*

**Napoleon Club.** A very attractive and very popular gay club with piano music downstairs every night and disco with a DJ Friday and Saturday, 9 PM–2 AM. You must be 21 years of age. *52 Piedmont St., tel. 617/338–7547. Open daily 5 PM–2 AM. Cover charge weekends for dancing. No credit cards.*

**Chatterly's.** The huge outdoor patio overlooking Boston Harbor is a favorite watering hole in the summer. *Long Wharf, 200 Atlantic Ave., tel. 617/227–0828. Open daily 11:30 AM–1 AM. No cover charge. AE, DC, MC, V.*

## Other Attractions

**Medieval Manor** offers a 2½ hour, fixed-price, 12th-century dining orgy that features a six-course meal, serving wenches, strolling minstrels, court jesters dictating when you are permitted to use the bathroom, and a lot of good, messy fun (there's no silverware). The food is not gourmet cuisine, but it is plentiful. *246 E. Berkeley St., tel. 617/423–4900. Open for dinner only Mon.–Fri. 7:30, Sat. 5 and 9:30, Sun. 6. Reservations are necessary. $20–$32 per person, depending on the day of the week and which show or meal you attend. MC, V.*

Boston's nude-dancing bars, peep shows, and "adult" bookstores and movie houses are largely confined to the **Combat Zone,** a two-block area of lower Washington Street. While it is quite safe to explore the area during the day, its name takes on significance at night. If you venture there, use caution; leave your valuables at home or in the hotel safe.

# 9 Cambridge

# Exploring Cambridge

Cambridge is an independent city faced with the difficult task of living in the shadow of its larger neighbor, Boston, while being overshadowed as well by the giant educational institutions within its own borders. It provides the brains and the technical know-how that, combined with Boston's financial prowess, has created the vibrant high-tech economy of which Massachusetts is so proud. Cambridge also continues to function as the conscience of the greater Boston area; when a new social experiment or progressive legislation appears on the local scene, chances are it came out of the crucible of Cambridge political activism.

Cambridge dates from 1630, when the Puritan leader John Winthrop chose this meadowland as the site of a carefully planned, stockaded village he named New Towne. Eight years later the town was renamed Cambridge in honor of the university at which most Puritan leaders had been educated.

In 1636 the Great and General Court of the Massachusetts Bay Colony established the country's first college here. Named in 1638 for a young Charlestown clergyman who died that year, leaving the college his entire library and half his estate, Harvard remained the only college in the New World until 1693, by which time it was firmly established as a respected center of learning.

By the middle of the 17th century, Cambridge was the New World's publishing center, and through 350 years it has remained a place to which people come primarily to learn and to teach, to discuss, to lecture, to write, and to think. At the same time, Cambridge is a city of 95,000 people in which half the population has nothing whatsoever to do with its universities.

The old Cambridge that took shape around the 17th-century college was a considerable journey from the several villages that grew up within its 22-mile expanse. In time the other communities broke away to form Lexington, Watertown, Arlington, and other cities, and in 1846 the college town was itself incorporated as a city. It then became affiliated politically with the industrial communities of Cambridgeport and East Cambridge, which lie below it on the west bank of the Charles River. Settled primarily in the 19th century, they produced furniture, brushes, caskets, bricks, glass, and reversible collars. In the 1840s the population of the two communities, made up of Irish, Polish, Italians, and French Canadians, was eight times that of the Harvard end of town.

The academic and industrial sections were effectively joined when the Massachusetts Institute of Technology moved to Cambridge in 1916. The striking modern buildings that have since been designed by graduates of the MIT and Harvard schools of architecture are in themselves sufficient reason for a visit to Cambridge today.

*Numbers in the margin correspond with points of interest on the Cambridge map.*

Cambridge, just minutes from Boston by MBTA, is easily ❶ reached on the Red Line train to **Harvard Square.** Not a square

# Cambridge

Arthur M. Sackler Museum, **6**
Brattle House, **14**
Christ Church, **10**
Dawes Island, **9**
Dexter Pratt House, **13**
First Parish Church, **8**
Fogg Art Museum, **5**

Hart Nautical Museum, **20**
Harvard University Museums of Natural History, **7**
Harvard Square, **1**
Harvard Yard, **3**
Hayden Gallery, **21**
Kresge Auditorium, **17**

Longfellow National Historic Site, **12**
Massachusetts Institute of Technology, **16**
MIT Chapel, **18**
MIT Museum, **19**
Radcliffe College, **11**
The Square, **15**

Wadsworth House, **2**
Widener Library, **4**

at all, Harvard Square is where Massachusetts Avenue, coming from Boston, turns and widens into a triangle broad enough to accommodate a brick peninsula on which the MBTA station is located. Sharing the peninsula is a local institution, the out-of-town newsstand, which occupies the restored kiosk of 1928 that was the entrance to the MBTA station until its reconstruction when the Red Line was extended beyond Harvard Square.

The greater area of the square is a broad and busy one. The pedestrian flow is constant and varied, and wide sidewalks and miniparks encourage entertainers, promoters of causes, and those who want to share with you their religious convictions. Harvard Square is walled on two sides by banks, restaurants, and shops and on the third by Harvard University.

A good place to begin one's tour is the **Cambridge Discovery** information booth near the MBTA station entrance, where you will find maps, brochures, and information about the entire city. The walking tour brochures cover Old Cambridge, East Cambridge, and Revolutionary Cambridge. Cambridge Discovery also gives a rewarding tour of Old Cambridge conducted by a corps of well-trained high school students. *Cambridge Discovery, Inc., Box 1987, Cambridge 02238, tel. 617/497–1630. Open in winter, Mon.–Sat. 9–5, Sun. 1–5; in summer, Mon.–Sat. 9–6, Sun. 1–5.*

On the Harvard University side of Harvard Square stands ➋ **Wadsworth House,** a yellow clapboard structure built in 1726 as a home for Harvard presidents. It served as the first headquarters for George Washington when he arrived to take command of the Continental Army on July 2, 1775.

Step past Wadsworth House and through a gateway into ➌ **Harvard Yard.** While the college dates from 1636, the oldest buildings in Harvard Yard are of the 18th century; together the buildings chronicle American architecture from Colonial time to the present: **Holden Chapel,** built in 1744, is a Georgian gem. The graceful **University Hall** was designed in 1815 by Charles Bulfinch. **Memorial Hall,** completed in 1878 as a memorial to Harvard men who died in the Union cause, is High Victorian both inside and out. **Sever Hall,** designed in 1880 by Henry Hobson Richardson, represents the Romanesque revival that was followed by the Classical (note the pillared facade of Widener Library) and the Neo-Georgian, represented by the sumptuous brick houses along the Charles River. Harvard's four oldest buildings, Massachusetts Hall, Holden Chapel, Hollis Hall, and Harvard Hall, were occupied by the patriot regiments during the Revolution.

The Harvard University information office on the ground floor of Holyoke Center (1350 Massachusetts Ave.), run by students, offers a free hour-long tour of the Yard (once daily, Mon.–Sat.) and maps of the university area. The tour does not include visits to museums, but it provides a fine orientation and will give you ideas for further sightseeing.

➍ **Widener Library,** which boasts the country's second-largest collection of books, has a Gutenberg bible, a Shakespeare folio, and dioramas of Cambridge as it appeared in 1667, 1775, and 1936. Imagine what it must have been like to be here at the outbreak of the Revolution, when 16,000 patriots milled around

this town of 1,600 people. *Harvard Yard, tel. 617/495–2413.*
*Open during the academic year, weekdays 9 AM–10 PM, Sat.*
*9–5, Sun. noon–5; in summer, weekdays 9–4:45, Sat. 9–1,*
*Sun. 9–noon. Tours by appointment.*

**⑤** Harvard has two celebrated art museums, each a treasure in
itself. The most famous is the **Fogg Art Museum.** Founded in
1895, it now owns 80,000 works of art from every major period
and from every corner of the world. Its focus is primarily on
European, American, and Far Eastern works; it has notable
collections of 19th-century French Impressionist and medieval
Italian paintings. Special exhibits change monthly. *32 Quincy*
*St., tel. 617/495–5573. Admission: $4 adults, free under 18,*
*$2.50 senior citizens and students. Free Sat. 10–noon. Open*
*Tues.–Sun. 10–5.*

**⑥** When you purchase a ticket to the Fogg, you are entitled to tour
the **Arthur M. Sackler Museum** (tel. 617/459–9400) across the
street as well. It exhibits Chinese, Japanese, ancient Greek,
Egyptian, Roman, Buddhist, and Islamic works. The Sackler
keeps the same hours as the Fogg.

A ticket to the Fogg also gains you admission to Harvard's
**Busch-Reisinger Museum** (tel. 617/495–4544), now located in
the new Werner Otto Hall entered through the Fogg. The collection specializes in Central and Northern European art.
Hours are the same as at the Fogg and the Sackler.

**⑦** Harvard also maintains the **Harvard University Museums of**
**Natural History.** This vast brick building fulfills the plan
of the Swiss naturalist Louis Agassiz. His idea was to bring
under one roof the study of all kinds of life, plants, animals,
and humankind. It contains four distinct collections: comparative zoology, archaeology, botany, and minerals. The
most famous exhibit here is the display of glass flowers in the
*Botanical Museum.* Renting the taped tour will help you
to appreciate fully these models of more than 700 plant species, meticulously recreated in glass by a father and son who
worked continuously in Dresden, Germany, from 1871 to
1936.

The *Peabody Museum of Archaeology and Ethnology* holds one
of the world's outstanding anthropological collections; exhibits
focus on American Indian and Central and South American cultures. The *Museum of Comparative Zoology* traces the evolu-
tion of animals and man. The best known among its wealth of
exhibits are the whale skeletons; the largest known turtle
shell; the Harvard mastodon, Kronosaurus; the giant sea ser-
pent; George Washington's pheasants; and the world's oldest
reptile egg. The *Mineralogical Museum,* founded in 1784, has
an extensive collection of exotic crystals and meteorites; scale
models of volcanoes and well-known mountains are also on
show. *26 Oxford St., tel. 617/495–3045. Admission: $3 adults,*
*$1 children 5–15, $1 students and senior citizens. Open Mon.–*
*Sat. 9–4:30, Sun. 1–4:30. Free Sat. 9–11. Closed major holi-*
*days.*

**⑧** At the **Old Burying Ground** and **First Parish Church** on the corner of Church Street and Massachusetts Avenue, you can make
out through the locked iron railing of the cemetery a number of
17th-century and 18th-century tombstones of ministers, early
Harvard presidents, and Revolutionary War soldiers. The

wooden Gothic Revival church was built in 1833 by Isaiah Rogers. *3 Church St., tel. 617/876–7772. Open in winter, weekdays 9–5; in summer, weekdays 9–1. Sun. service at 10:30, church open until 1.*

**9** Cross to **Dawes Island** in the middle of Garden Street to read the history legends and to see the bronze horseshoes embedded in the sidewalk. The horseshoes were a Bicentennial gift from the descendants of William Dawes, a doctor who galloped through Cambridge spreading the alarm ("The British are coming") on the eve of the Battle of Lexington. Beyond the ornamental arch is **Cambridge Common,** a public park since 1631.

**10** Cross back to Garden Street and stroll along the Burying Ground to **Christ Church,** designed in 1761 by Peter Harrison, the country's first trained architect. During the Revolution the church was used as a soldier's barracks until Washington ordered it reopened for services on New Year's Eve 1775. Step into the vestibule to look for the bullet holes made by a British soldier marching to Concord. The interior is airy and elegant in its simplicity. *Zero Garden St. Open daily 7–6. Sun. services at 8, 10, 12:30, and 5.*

**11** At the next corner turn down Appian Way and take the first right through a small garden and into the yard of **Radcliffe College.** This is the heart of the college founded in 1897 "to furnish instruction and the opportunities of collegiate life to women and to promote their higher education." Still an independent corporation within Harvard University—to which it was wedded in 1977—Radcliffe maintains its own physical plant, including the Agassiz Theater. Exit through the gate next to the theater and continue down Mason Street to Brattle, where you turn right. Walk past the stone buildings and chapel of the Episcopal Divinity School.

**Brattle Street** is one of the country's most elegant. Elaborate mansions line both sides from this corner all the way to Elmwood, the great, square, mid-18th-century house that is the home of the Harvard president. In the 1770s this street was known as **Tory Row** because its mansions (then numbering seven), with their lands that stretched to the river, were owned by staunch supporters of King George. These properties were appropriated by the patriots when they took over Cambridge in the summer of 1775.

**12** Washington himself quickly moved from the humbler Wadsworth House to the stately home at 105 Brattle Street, now maintained as the **Longfellow National Historic Site.** The house was built in 1759 by the son of a wealthy West Indies plantation owner who fled town in 1774. George Washington lived here throughout the siege of Boston. The poet Henry Wadsworth Longfellow rented a room here in 1837 and later received the house as a gift from his new father-in-law on his marriage to Frances Appleton, who burned to death here in a fluke accident. Longfellow filled the house with the exuberant spirit of his own work and that of his literary circle, which included Emerson, Thoreau, Holmes, Dana, and Parkman. This was the period in which Harvard students began shedding traditional theology and rote learning. Harvard's Tyrell Channing was probably the first university professor in this country to teach that the most important discipline is thinking. *105 Brattle St.,* *tel. 617/876–4491. Admission: $2 adults, free under 16 and over 62. Last tour departs at 4. Open daily 10–4:30.*

The absorption with ideas that still pervades old Cambridge can be savored in the dozen cafes and the half-dozen outstanding bookstores to be found around Harvard Square. Walk back ⑬ along Brattle Street to reach the yellow **Dexter Pratt House,** immortalized in Longfellow's "The Village Blacksmith." It is now owned by the Cambridge Center for Adult Education. *56 Brattle St., tel. 617/547–6789. Admission free. Open Mon.–Sat. 9–7.*

⑭ **Brattle House** is an 18th-century gambrel-roofed Colonial that once belonged to the Loyalist William Brattle, who left Boston in 1774. From 1840 to 1842 it was the residence of Margaret Fuller, the feminist editor of *The Dial;* today it is headquarters for the Cambridge Center for Adult Education, and it is listed in the National Register of Historic Places. *42 Brattle St., tel. 617/547–6789. Admission free. Open Mon.–Thurs. 9–9, Fri. 9–7, Sat. 9–2.*

You can easily take an hour to walk this short block crammed ⑮ with shops and restaurants that locals call **The Square,** which is formed by the juncture of Massachusetts Avenue and John F. Kennedy Drive. An extension of it, the commercial end of Brattle Street, includes the stretch of Kennedy Drive that runs on to the Charles River. Give or take a few sidestreets, you can count 150 shops and an equal number of eating spots within this extended space.

An exploration of Cambridge would not be complete without a ⑯ visit to the **Massachusetts Institute of Technology.** The 135-acre campus of MIT borders the Charles River, 1½ miles south of Harvard Square.

No one could have guessed that the founding of a small technological school in 1861 in Boston's Copley Square would one day meld the academic and industrial communities of Cambridge into an entirely new entity. Despite the pleas of the Harvard president that the school relocate in Allston, just across the river from its own campus (and thereby conveniently in Harvard's shadow), MIT President Richard MacLaurin opted for the new landfill at the opposite end of the city, abutting the riverside factories of East Cambridge.

The Massachusetts Institute of Technology moved to Cambridge in 1916 with great panoply, and it has long since fulfilled the predictions of its founder, the geologist William Barton Rogers, that it would surpass "the universities of the land in the accuracy and the extent of its teachings in all branches of positive science." Yet it has always been "the factory," even to its students, lacking as it does Harvard's ivy and aura.

In the 1930s there was a shift in focus from practical, applied engineering and mechanics to the outer limits of scientific fields. With the outbreak of World War II, the significance of such research became apparent. An emergency office of scientific research and development was set up, free of red tape, and manned by scientists from both Harvard and MIT. Here many of the components of modern warfare were developed and refined. The laboratories founded in wartime have since produced instrumentation and guidance devices for NASA flights and for nuclear submarines.

It can be argued that MIT (9,500 graduate and undergraduate students) has as much impact on Cambridge and Boston today as does Harvard (16,900 graduate and undergraduate students). In fact, one in five MIT graduates goes to work in the immediate area, many of them in the high-tech companies founded by fellow alumni that now fill many former industrial complexes in Cambridge.

Obviously designed by and for scientists, the MIT campus is divided by Massachusetts Avenue into the West Campus, which is devoted to student leisure life, and the East Campus, where the heavy work is done. The West Campus has some extraordinary buildings. The **Kresge Auditorium,** designed by Eero Saarinen with a curving roof and unusual thrust, rests on three instead of four points. The **MIT Chapel,** another Saarinen design, is lit primarily by a roof oculus that focuses light on the altar, as well as by reflections from the water in a small moat surrounding it, and it is topped by an aluminum sculpture by Theodore Roszak. **Baker House** was designed in 1947 by the Finnish architect Alvar Aaltoa in such a way as to give every room a view of the Charles River.

The East Campus, which has grown around the university's original neoclassical buildings of 1916, also boasts outstanding modern architecture and sculpture, notably the high-rise Earth Science Building by I. M. Pei and the giant stabile that Alexander Calder designed as a baffle for the wind so that the revolving doors in Pei's building can function (when the building first opened, they could not). MIT's East Campus buildings are connected by a five-mile "infinite corridor," touted as the second-longest corridor in the country.

The Institute maintains an Information Center and offers free tours of the campus Monday–Friday at 10 and 2. *Building Seven, 77 Massachusetts Ave., tel. 617/253–4795. Open weekdays 9–5.*

MIT has several fine museums. The **MIT Museum** contains photos, paintings, scientific instruments, and memorabilia relating to the Institute. *265 Massachusetts Ave., tel. 617/253–4444. Admission free for MIT students, $2 non–students. Open Tues.–Fri. 9–5, weekends 1–5.*

The **Hart Nautical Museum** harbors a small but outstanding collection of ships' models. *55 Massachusetts Ave., tel. 617/253–5942. Admission free. Open daily 9–8.*

**Albert & Vera List Visual Art Center** (The **Hayden Gallery** and Bakalar Gallery) shows selections from the university's collection of 800 works of art; there are also changing exhibits and gallery talks. *20 Ames St., tel. 617/253–4680. Admission free. Open weekdays noon–6, weekends 1–5. Closed in summer.*

# Shopping

The majority of Cambridge's stores are clustered around Harvard Square. Within a few blocks more than 150 stores have clothes, books and records, furnishings, and a surprising range of specialty items. Three small weatherproofed shopping complexes are located just off the square: The Garage (38 John F. Kennedy St.), The Galleria (57 John F. Kennedy St.), and

Charles Square (Bennett and Eliot Sts.). The late shopping night in Harvard Square is Thursday.

A few of the city's most original shops avoid the high rents in Harvard Square; you will find them on Massachusetts Avenue south of Porter Square and on Huron Avenue. Many of the city's stores now have branches on the Boston waterfront and in New York City.

**Antiques** **Bernheimer's Antique Arts** (52C Brattle St., tel. 617/547–1177). European, Asian, Islamic, pre-Columbian, and native American art and antique jewelry are this dealer's specialties.
**Fleur de Lys** (52 Brattle St., tel. 617/864–7738). Here is an eclectic collection of French and European china, antiques, jewelry, and furniture from the period 1880–1930.
**The Music Emporium** (2018 Massachusetts Ave., tel. 617/661–2099) offers one of New England's best selections of new, old, and antique stringed instruments, including some from the 19th century. Contemporary acoustic and folk-related music and instruments are also available.

**Books** Cambridge is a book lover's paradise; shops selling new and secondhand books are tucked away on every side street.
**The Bookcase** (42 Church St., tel. 617/876–0832). The basement is filled with an enormous selection of secondhand books.
**Pangloss Bookshop** (65 Mt. Auburn St., tel. 617/354–4003) stocks scholarly monographs in the humanities and social sciences and literary magazines and journals.
**Reading International** (47 Brattle St., tel. 617/864–0705) has academic and nonacademic books, foreign newspapers and magazines, and a diverse collection of scholarly journals; the store is open daily from 7:30 AM to 11 PM or later.

**Clothing** **Jasmin** (37 Brattle St., tel. 617/334–6043). Current designers from New York and Los Angeles sell their funky collections here.
**Pepperweed** (1684 Massachusetts Ave., tel. 617/547–7561) offers contemporary and unusual fashions from American, European, and Japanese designers.
**Serendipity** (1312 Massachusetts Ave., tel. 617/661–7143). The moderately priced imports of women's clothing are from India, Mexico, and South America, and the shop has jewelry, shoes, and accessories.

**Department Store** **Harvard Coop Society** (1400 Massachusetts Ave., tel. 617/492–1000; at MIT, 3 Cambridge Center, tel. 617/491–4230). Begun in 1882 as a nonprofit service for students and faculty, the Coop is now a full department store known for its extensive selection of records and books. It has good assortments of men's clothing, women's shoes, and stationery.

**Food** **Blacksmith House Bakery** (56 Brattle St., tel. 617/354–3036). Rich German tortes, Viennese-style pastries, and *bouche de Noël* at Christmas are the major temptations.
**Cardullo's** (6 Brattle St., tel. 617/491–8888) is good for exotic imports, sandwiches to go, cheese, wines, and more than 270 varieties of beer.

**Ice Cream** **Emack & Bolio's** (1310 Massachusetts Ave., tel. 617/497–5362; 1726 Massachusetts Ave., tel. 617/354–8573). The homemade ice cream is so good that it's popular even in New York.
**Steve's** (31 Church St., tel. 617/354–9106; 95 Massachusetts Ave., tel. 617/247–9401). The original Steve's, which started

out in Somerville, was one of the first homemade ice-cream parlors to offer "mix-ins." Some say this is *the best* ice cream.

**Newspapers and Periodicals** **Out-of-Town News** (Harvard Square, tel. 617/354–7777). A staggering cross section of the world's newspapers and magazines is on sale here daily 6 AM–11:30 PM. Also serves as a ticket agency.

**Pottery** **Fresh Pond Clay Works** (368 Huron Ave., tel. 617/492–1907). Here are bright and beautiful lamps, vases, and other pottery made on the spot.

**Records** **Briggs and Briggs** (1270 Massachusetts Ave., tel. 617/547–2007). The selection includes classical, folk, blues, ethnic, early music, new music, and jazz recordings.
**Cheapo Records** (645 Massachusetts Ave., tel. 617/354–4455). New and used R&B, rock, and jazz LPs and 45s are available.

**Shopping Center** **Cambridgeside Galleria** (100 Cambridgeside Place, tel. 617/621–8666). Located in East Cambridge, accessible by the Green Line Lechmere stop, this new three-story mall opened in September 1990. It has over 60 shops including the anchor stores of Filenes, Lechmere, and Sears. The first 90 minutes of parking are 99¢.

# Dining

*The restaurants were selected by Mary H. Frakes.* Few small cities of comparable size offer as wide a choice of dining options as does Cambridge. There are more than 150 restaurants to choose from here, and because of the city's diversity of cultures, most of the major ethnic cuisines are represented.

As a general rule, you can expect to tip about 15% on a check of less than $60, about 20% on a check larger than $60.

The following price categories are based on the average cost of a three-course dinner for one person, food alone, not including beverages, tax, and tip.

| Category | Cost* |
|---|---|
| Very Expensive | over $35 |
| Expensive | $20–$35 |
| Moderate | $10–$20 |
| Inexpensive | under $10 |

*per person; add 5% tax*

The following credit card abbreviations are used: AE, American Express; CB, Carte Blanche; D, Discover Card; DC, Diners Club; MC, MasterCard; V, Visa.

The most highly recommended restaurants are indicated by a star ★.

### American

**Rarities.** The subdued contemporary decor complements a New American cuisine based on regional cooking and seasonal ingredients. The à la carte menu includes porterhouse of veal with vegetable strudel and a Rhode Island wine-based sauce.

*Hotel Charles, 1 Bennett St., tel. 617/864–1200. Reservations advised. Dress: casual. AE, CB, DC, MC, V. No lunch. Closed Sun. Expensive.*

★ **798 Main.** Bruce Frankel, the owner and chef, has revamped what used to be the nouvelle-cuisine Panache, and the new restaurant features a more casual, neocolonial look. The menu, which changes frequently, updates New England fare with such entrees as grilled veal loin chop with fennel and garlic potatoes and desserts like hard apple cider sorbet with raspberries. At the same time, Frankel has retained several Panache favorites, including the Hubbardston chevre with sun-dried tomatoes and grilled flatbread. *798 Main St., tel. 617/876–8444. Reservations advised. Dress: casual but neat. AE, MC, V. No lunch. Closed Sun. and Mon. Moderate–Expensive.*

**33 Dunster St.** Decorated effectively with stained glass, books, antiques, and bentwood, this is a surprisingly reasonable place to dine. The salad bar is a specialty, and the large international menu features the likes of quiche, steak sandwich, fettucini Alfredo, chicken teriyaki, broiled swordfish, and stuffed shrimp. The Sunday brunch has live jazz and over 100 items to chose from. Nightly specials add to the variety. *33 Dunster St., tel. 617/354–0636. Reservations for large parties only. Dress: informal. MC, V. Moderate.*

**Bartley's Burger Cottage.** Famed for its 42 varieties of burgers and fried onion rings, Bartley's is good, too, for salads and sandwiches. Daily specials might include baked meatloaf with mashed potatoes and a vegetable. The small, crowded tables and bustling waitresses qualify the place as a real burger joint. And it's popular with students. *1246 Massachusetts Ave., tel. 617/354–6559. No reservations. Dress: informal. No credit cards. Closed Sun. Inexpensive.*

**Elsie's Deli.** Elsie has retired, but the quality of her revered sandwiches persists. We recommend the hot pastrami, the roast beef, and the super salads. *71A Mount Auburn St., tel. 617/354–8362. No reservations. Dress: informal. No credit cards. Inexpensive.*

## Cajun

**Cajun Yankee.** After eating the crawfish étouffée or the spicy jambalaya here, you'll begin to understand why Paul Prudhomme weighs as much as he does. Utility paneling, whitewashed walls, and metal chairs foster a down-home atmosphere for the most authentic Louisiana cooking in Boston. *1193 Cambridge St., tel. 617/576–1971. Reservations suggested. Dress: casual. AE, CB, DC, MC, V. No lunch. Closed Sun. and Mon. Moderate.*

## Chinese

**Sally Ling's.** Boston's most expensive Chinese restaurant is now on the 14th floor of the Hyatt Regency Hotel, where the view is spectacular and the food excellent. Among the house's Szechuan specialties are the peony blossom beef, garlicky steamed prawns, and lobster sauteed with ginger and scallions. *575 Memorial Dr., tel. 617/868–1818. Reservations recommended. Jacket and tie required. AE, DC, MC, V. No lunch weekends. Expensive.*

**Joyce Chen Restaurant.** Joyce Chen offers a gracious setting

# Cambridge Dining

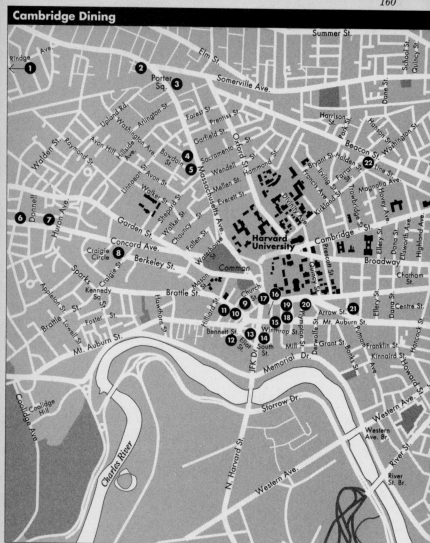

Acropolis, **5**

Averof, **2**

Bartley's Burger Cottage, **20**

Bertucci's, **10**

The Border Cafe, **9**

Cafe Sushi, **21**

Cajun Yankee, **33**

Casa Mexico, **15**

Casa Portugal, **32**

Chez Nous, **7**

Cottonwood Cafe, **3**

Daily Catch, **30**

Dali, **22**

East Coast Grill, **31**

Elsie's Deli, **18**

Goemon, **29**

Green Street Grill, **24**

Grendel's Den, **13**

Harvest, **11**

India Pavilion, **23**

Iruna, **14**

Joyce Chen Restaurant, **1**

La Groceria, **26**

Legal Sea Foods, **28**

Lucky Garden, **6**

Mary Chung, **25**

Mexican Cuisine, **4**

Michela's, **29**

The Peacock, **8**

Rarities, **12**

Sally Ling's, **34**

798 Main, **27**

33 Dunster St., **16**

Upstairs at the Pudding, **19**

Wursthaus, **17**

and an extensive menu of Mandarin, Shanghai, and Szechuan food. Specialties include hot and cold soups, Szechuan scallops, and moo shu dishes. *390 Rindge Ave., tel. 617/492-7373. Reservations suggested for large parties. Dress: informal. AE, MC, V. Moderate.*

**Lucky Garden.** Cambridge's first Szechuan restaurant offers hot-and-sour soup, scallops, Peking duck, and fried dumplings in a pleasant, comfortable atmosphere. No liquor. *282 Concord Ave., tel. 617/354-9514. Reservations accepted, but there's often a wait anyway. Dress: informal. MC, V. Moderate.*

**Mary Chung.** Here is one of the finest Chinese restaurants in the Boston area. Manadarin and Szechuan specialties—such as pork-filled dumplings with chili oil and bean curd with hot sauce—are served in a relaxed, casual setting. No liquor. *447 Massachusetts Ave., tel. 617/864-1991. No reservations. Dress: informal. No credit cards. Closed Tues. Moderate.*

## Contemporary (Mixed Menu)

**Chez Nous.** The menu changes daily in this small, storefront dining room, simply decorated. Dinner might begin with smoked salmon, followed by roast free-range chicken and oven-poached halibut, then chocolate almond torte and raspberries for dessert. *147 Huron Ave., tel. 617/864-6670. Reservations recommended. Jacket and tie suggested. MC, V. No lunch. Closed Sun. and Mon. Very Expensive.*

★ **East Coast Grill.** The chef calls his food "equatorial cuisine" to acknowledge the hot pepper and spices common in fare served near the equator. A number of ethnic dishes such as grilled tuna with West Indies sofrito, grilled sweetbreads, jerk chicken, and "pasta from Hell"—a pasta livened with inner beauty hot sauce—share the menu with southern regional specialties such as North Carolina barbecue. The dining room is small, bright, and very busy. *1271 Cambridge St., tel. 617/491-6568. No reservations; go early or late to avoid a long wait. Dress: informal. MC, V. No lunch. Expensive.*

★ **Green Street Grill.** The tables are small, the room very plain, the service casual, yet the chef is turning out some of the city's most imaginative dishes. Reflecting his West Indian background, the food tends to be hot and spicy. Among the specialties are West Indian conch stewed with hot chile in a tomato and thyme lemon butter sauce, and grilled swordfish with a spicy white rum passion fruit lime and thyme dressing. The dishes use lots of sauces, many of which show a decidedly French influence. *280 Green St., tel. 617/876-1655. No reservations. Dress: informal. AE, MC, V. No lunch. Expensive.*

**Harvest.** This is the sort of place where junior Harvard faculty might come to celebrate getting a fellowship. It adopted nouvelle American cuisine early on, hosting a game festival in January or February every year that features the likes of elk and antelope. The leafy patio is a good choice for an outdoor meal in summer, and the bar attracts young, brainy singles. The less expensive cafe section doesn't take reservations. *44 Brattle St., tel. 617/492-1115. Reservations suggested. Jacket and tie suggested. AE, CB, D, DC, MC, V. Expensive.*

**Cottonwood Cafe.** This Southwestern eatery is to Tex-Mex what Ralph Lauren is to Wrangler jeans. Sweet corn tamales, a terrific smoked tomato sauce, and seafood posole draw a trendy crowd. There is outdoor seating during warm weather. It's reached at the Porter Square stop on the T's Red Line. *1815*

*Massachusetts Ave., tel. 617/661-7440. Reservations suggested. Dress: casual but neat. AE, MC, V. Moderate-Expensive.*

**Grendel's Den.** Housed in a former Harvard College fraternity building, Grendel's has an unusually warm, clubby atmosphere, a downstairs bar, and an eclectic assortment of cuisines, including Middle Eastern, Greek, Indian, Italian, and French. Diners are welcome to mix and match small-portion dishes, which generally include such diverse items as shish kebab, fettuccine, spareribs, moussaka, hummus, and broiled fish. And there's a large salad bar. *89 Winthrop St., tel. 617/491-1160. Reservations accepted, recommended on weekends. Dress: informal. AE, CB, DC, MC, V. Moderate.*

**The Border Cafe.** Good, reasonably priced Sunbelt fare—Tex-Mex with Cajun and Caribbean touches—brightly painted murals advertising Tabasco and Dixie beer, and a lively bar scene has the Harvard Square crowds packed in on weekends. And what would a restaurant like this be without a recording of El Paso in the background? *32 Church St., tel. 617/864-6100. No reservations. Dress: casual. AE, CB, MC, V. Inexpensive-Moderate.*

## French

**The Peacock.** This basement restaurant in a residential side street north of Harvard Square provides its loyal following with a romantic setting and a French provincial menu that changes every other week. The specialties are chicken liver pâté, sole suchet, and meringues. Beer and wine (including ports and sherries) only. *5 Craigie Circle, tel. 617/661-4073. Reservations suggested. Jacket and tie optional. MC, V. No lunch. Closed Sun. and Mon. Expensive.*

## German

**Wursthaus.** This Harvard Square landmark has wood booths in the beer-hall style, decorative steins, 160 beers, and 38 sandwiches. The menu may mix its languages to describe what is basically hefty German fare: "schnitzel served mit mushroom sauce aux sherry," for example. Try the sauerbraten, available Tuesday, Thursday, and Sunday, or the generous hot pastrami sandwich. *4 John F. Kennedy St., tel. 617/491-7110. No reservations. Dress: casual. AE, DC, MC, V. Inexpensive-Moderate.*

## Greek

**Acropolis.** At the Acropolis you'll find a basic blue-and-white Aegean decor with predictable lamb dishes and Greek wines. The daily specials are a good value. *1680 Massachusetts Ave., tel. 617/354-8335. Dress: informal. AE, CB, DC, MC, V. Moderate.*

## Iberian

**Casa Portugal.** Here is a small, intimate, genuinely Portuguese restaurant near Inman Square whose specialties include pork with clams, squid stew, seafood dishes, and native wines. *1200 Cambridge St., tel. 617/491-8880. Reservations for weekends. Dress: informal. AE, MC, V. No lunch. Moderate.*

**Iruna.** This Spanish restaurant, popular with students for years, specializes in paellas and seafoods and has great salads. Outdoor dining is possible in warm weather. Wine, beer, and sangria only. *56 John F. Kennedy St., tel. 617/868-5633. Reservations accepted. Dress: informal. No credit cards. Closed Sun. Moderate.*

★ **Dali.** Situated just outside Harvard Square, this gem offers a wide selection of Spanish tapas and entrees and the best list of Spanish wines and sherries in the area. *415 Washington St., tel. 617/661-3254. Dress: casual but neat. AE, MC, V. No lunch. Inexpensive-Moderate.*

## Indian

**India Pavilion.** This is perhaps the best Indian restaurant in the Boston area. The food is authentically spicy; if you like it hot, try the *vindaloo* lamb, chicken, or fish. For those with tamer palate, the lamb *jalfrazie*, with green vegetables and onions, is a winner. There are vegetarian specialties as well, and beer and wine. *17 Central Sq., tel. 617/547-7463. Reservations accepted. Dress: informal. MC, V. No lunch Sun. Moderate.*

## Italian

★ **Michela's.** One of the city's most popular restaurants, Michela's boasts a menu that changes every eight weeks or so. It promises imaginative dishes such as pizza *vongole* (with clams and fresh oregano), house-cured *bresaola* (air-dried beef served with blackened mushrooms and ricotta), and lobster and Taylor bay scallops in a broth with fennel, black pasta, and hot red peppers. All sauces, breads, and pastas are made fresh daily. The decor combines the building's industrial past (with exposed heating ducts) and soft, Tuscany colors. An atrium cafe serves a lighter menu, with all dishes under $12 Monday-Friday. *1 Atheneum St. (lobby of the former Carter Ink Bldg.), tel. 617/225-2121. Reservations advised. Jacket and tie optional. AE, CB, DC, MC, V. No lunch Sat. Closed Sun. Expensive.*

★ **Upstairs at the Pudding.** The Harvard Club, famed for its theatrical presentations and other high jinks, is home to this elegant restaurant featuring Northern Italian cuisine. The walls are a deep ivy green, the tablecloths pink, the setting intimate. The four-course fixed-price dinner ($40) offers an opportunity to choose from among 10 items in each course—the best way to sample Chef Deborah Hughes' diverse talents. Some examples: for the first course, *tagliatelle* with sun-dried tomatoes, French goat cheese, artichoke hearts, and Moroccan lemons; for the main course, veal scallopini with a hazelnut Marsala sauce; and for the third course, salad or a dessert such as charlotte au chocolat. All main courses are served with an array of fresh vegetables. An à la carte menu is also available. Sunday brunch menu includes Belgian waffles, Welsh rarebit, and sweet red pepper corned beef hash. *10 Holyoke St., tel. 617/864-1933. Reservations advised. Jacket and tie optional. AE, MC, V. No lunch. No dinner Sun. Very Expensive.*

**La Groceria.** The atmosphere here is informal, that of a real Italian trattoria; the restaurant is composed of several small rooms. Specialties include homemade pasta, antipasto, veal dishes, and homemade cheesecake and cannoli. *853 Main St., tel. 617/547-9258 or 617/876-4162. Reservations for large*

*groups only. Dress: informal. AE, CB, DC, MC, V. No lunch
Sun. Moderate.*

**Bertucci's.** Part of a small local chain, Bertucci's turns out some
of the best pizza in Boston. The ingredients are fresh and interesting, and the pies are baked over a wood flame in brick ovens,
which gives them a unique flavor. Also available are salads,
pasta, and calzones. There are several branches throughout the
Boston area. *21 Brattle St., tel. 617/864-4748. No reservations.
Dress: casual. MC, V. Inexpensive–Moderate.*

## Japanese

★ **Cafe Sushi.** Here is an exceptional sushi bar that will please
devotees. Try the *kaki* (oyster sushi) or *anago* (broiled eel). An
introductory platter is available for novices. *1105 Massachusetts Ave., tel. 617/492-0434. No reservations. Dress: informal. MC, V. Moderate.*

★ **Goemon's Japanese Noodle Restaurant.** Large bowls of Japanese noodles in broth, with a mix-and-match selection of meats
and vegetables, are filling fare and a considerable bargain. The
contemporary decor features sleek black lacquer, yet the atmosphere is relaxed, not cold, and the service attentive. Dining
at the counter lets you study the chefs at work. *1 Kendall Sq.,
tel. 617/577-9595. Reservations required for parties of 5 or
more. Dress: casual. AE, MC, V. Inexpensive.*

## Mexican

**Casa Mexico.** The attractive basement dining room has Mexican tiles set in the brick walls. Among the specialties are *mole
poblano*, enchiladas, and tostadas. *75 Winthrop St., tel. 617/
491-4552. Reservations Mon.–Thurs. only. Dress: informal.
AE, CB, DC, MC, V. No lunch Sun. Moderate.*

**Mexican Cuisine.** The Mexican Cuisine restaurant features authentic regional seafood specialties such as *camarones
borrachos* (shrimp in a "drunken" tequila sauce), Tampico-
style scallops, and tuna *en pipian* (sauce made with pumpkin
seeds). There's little ambience, a high noise level, and lots of
customers. *1682 Massachusetts Ave., tel. 617/661-1634. No
reservations (to avoid waiting, arrive before 6). Dress: informal. AE. No lunch Sun. Moderate.*

## Middle Eastern

**Averof.** A large restaurant specializing in Lebanese and Greek
cuisine, Averof caters to groups. The house features a char-
coal-grilled shish kebab with onions, tomatoes, and Greek peppers; fried calamari (squid); and *moussaka*—layers of
eggplant, chopped beef, and melted cheese. For dessert, try
the baklava. Belly dancers try to draw you into their act from
8:30 nightly. *1924 Massachusetts Ave., tel. 617/354-4500. Reservations accepted. Dress: casual. AE, CB, DC, MC, V. Moderate.*

## Seafood

**Legal Sea Foods.** Located in the Kendall Square area near MIT,
this Cambridge-born restaurant is so popular that it now has
branches in the Boston Park Plaza Hotel, the Copley Place
Mall, and in Chestnut Hill. More than 30 varieties of fish—

broiled, baked, fried, and raw—are served daily in the mahogany dining room. Don't miss the chowder and homemade
desserts. There's an oyster bar, too. The policy here is to
serve food as soon as it's ready, which may leave some people
at the table eating while others wait. *5 Cambridge Center,
tel. 617/864–3400. No reservations; go early or be prepared
to wait. Dress: informal. AE, MC, V. No lunch Sun. Moderate.*

# Lodging

Hotel facilities in Cambridge are severely limited and tend to
be fully booked well in advance of such periods as student regis-
tration, football weekends, university reunions and commence-
ments, and the autumn turning of the leaves. Three major
hotels are located near the river, an awkward distance from
public transport but easily accessible by car (and the views are
fine).

A growing number of bed-and-breakfasts offer comfortably
modest accommodations, and there are single rooms at the
Cambridge YMCA.

## Hotels

The hotel reviews here are grouped according to the following
price categories, which apply to regular weekday rates for a
double room for two persons and do not reflect special weekend
or package rates. A Massachusetts occupancy tax of 9.7% is
added to all hotel bills.

| Category | Cost* |
|---|---|
| Very Expensive | over $170 |
| Expensive | $130–$170 |
| Moderate | $80–$130 |
| Inexpensive | under $80 |

*\*double room, add 9.7% state tax*

The following credit card abbreviations are used: AE, American Express; CB, Carte Blanche; D, Discover Card; DC, Diners
Club; MC, MasterCard; V, Visa.

The most highly recommended properties are indicated by a
star ★.

**Very Expensive**   **Cambridge Center Marriott Hotel.** The new 25-story hotel is two
miles from downtown Boston in Kendall Square. All rooms
have either two double beds or one king-size bed, plus color TV
with free HBO. Two floors are designated Concierge Level—
more services at a higher price. Children under 18 stay free in
their parents' room. *2 Cambridge Center, tel. 617/494–6600 or
800/228–9290. 432 rooms. Facilities: indoor pool with whirlpool, Universal gym with sauna, lockers, stationary bikes,
sundeck in season, restaurant, nightclub. AE, CB, DC, MC,
V.*

★   **Hyatt Regency.** Shaped like a ziggurat, the Hyatt Regency is a
dramatic building on the Charles River. A glass-sided elevator
hoists you through the 14-story atrium at its center. Some

rooms have private balconies, and most rooms have views of Boston directly across the river. There are three restaurants, a revolving rooftop lounge, and shops. *575 Memorial Dr., tel. 617/492-1234. 469 rooms. Facilities: indoor pool and Universal Health Club with whirlpool, steam bath, and sauna; bath amenities, nightly turndown, concierge, baby-sitting service, complimentary shuttle to points of interest. AE, CB, DC, MC, V.*

**Expensive** **The Charles Hotel.** The 296-room Charles anchors one end of
★ the Charles Square development, which is set around a brick plaza facing the Charles River. The architecture is sparse and modern, softened by New England antiques and paintings by local artists. Guest rooms have quilts, TV in the bathroom, and an honor bar. Though a new hotel, furniture and carpeting at the Charles were entirely refurbished in 1991. The dining room, Rarities, serves New American cuisine. A Sunday buffet brunch is served in the Bennett Street Cafe. The Regattabar is one of the city's hottest spots for jazz. Children under 18 stay free in their parents' room. Small pets allowed. *1 Bennett St., tel. 617/864-1200 or 800/882-1818. 296 rooms. Facilities: full spa services, swimming pool, 24 shops, 24-hour room service, paid parking. AE, CB, DC, MC, V.*

**Royal Sonesta Hotel.** A high-rise building near the Museum of Science, the Royal Sonesta has superb views of Boston's Beacon Hill just across the Charles River. A West Wing liberally decorated with modern art was recently added. All newly decorated rooms have color TV, air-conditioning, and a refrigerator. A business center provides computers, secretarial service, and telexes. Children under 12 stay free in their parents' room. *5 Cambridge Pky., tel. 617/491-3600 or 800/343-7170. 400 rooms. Facilities: 2 restaurants, indoor heated swimming pool, courtesy van to Government Center and the Faneuil Hall Marketplace 7 times daily, free parking, baby-sitting service. AE, CB, DC, MC, V.*

★ **Sheraton Commander.** A nicely maintained older hotel on Cambridge Common, its rooms are furnished with Boston rockers and four-posters. All rooms have color TV and air-conditioning, and some have kitchenettes. *16 Garden St., tel. 617/547-4800 or 800/325-3535. 175 rooms and suites. Facilities: new fitness room with rowing machines and exercise cycles, restaurant, lounge, multilingual staff, valet service, free parking. AE, CB, DC, MC, V.*

**Moderate** **Harvard Manor House.** This modern five-story motel in Brattle
★ Square is the nearest lodging to Harvard Square shops, restaurants, and tourist sites. All rooms have color TV and air-conditioning, and the rate includes a complimentary Continental breakfast. Children under 16 stay free in their parents' room. *110 Mt. Auburn St., tel. 617/864-5200 or 800/458-5886. 72 rooms. Facilities: free parking. AE, DC, MC, V.*

**Howard Johnson's Cambridge.** This is a modern 16-story hotel overlooking the Charles River; some rooms have private balconies, and all rooms have views, some of them better than others. Children under 18 stay free in their parents' room. Pets allowed. *777 Memorial Dr., tel. 617/492-7777 or 800/654-2000. 205 rooms. Facilities: indoor pool, free parking, 2 restaurants, bar, baby-sitting service. AE, CB, DC, MC, V.*

**Quality Inn-Cambridge.** The standard Quality Inn has an agreeable location: a pleasant shopping and residential neighborhood north of Harvard Square, handy to Harvard Law

School. It's on a bus line, and it's a 10-minute walk from Harvard Square. All rooms have color TV and air-conditioning. Children under 17 stay free in their parents' room. *1651 Massachusetts Ave., tel. 617/491–1000 or 800/228–5151. 135 rooms. Facilities: outdoor pool, free parking, baby-sitting service. AE, CB, DC, MC, V.*

**Inexpensive**  **Suisse Chalet Inn.** This is a typical Suisse Chalet, clean, economical, and sparse. It's isolated from most shopping or sites, a 10-minute drive from Harvard Square, but it is within walking distance of the Red Line terminus, offering T access to Boston and Harvard Square. All rooms have color TV, air-conditioning, and direct-dial phones. *211 Concord Tpk., 02140, tel. 617/661–7800 or 800/258–1980. 79 rooms. Facilities: free parking. AE, DC, MC, V.*

### Bed-and-Breakfasts

A bed-and-breakfast is overnight lodging and breakfast in a private residence. Bed-and-breakfasts are becoming increasingly popular in Cambridge, and the homes listed by the reservations services named here are inspected regularly and must meet specific standards. All are in the *Inexpensive–Moderate* price range.

**Bed and Breakfast Cambridge and Greater Boston** (Box 665, Cambridge 02140, tel. 617/576–1492) lists rooms in 30 Cambridge homes.
**Cambridge Discovery** (tel. 617/497–1631). The kiosk in Harvard Square lists a dozen B&Bs in the Cambridge area.
**Cambridge House Bed and Breakfast** (2218 Massachusetts Ave., Cambridge 02140, tel. 617/491–6300 or 800/232–9989). A gracious old home listed on the National Register of Historic Places, Cambridge House has 7 antique-filled guest rooms and five in its carriage house. All are convenient to the T and buses. There is also a reservations center here for host homes in the metropolitan Boston area.

### YMCAs

**Cambridge YMCA.** The accommodations are single rooms for men only, with a maximum stay of seven days. *820 Massachussetts Ave., tel. 617/661–9622. 140 rooms. Access to pool and sports facilities. Pay parking. No credit cards. No children. No pets.*

# The Arts and Nightlife

The Thursday *Boston Globe* Calendar, the weekly *Boston Phoenix*, and the monthly *Boston* magazine are excellent sources of information about happenings around Cambridge. Because many events are associated with local colleges, admission costs are often less than those in Boston.

### Theater

Cambridge boasts a nationally respected resident theater company, stagings of off-Broadway plays, and a dependable stream of classic productions by the MIT and Harvard companies.

**The Gilbert and Sullivan Players** (Office for the Arts at Harvard, tel. 617/493–2736) produce one operetta each semester in the Agassiz Theater at Harvard.

**Harvard's Hasty Pudding Theatricals** (12 Holyoke St., tel. 617/495–5205), the "oldest theatrical organization in the United States," produces one show annually; it usually runs from late February to the end of March, then goes on tour.

**The Loeb Drama Center** (64 Brattle St., tel. 617/495–2668) has two theaters, the main one an experimental stage. This is the home of the highly regarded American Repertory Theater, which performs here from November to mid-June. The Harvard-Radcliffe Drama Club stages its productions here in October, April, July, and August. Various other presentations are scheduled around these two seasons.

**MIT's Community Players** (tel. 617/253–2530) and the **Shakespeare Ensemble** (tel. 617/253–2903) perform throughout the academic year. See local newspaper listings or the school paper, *Tech Talk*, for schedules.

## Concerts

The quality and range of music is predictably high in Cambridge, but the groups change constantly.

**Harvard's Sanders Theater** (Cambridge and Quincy Sts., tel. 617/495–2420) and **MIT's Kresge Auditorium** (77 Massachusetts Ave., tel. 617/253–2826 or 617/253–9800) provide fine stages for local and visiting classical and folk performers.

**Harvard musical groups** (tel. 617/495–2791), ranging from the Harvard-Radcliffe Orchestra (the oldest continuously performing symphony in the country) to the Kuumba Singers, a group of outstanding black gospel singers, perform throughout the year.

**Longy School of Music** (27 Garden St., tel. 617/876–0956) and **New School of Music** (25 Lowell St., tel. 617/492–8105) both offer frequent free classical music concerts.

## Dance

**Cambridge Multicultural Arts Center** (41 Second St., tel. 617/577–1400) hosts local performers in ethnic music and dance, and two galleries show the visual arts.

**Folk Arts Center of New England** (1950 Massachusetts Ave., tel. 617/491–6083) sponsors participatory international folk dancing at locations throughout the city on Friday and Saturday nights. Admission: $5.

**Harvard Summer Dance Center** (Sanders Theater, tel. 617/495–5535) presents a dance series two weekends in July. Performers include faculty members and choreographers from Boston and New York and their companies.

## Film

Cambridge is the best place in New England for finding classic, foreign, and nostalgia films.

**The Brattle Theater** (40 Brattle St., tel. 617/876–6837) is a landmark cinema for classic-movie buffs.

**The Blacksmith House** (56 Brattle St., tel. 617/547–6789) shows classic movies on Friday evening, from spring to fall.

**Loews Harvard Square Theater** (1438 Massachusetts Ave., tel. 617/864–4580) shows both first-run and revival films.

**Loews Janus Cinema** (57 John F. Kennedy St., tel. 617/661–3737) programs first-run movies only.

**Somerville Theater** (55 Davis Sq., Somerville, tel. 617/625–5700), just two stops from Harvard Square on the Red Line, shows classics, foreign films, and first-run movies in a classic theater.

## Cafes and Coffeehouses

Cambridge boasts one of the best concentrations of cafes and coffeehouses in the New World. Whether they serve wine or coffee, pastries or full meals, the atmosphere in these places is unhurried, geared to the single diner who may read while dining, and to the couple locked in discussion. Poetry readings and music are featured at a few locations, but basically they are low-key, genial lingering spots, endemic to an academic setting and rarely found in American cities.

**Au Bon Pain** in the center of Harvard Square is the ideal spot for people-watching. Some tables are reserved for chess players who challenge all comers. Croissants are the speciality, with a choice of fillings, and salads and light fare are available, cafeteria style. *1360 Massachusetts Ave., tel. 617/497–9797. Open Sun.–Thurs. 7 AM–midnight, Fri.–Sat. 7 AM–1 AM. No credit cards.*

**The Blacksmith House.** This is the original 18th-century house where Longfellow's blacksmith lived (a nearby stone commemorates the long-gone chestnut tree). Now operated by the Cambridge Center for Adult Education, it houses an outstanding German bakery with indoor tables and a warm-weather streetside cafe. Poetry readings, concerts, films, and plays are staged in the Spiegel Performance Center, a modern addition at the rear of the building. *56 Brattle St., tel. 617/354–3036. Open weekdays 9–7, Sat. 9–5. Closed Sun. The outdoor cafe is open in summer until 9 PM. No credit cards.*

**Cafe Algiers** is a genuinely Middle Eastern cafe with a choice of strong coffees and tea and pita-bread lunches. It's dark and quiet, a good place to meet for a serious conversation. *40 Brattle St., tel. 617/492–1557. Open daily 9 AM–midnight. No credit cards.*

**Modern Times Cafe.** Up front are a lunch counter and five booths, in the back an inviting room with a dozen tables. The menu is light: omelets, salads, sandwiches, and such daily specials as *spanikopita* (spinach-cheese pie). The cafe makes its desserts; there are beers and house wines. Local musicians perform occasionally. *134 Hampshire St., tel. 617/354–8371. Open Tues.–Fri. 11:30 AM–10 PM, weekends 9:30 AM–10 PM.*

**Passim's.** One of the country's first and most famous venues for live folk music, Passim's by day is a quiet basement setting for a light lunch or a coffee break, a good spot to buy a card or attractive jewelry. By night it's a gathering place for folk and bluegrass music or poetry readings. *47 Palmer St., tel. 617/492–7679. Open 12–5:30 Tues.–Sat. and 8 or 8:30 PM until closing Tues.–Sun. Closed Sun. May–Aug. No credit cards.*

**Woven Hose Cafe.** The Woven Hose has light meals, daily dinner specials, and outdoor dining in season. *1 Kendall Sq., tel. 617/577–8444. Call for hours. MC, V.*

## Nightclubs and Bars

**Cantab Lounge.** A local band plays rock, blues, and jazz Wednesday–Sunday from 9:30 until closing in this friendly and informal lounge. Downstairs there's a comedy-mystery theater and dinner Thursday–Sunday. *738 Massachusetts Ave., tel. 617/354–2685. No credit cards.*

**Casablanca.** Ceiling fans, wicker furniture, deep seats, and Omar White's murals create an unbeatable atmosphere for a quiet drink. *40 Brattle St., tel. 617/876–0999. Open Sun.–Wed. 5 PM–1 AM, Thurs.–Sat. 5 PM–2 AM. No credit cards.*

**Indigo.** This predominately lesbian bar plays new wave and rock on a small dance floor lit in purple neon. Upstairs is a larger dance floor, and Wednesday is movie night. *823 Main St., tel. 617/497–7200. Downstairs open Wed. 8–1, Thurs. and Fri. 4–1, Sat. 9–1. Upstairs open Fri. and Sat. Cover charge weekends. AE, DC, V.*

**Man Ray.** This art gallery and progressive rock bar is connected to **Campus,** a predominantly gay jukebox bar. *21 Brookline St., tel. 617/864–0400. Open Wed.–Sun. 8 PM–1 AM. Cover charge. No credit cards.*

**Nightstage.** The club's two levels present top names in blues, jazz, folk, Latin, pop, and bluegrass. National and local talent are featured. *823 Main St., tel. 617/497–8200. Admission varies; tickets recommended in advance. Open Sun.–Wed. 8 PM–1 AM, Thurs.–Sat. 8 PM–2 AM. AE, MC, V.*

**Plough & Stars.** This traditional Irish bar has Guinness and Bass on tap and Irish, country, and bluegrass music daily from 9 PM to 1 AM. It's a comfortable, friendly, noisy place, popular with students and neighborhood people. *912 Massachusetts Ave., tel. 617/492–9653. Open daily noon–1 AM. No cover, no minimum. No credit cards.*

**Regattabar.** Some top names in jazz perform at this spacious and elegant club in the Charles Hotel. Even when there's no entertainment, it's a pleasant place for a drink (and drinks are expensive). *Bennett & Eliot Sts., tel. 617/864–1200. Shows Tues.–Thurs. at 8, Fri. at 8 and 10, Sat. at 9 and 11. Proper dress required. Cover charge varies. AE, MC, V.*

**Ryles.** Soft lights, mirrors, and greenery set the mood for first-rate live jazz by local and national groups. The lounge and restaurant downstairs has a jukebox and light fare. *212 Hampshire St., tel. 617/876–9330. Open Sun.–Thurs. 5 PM–1 AM, Fri.–Sat. 5 PM–2 AM. No reservations. Cover charge, no minimum. Sun. brunch. AE, MC, V.*

**Scullers.** This new 100-seat place has made a very strong name for itself by hosting such well-knowns as Herb Pomeroy and the Victor Mendoza Quintet. On the second floor of the Guest Quarters Suite Hotel, this is a cozy place to relax; all but two or three tables has a direct view of the performers. *400 Soldier's Field Rd., tel. 617/783–0811. Reservations strongly suggested. Admission varies from $5–$12 depending on the performer and the night. Shows Tues.–Sat. at 8:30 and 10:30. Special Sunday jazz brunch 11:30–2:30. AE, DC, MC, V.*

**The Willow.** Even though it's not in Cambridge, the Willow cannot be overlooked. This small club seats only 100 people or so, and its devoted patrons come to hear excellent local jazz ensembles jam. *699 Broadway, Somerville, tel. 617/623–9874. No reservations. Shows nightly at 9 and 11. Admission varies from $6–$10. No credit cards.*

**Comedy Club**

**Catch a Rising Star.** A New York club of the same name owns and operates this venue, where comedy is the fare seven nights a week. Nationally known acts appear Wednesday–Sunday, new talents are showcased Monday and Tuesday. *30 John F. Kennedy St., tel. 617/661–9887. Shows Mon.–Thurs. and Sun. at 8:30, Fri. at 8:30 and 11, Sat. at 7:30, 9:45, and midnight. All ages admitted. Cover charge. AE, MC, V.*

# 10 Excursions

# West of Boston: Lexington and Concord

The events of April 19, 1775, the first military encounters of the American Revolution, are very much a part of present-day Lexington and Concord. In these two quintessential New England towns, rich in literary and political history, one finds the true beginning of America's freedom trail on the very sites where a colonial people began their fight for freedom and a new nation.

## Getting Around

**By Car** Cross the Charles River at the Massachusetts Avenue Bridge and proceed through Cambridge, bearing right for Arlington at Harvard Square. Continue through Arlington Center on Massachusetts Avenue to the first traffic light, turn left into Jason Street, and begin your tour. Travel time is 25 minutes one-way.

**By Train** Boston and Maine trains run from North Station (150 Causeway St., tel. 617/227–5070 or 800/392–6099) to Concord and beyond. Travel time is one hour one-way.

**By Bus** The **MBTA** (tel. 617/722–3200) operates buses to Lexington and Boston's western suburbs from Alewife Station in Cambridge. Travel time is about one hour one-way.

## Guided Tours

**Brush Hill Bean-Town Trolley Tours** (109 Norfolk St., Boston 02124, tel. 617/986–6100 or 800/647–4776) has daily motorcoach tours to Lexington's Battle Green and Concord's Old North Bridge area from mid-February to mid-December.

**The Gray Line** (275 Tremont St., Boston 02116, tel. 617/426–8805) offers two tours west of Boston from mid-April to mid-October: "The Grand Combination" lasts seven hours and covers 75 miles, including Boston, Concord, and Lexington; the "Lexington, Concord, Cambridge" tour lasts about three hours.

## Exploring Lexington

*Numbers in the margin correspond with points of interest on the Lexington map.*

As the Redcoats retreated from Concord on April 19, 1775, the Minutemen peppered the British with musket fire from behind low stone walls and tall pine trees before marching to the safety of Charlestown's hills. "The bloodiest half mile of Battle Road," now Massachusetts Avenue in Arlington, began in front of the **Jason Russell House.** Russell, along with 10 other Minutemen, was killed here during the Battle of the Foot of the Rocks, which involved about 1,700 Minutemen and militia and a similar number of British soldiers, near the intersection of today's Lowell Street and Massachusetts Avenue. Another 10 Minutemen and more than 20 British soldiers were killed outside. Bullet holes are still visible in the house. *7 Jason St., Arlington,*

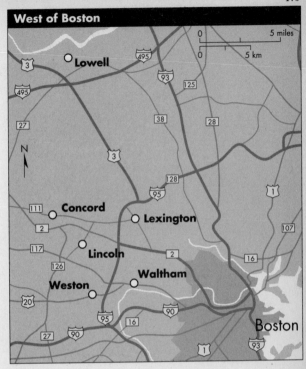

## West of Boston

0          5 miles
0       5 km

3  Lowell

495

93

125

27

38

28

N

3

128

95

111  Concord        Lexington

2                          107

117  Lincoln        2

126                16

Weston  Waltham

20

95   16        90

27  90        Boston

16

1

93

*tel. 617/648–4300. Admission: $2.50 adults, 50¢ children over
12. Open Apr. 19–Nov. 1, Tues.–Sat. 2–5. 30-min tours.*

Continue west on Massachusetts Avenue through Arlington
Heights to the **Old Schwamb Mill** (turn off Massachusetts onto
Lowell, then take the second right to Mill Lane). In 1650 this
was the site of a gristmill; during the Revolution, the Battle of
the Foot of the Rocks on Mill Brook took place here. Today private craftsmen produce and sell Shaker reproductions of furniture, rugs, baskets, and boxes. *17 Mill Lane, tel. 617/643–0554.
Admission: free for drop-ins, $35 for a group of 6–10 with a full
tour. Open weekdays 10–4.*

Where Massachusetts Avenue meets Route 2A in East Lexington is the **Museum of Our National Heritage.** The contemporary
brick and glass building, built and supported by the Scottish-
Rite Masons, houses changing exhibits in a tasteful and subdued setting. The displays focus on America's heritage as seen
through its artifacts, and there are events, lectures, and films.
*33 Marrett Rd., tel. 617/861–6559. Admission free. Open
Mon.–Sat. 10–5, Sun. noon–5. Closed major holidays.*

Less than a quarter of a mile west on Massachusetts Avenue,
the **Munroe Tavern,** built in 1635 as a pub, is open to the public
as a historic site. The Munroe family hid in nearby woods while
the dazed and demoralized British rested and regrouped here
on their retreat to Boston following their second encounter of
the day with the rebels at Concord's Old North Bridge. *1332
Massachusetts Ave., tel. 617/861–0928. Admission: $2 adults,*

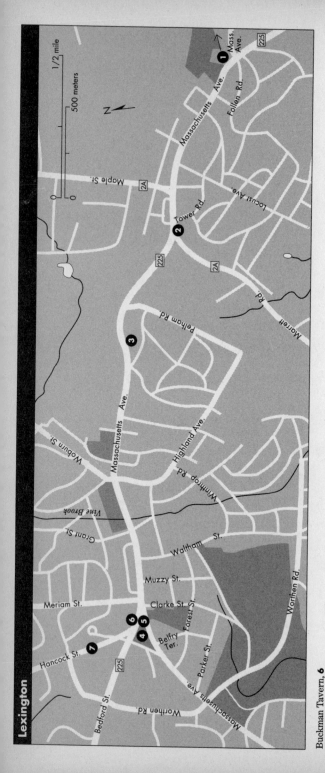

**Lexington**

1/2 mile

500 meters

N

Mass. Ave.

225

Follen Rd.

Massachusetts Ave.

Maple St.

2A

Tower Rd.

Locust Ave.

2

225

2A

Morrell Rd.

Pelham Rd.

3

Massachusetts Ave.

Highland Ave.

Winthrop Rd.

Woburn St.

Vine Brook

Grant St.

Waltham St.

Muzzy St.

Meriam St.

Clarke St.

Forest St.

6

5

4

Belfry Ter.

7

Hancock St.

225

Parker St.

Worthen Rd.

Bedford St.

Massachusetts Ave.

Worthen Rd.

Buckman Tavern, **6**
Hancock-Clarke
House, **7**
Lexington Green, **4**
Minuteman Statue, **5**
Munroe Tavern, **3**
Museum of Our
National Heritage, **2**
Old Schwamb Mill, **1**

*50¢ children 6–16. Open weekend nearest Apr. 19–Oct. 31, Mon.–Sat. 10–5, Sun. 1–5.*

❹ Massachusetts Avenue continues to **Lexington Green**, a two-acre, triangular piece of land bounded by Harrington Road, Bedford Street, and Massachusetts Avenue. Here on the Battle Green the Minuteman Captain John Parker assembled his men to await the arrival of the British, who marched from Boston to Concord to "teach rebels a lesson" on the morning of April 19. Henry Hudson Kitson's renowned statue of Parker, the ❺ **Minuteman Statue,** stands at the tip of the Green, facing downtown Lexington. The **Revolutionary Monument** marks the site where seven of the Minutemen killed that day are buried. Captain Parker's command that morning to his 77 men, who formed two uneven lines of defense, is emblazoned on the **Line of Battle boulder,** to the right of the Minuteman Statue: "Stand your ground, don't fire unless fired upon; but if they mean to have war, let it begin here." *Visitors Center (Lexington Chamber of Commerce), 1875 Massachusetts Ave., tel. 617/862–1450. Open June 1–Oct. 31, daily 9–5; Nov. 1–May 31, daily 10–4.*

The British Major John Pitcairn was equally emphatic that morning, ordering his troops to surround the Minutemen and disarm them but not to shoot. A shot did ring out, and the rest is history. Word of the bloodshed in Lexington spread rapidly to surrounding towns. When the British marched into Concord later that day, more than 400 Minutemen were waiting on Punkatasset Hill, the high ground overlooking the Concord River and the Old North Bridge. A rectangular marker in the stone wall along Liberty Street, behind the Old North Bridge Visitors Center, announces: "On this field the minute men and militia formed before marching down to the fight at the bridge."

Two questions remain unanswered. Who fired first? Why did Parker, a 45-year-old veteran of the French and Indian War, place his men behind the two-story, barnlike meetinghouse that stood where the Minuteman Statue stands today? (A memorial behind the statue marks the meetinghouse site.) The Minutemen couldn't see the advancing British, much less make a show of resistance. Indeed, why didn't Captain Parker tell his men to take to the hills overlooking the British route? It was an absurd situation, 77 men against 700, one of history's most celebrated accidents.

❻ On the right side of the Green is **Buckman Tavern,** built in 1690, where the Minutemen gathered initially to wait for the British on April 19. A 30-minute tour visits the tavern's seven rooms. *1 Bedford St., tel. 617/862–5598. Admission: $2.50 adults, 50¢ children 6–16. Open weekend nearest Apr. 19–Oct. 31, Mon.–Sat. 10–5, Sun. 1–5.*

A quarter mile north of the Green stands the eight-room ❼ **Hancock-Clarke House,** built in 1698. Here the patriots John Hancock and Sam Adams, who were attending the Provincial Congress in session in Concord, were roused from their sleep by Paul Revere, who had ridden out from Boston to "spread the alarm through every Middlesex village and farm" that the British were marching to Concord. Both Hancock and Adams fled to avoid capture. A 20-minute tour is offered. *35 Hancock St., tel. 617/861–0928. Admission: $2.50 adults, 50¢ children 6–16. Open weekend nearest Apr. 19–Oct. 31, Mon.–Sat. 10–5, Sun. 1–5.*

*Note: The Lexington Historical Society offers a combination ticket of $5 for admission to the Munroe Tavern, the Buckman Tavern, and the Hancock-Clarke House.*

The town of Lexington comes alive each *Patriot's Day* (the Monday nearest April 19) to celebrate and recreate the events of April 19, 1775, beginning at 6 AM, when "Paul Revere" rides down Massachusetts Avenue shouting "The British are coming! The British are coming!" "Minutemen" groups in costume participate in events throughout the day.

## Exploring Concord

*Numbers in the margin correspond with points of interest on the Concord map.*

To reach Concord from Lexington, take routes 4/225 through Bedford and Route 62 west to Concord; or Route 2A west, which splits from routes 4/225 at the Museum of Our National Heritage. The latter route will take you through parts of **Minute Man National Historical Park,** whose more than 750 acres commemorate the events of April 19; it includes Fiske Hill and the **Battle Road Visitors Center,** approximately one mile from the Battle Green on the right off Route 2A. *Tel. 617/862–7753. Admission free. Open Apr.–Dec., daily 8:30–5. Audiovisual programs; printed material; lectures in summer.*

**1** As you enter Concord, the Chamber of Commerce **tourist information kiosk** is a handy place to get your bearings; maps and brochures are available here. *Heywood St., tel. 508/369–3120. Open mid-Apr.–May, weekends 9:30–4:30; June–Oct., daily 9:30–4:30. Hours vary in winter.*

**2** Now a series of rotating art exhibits, the **Jonathan Ball House,** built in 1753, was a station on the underground railroad for runaway slaves during the Civil War. Ask to see the secret room. The garden and waterfall are refreshing. *Concord Art Association, 37 Lexington Rd., tel. 508/369–2578. Admission: $2 adults, free for senior citizens. Open Tues.–Sat. 11–4:30, Sun. 2–4:30.*

Memorials to the Civil War dead will be found on Monument Square, across from the Colonial Inn in downtown Concord.
**3** The **Wright Tavern,** just off the square, was headquarters first for the Minutemen, then the British, on April 19. The tavern was built in 1747; information is available from the Tri-Con Gift Shop next door.

**4** At the **Old North Bridge** the tables were turned on the British later in the day on April 19. Here Minutemen from Concord and surrounding towns fired "the shot heard round the world," signaling the start of the American Revolution, and here Daniel Chester French's Minuteman Statue honors the country's first freedom fighters. The National Historical Park's North Bridge Visitors Center is a half-mile down Monument Street. *174 Liberty St., tel. 508/369–6993. Open daily 8:30–5. Audiovisual programs Jan.–Mar., printed material, lectures in summer.*

**5** The Reverend William Emerson watched rebels and Redcoats do battle from the back meadow of his home, the **Old Manse,** on Monument Street. The house, built in 1769–1770, was occupied by the family except for the 3½ years Nathaniel Hawthorne rented it. A 30-minute tour shows visitors Hawthorne's win-

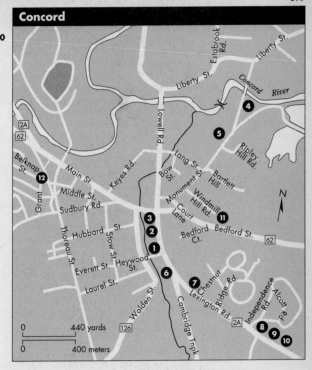

dowpane writings and original wallpaper of 1769. *Monument St., tel. 508/369–3909. Admission: $4 adults, $3.50 senior citizens, $2.50 children 6–12. Open the weekend nearest Apr. 19– late Oct., Mon. and Wed–Sat. 10–4:30; Sun. and holidays 1– 4:30.*

**⑥** The 19th-century essayist and poet Ralph Waldo Emerson, grandson of William Emerson, lived briefly in the Old Manse in 1834–1835, then moved to what we know as the **Ralph Waldo Emerson House** at 28 Cambridge Turnpike. Here he wrote the famous *Essays* ("To be great is to be misunderstood"; "A foolish consistency is the hobgoblin of little minds, adored by little statesmen and philosophers and divines"). Emerson is even better remembered for the words from his "Concord Hymn" (1837): "Here once the embattled farmers stood And fired the shot heard round the world." (The lines are inscribed at the foot of the Minuteman Statue at the Old North Bridge.) The Emerson House furnishings are pretty much as Emerson left them, even down to his hat on the banister newel post. *28 Cambridge Turnpike, on Route 2A, tel. 508/369–2236. Admission: $3 adults, $1.50 children 6–17. Open the weekend nearest Apr. 19–mid–Oct., Thurs.–Sat. 10–4:30, Sun. 2–4:30. 30-min tours.*

**⑦** The original contents of Emerson's study are in the **Concord Museum**, one-half mile southeast on Route 2A heading into Concord (with additional Emerson material at Harvard University's Houghton Library). The museum houses 15 period rooms, from Colonial to Empire; the bed in which Thoreau slept at Walden; powder horns; a diorama of the battle at the Old

North Bridge; and one of the two lanterns hung at the Old
North Church on the night of April 18, 1775. The bulk of the
museum's belongings were acquired from an "incurable collector," Cummings Davis, who in 1851 began a lifelong hunt in
Concord and the surrounding area for all manner of collectibles
from textiles to furniture. In 1887 the Concord Antiquarian Society was formed to take charge of Davis's treasures. The museum, in an attractive country setting, occupies a 1930 Colonial
Revival house. *200 Lexington Rd., tel. 508/369–9609. Admission: $5 adults, $4 students and senior citizens, $1.50 children
under 15. Open Mar.–Dec., Mon.–Sat. 9:30–3:30, Sun. 1:30–
3:30.*

**8** Louisa May Alcott's family home, **Orchard House,** is named
for the apple orchard that once surrounded it. This was home
for the Alcott family from 1857 to 1877. Here Louisa wrote *Little Women* and her father, Bronson, founded his school of
philosophy. (Fourteen years earlier, Bronson, with the English
reformer Charles Lane, Emerson, and Thoreau, tried to establish a Utopian community at an 18th-century farm, Fruitlands,
in rural Harvard; today the Fruitlands Museum houses memorabilia associated with the venture, along with a Shaker House
and an Indian artifact collection.) Nothing is roped off in Orchard House, allowing one a better sense of what life was like
for the Alcotts. *399 Lexington Rd., tel. 508/369–4118. Admission: $4 adults, $2 children 6–12, free under 6, $3 students and
senior citizens. Open Apr. 1–Oct. 31, Mon.–Sat. 10–4:30,
Sun. 1–4:30; Nov. and Mar., weekends only 1–4:30.*

Nathaniel Hawthorne lived at the Old Manse in 1842–1845,
working on stories and sketches, then moved to Salem (where
he wrote *The Scarlet Letter*) and Lenox (*The House of the Seven
Gables*). In 1852 he returned to Concord, bought a rambling
**9** structure called **The Wayside,** and lived here until his death in
1864. The subsequent owner, Margaret Sidney (author of *Five
Little Peppers and How They Grew*), kept Hawthorne's tower
study intact. *455 Lexington Rd. (Rte. 2A), tel. 508/369–6975.
Admission: $2 adults, free under 16 and over 62. Open mid-
Apr.–Oct. 31, Fri.–Tues. 10–5:30 (last tour leaves promptly at
5). A unit of Minute Man National Historical Park.*

**10** Next door to The Wayside, the yard of **Grapevine Cottage** (491
Lexington Rd., not open to the public) has the original Concord
grapevine, the grape the Welch's jams and jellies company
made famous. Welch's moved its headquarters from New York
to downtown Concord in 1983 to bring the company "back to its
roots." A plaque on the fence tells how Ephraim Wales Bull began the Concord grape.

**11** Each Memorial Day, Louisa Alcott's grave in the nearby **Sleepy
Hollow Cemetery** (entrance on Route 62 West) is decorated.
Along with Emerson, Thoreau, and Hawthorne, she is buried
in a section of the cemetery known as Author's Ridge. A huge
quartz stone marks Emerson's grave; its bronze tablet reads,
"The passive master lent his hand To the vast soul o'er which
him planned." *Open weekdays 7–3:30.*

A short drive from Monument Square on Main Street to Thoreau Street, then left onto Belknap Street, takes you to the
**12** **Thoreau Lyceum,** where the writer and naturalist's survey
maps, letters, and other memorabilia are housed. A replica of
his Walden Pond cabin is here. *156 Belknap St., tel 508/369–*

*5912. Admission: $2 adults, $1.50 students, 50¢ children under 12. Open Mar.–Dec., Mon.–Sat. 10–5, Sun. 2–5. Closed holidays.*

## Exploring Waltham, Weston, Lincoln

Other communities west of Boston, lacking Lexington and Concord's historical and literary significance, have different attractions for the visitor.

In downtown **Waltham,** a stone's throw from the Charles River and Route 20, approximately 12 miles west of Boston, the Boston Manufacturing Company experimented in 1813 with its own "industrial revolution": making a product from start to finish under one roof. The **Charles River Museum of Industry,** which opened in the fall of 1988, houses a history of American Industry from 1800 to the present that emphasizes steam power machinery. Exhibits include automaking and watchmaking, electronic equipment, and records on all the industries. *154 Moody St., tel. 617/893–5410. Admission: $2.50 adults, $1.50 children and senior citizens. Open Thurs. and Sun. by appointment. Closed major holidays.*

When it was obvious that the waters of the Charles were inadequate to supply enough energy to make cloth on the scale intended, the company moved its operations to Lowell, on the Merrimack River.

The other side of Waltham's industrial past can be found in two well-preserved pieces of architecture. One, the **Lyman Estate,** or The Vale, was built in 1793 by Theodore Lyman, a wealthy Boston merchant and entrepreneur. The Salem architect Samuel McIntire designed the elegant country house and laid out the surrounding grounds according to English design principles. An enthusiastic horticulturalist and gentleman farmer, Lyman erected greenhouses for the cultivation of exotic fruits and flowers. The camellias and grapevines that can be seen today are more than 100 years old. Today the property is under the supervision of the Society for the Preservation of New England Antiquities (SPNEA), which has a Conservation Center here. The house, substantially enlarged in 1882, is rented out for functions. *185 Lyman St., tel. 617/891–7095 (greenhouse) or 617/893–7232 (house). Admission: $2. Greenhouses open daily 10–4; house open by appointment for groups of 10 or more.*

**Gore Place,** built nearby in 1805, is a 22-room Federal period mansion accented by a "flying staircase" that spirals three full flights upward. Built originally as the country house of Governor Christopher Gore, it now houses a museum of Early American, European, and Oriental antiques. The 40 acres of grounds includes cultivated fields, gardens, and woodlands. *52 Gore St., tel. 617/894–2798. Admission including a guided tour: $4 adults, $2 under 15, $3 senior citizens. Open Apr. 15–Nov. 15, Tues.–Sat. 10–4, Sun. 2–4. The grounds are open daily, free of charge.*

In **Weston,** further out Route 20, the **Case Estates** is a smaller version of Jamaica Plain's 265-acre Arnold Arboretum.

The **Cardinal Spellman Philatelic Museum** (tel. 617/894–6735), on the campus of Regis College, displays more than 300,000 stamps. Still farther out on Route 20 is **Longfellow's Wayside Inn,** restored by Henry Ford beginning in 1923. Known originally as John How's Black Horse Tavern in 1661, the tavern's name became linked forever with that of the poet Henry Wadsworth Longfellow in 1863, when his *Tales of a Wayside Inn* was published. The Inn still offers "Food, Drink and Lodging for Man, Woman, and Beast."

A working 18th-century **gristmill** reproduction; the **schoolhouse** that "Mary" and her "little lamb" reportedly attended (moved here from Sterling by Henry Ford in 1926); and the **Mary Martha Chapel** are nearby.

To the north of Weston is **Lincoln,** located west of I–95 and south of Route 2, an elegant suburban hamlet that preserves more than 7,000 acres of land in conservation areas and is home to several interesting sites.

The Massachusetts Audubon Society's **Drumlin Farm** is a 180-acre working New England farm with domestic and wild animal exhibits, nature trails, and a gift shop. *South Great Rd., Rte. 117, tel. 617/259–9807. Admission: $5 adults, $3 children and senior citizens. Open Tues.–Sun. 9–5 in summer, 9–4 in winter.*

The **DeCordova & Dana Museum Park** is a cultural center set on 30 acres of parkland overlooking Sandy Pond. It offers modern art exhibitions and outdoor concerts on Sunday summer afternoons. *Sandy Pond Rd., tel. 617/259–8355. Admission: $4 adults, $2 children and senior citizens. Open Tues.–Fri. 10–5, weekends noon–5.*

The **Codman House,** originally a two-story, L-shaped Georgian building set amid agricultural land, was more than doubled in size in 1797–1798 by John Codman. (The design for the expansion is attributed to Charles Bulfinch.) The house is preserved with evidence of every period from the original Georgian paneled rooms to a Victorian dining room, and it is under the supervision of SPNEA. Codman also landscaped the grounds to resemble those of an English country estate. *Codman Rd., tel. 617/259–8843. Admission: $3 adults, $2.50 senior citizens, $1.50 children 5–12. Open June 1–Oct. 15, Wed.–Sun. for hourly tours noon–5.*

The **Gropius House** was the family home of the architect Walter Gropius (1883–1969), director of the Bauhaus in Germany from 1919 to 1928. This was the first building he designed on his arrival in the United States in 1937; he used components available from catalogues and building supply stores in a manner that was revolutionary in appearance and expressed Bauhaus principles of function and simplicity. The house is under the supervision of SPNEA. *68 Baker Bridge Rd., tel. 617/259–8843. Admission: $3 adults, $2.50 senior citizens, $1.50 children 5–12. Open June 1–Oct. 15, Fri.–Sun. noon–5; Nov. 1–May 30, the first full weekend of the month, noon–5.*

Route 2 from Lincoln will return you to Boston.

## Dining

The restaurant price categories are based on the average cost of a three-course dinner (à la carte) for one person, food alone, not including beverages, tax, and tip.

The following credit card abbreviations are used: AE, American Express; CB, Carte Blanche; D, Discover Card; DC, Diners Club; MC, MasterCard; V, Visa.

| Category | Cost* |
| --- | --- |
| Very Expensive | over $20 |
| Expensive | $12–$20 |
| Moderate | $8–$12 |
| Inexpensive | under $8 |

*per person; add 5% tax*

**Concord**  **Colonial Inn.** Traditional fare—from prime rib to scallops—is served in the gracious dining room of an inn of 1718. Overnight accommodations are available in 57 rooms. *48 Monument Sq., tel. 508/369–9200. Reservations suggested for dinner. Jacket and tie advised at night. AE, CB, DC, MC, V. Expensive.*

**Different Drummer.** Shrimp scampi, baked stuffed shrimp, fresh veal, and pasta are the highlights of the menu of a restaurant located inside the B&M train station. *86 Thoreau St., tel. 508/369–8700. Reservations suggested. Dress: casual. AE, MC, V. Open Mon. for lunch only. Moderate–Expensive.*

**Walden Station.** A casual restaurant situated in an old brick firehouse, Walden Station prepares new American cuisine such as fresh seafood, beef roulades, and beef filets. The fresh desserts are made on premises. *24 Walden St., tel. 508/371–2233. Reservations only for 5 or more. Dress: informal. AE, MC, V. Moderate.*

**Lexington**  **Le Bellecour.** Here the ambience is that of a country inn, and the cuisine is French. A new café serves lighter international cuisine. *10 Muzzey St., tel. 617/861–9400. Reservations preferred in the main dining room. Jacket and tie suggested in the main dining room. AE, MC, V. No lunch Sat. Sunday brunch in the cafe. Expensive.*

**Versailles.** An intimate French restaurant, the Versailles serves such specialties as cold poached salmon and quiche Lorraine for lunch, rack of lamb and veal Oscar for dinner. *1777 Massachusetts Ave., tel. 617/861–1711. Reservations recommended. Jacket and tie optional. AE, DC, MC, V. No lunch Sun. Expensive.*

**Yangtze River.** The Yangtze is a big, contemporary-style Chinese restaurant with a particularly good luncheon on weekdays and a dinnertime buffet Sunday through Thursday. *25 Depot Sq. tel. 617/861–6030. Reservations only for 5 or more. Dress: informal. AE, MC, V. Moderate.*

# Lowell

Everyone knows that the American Revolution began in Massachusetts. Until recently, however, little attention was paid to the fact that this state, and in particular the Merrimack Valley, was the nurturing ground of another great change in our national life: the Industrial Revolution that transformed a nation of farmers, merchants, and small tradesmen into a manufacturing colossus. The story of America's industrialization is vividly

recalled in the quintessential mill town of Lowell, the site of
state and national historic parks dedicated to the memory of
the day when the power loom was king along the Merrimack.

## Getting Around

**By Car** Lowell lies at the intersection of Routes 459 and 3. Take the
Mystic Bridge to I–93 and stay on I–93 to the junction of I–95.
Go south on I–95 until you see the exit for Route 3–Lowell.
Travel time is one hour.

**By Train** Trains operated by the Boston and Maine Railroad (tel. 617/
227–5070 or 800/392–6099) leave daily from North Station.
Travel time is one hour.

## Exploring Lowell

On arrival in Lowell, head for the **National and State Parks Visitor Center** in the downtown Market Mills Complex for a thorough orientation and informative films. The center is located in
what was the headquarters of the Lowell Manufacturing Company in the days when Lowell was "spindle city." You can follow
a walking tour that highlights the city's history from "mill
girls" to its 5.5 miles of canals. (The canals' gatehouses have
their original equipment, and costumed gatekeepers play roles
typical of the 1850s.) Tours June 30 to early September last one
to 2½ hours. Barge rides on the canals and a trolley service,
complete with replicas of turn-of-the-century cars (operates
June 30 to early September), are available. *246 Market St., tel.
508/459–1000. Open daily 8:30–5. Admission: boat tours $2;
trolley tours $2 adults, $1 senior citizens, free under 16.*

**Market Mills** is a restored mill complex with gift shop, restaurants, an art gallery, and artists' studios. *Market St., tel. 508/
459–7819. Art gallery open Tues.–Sun. 11–5.*

The **New England Quilt Museum** on Market Street displays historical and contemporary examples of the art of quilting. *Tel.
508/452–4207. Admission: $2 adults, $1 students and senior
citizens. Open Tues.–Sat. 10–4, Sun. noon–4.*

The **Lowell Heritage State Park** boasts a major waterpower exhibit, visitors programs, walking tours, boating, fishing, and
picnicking. *25 Shattuck St., tel. 508/453–1950. Admission free.
Call in advance for times; budget cuts have limited park hours.*

Part of the fascination of Lowell is its amazing ethnic diversity,
a legacy of the days when immigrants from throughout North
America and Europe came here to work in the textile mills. (Today a major influx is from Cambodia, and it was a Chinese immigrant, Dr. An Wang, who made Lowell a center of computer
manufacturing.) One major ethnic group to migrate to Lowell
in the heyday of the mills was the French Canadians. The most
famous son of French-Canadian Lowell was the poet and novelist Jack Kerouac, who was born here in 1922. Kerouac's memory is honored in the new **Eastern Canal Plaza,** where plaques
bear quotes from his Lowell novels and from *On the Road*.

Two blocks from the Market Mills entrance to the Lowell National Historical Park is the birthplace and museum of another
native son, James McNeill Whistler. Although the artist, who
painted the classic *Arrangement In Grey and Black #1: Portrait of the Artist's Mother*, popularly known as *Whistler's*

*Mother*, claimed to have been born in Baltimore, the Lowell Art Association purchased the gray clapboard house (built in 1823) to preserve Whistler's Lowell roots. The first floor of The Whistler House Museum of Art has a gallery; the upper floors house the collection of the society. *243 Worthen St., tel. 508/452-7641. Admission: $2 adults, free under 16. Open Tues.–Sat. 11–4, Sun. 1–4. Tours last about an hour.*

## Dining

The restaurant price categories are based on the average cost of a three-course dinner (à la carte) for one person, food alone, not including beverages, tax, and tip.

| Category | Cost* |
| --- | --- |
| Very Expensive | over $20 |
| Expensive | $12–$20 |
| Moderate | $8–$12 |
| Inexpensive | under $8 |

*per person; add 5% tax*

The following credit card abbreviations are used: AE, American Express; CB, Carte Blanche; D, Discover Card; DC, Diners Club; MC, MasterCard; V, Visa.

**Town House Inn.** The Town House serves all-American favorites—pork chops, prime ribs, baked scrod—in a Colonial setting. *850 Chelmsford St. (Rte. 110), tel. 508/454-5606. Dinner served only until 7 Mon.–Fri. Live entertainment Thurs.–Sat. 9 PM–1 AM. Dress: informal. AE, DC, MC, V. Closed Sun. Moderate.*

# North of Boston: The North Shore and Cape Ann

The area known as North of Boston is diverse and beautiful, as significant historically and culturally as any other part of the country. It stretches from the northern border of Boston to the southern border of New Hampshire, encompassing such fascinating towns as Marblehead, Salem, and Rockport. To the east is the Atlantic Ocean, to the west are orchards, forests, and rolling hills.

## Getting Around

**By Car** Head out of Boston by the Callahan Tunnel, staying on Route 1A through Revere Beach and Lynn. Just past Lynn is Swampscott; here, bear right on Route 129 and continue to Marblehead. Driving time to Marblehead is one hour.

**By Train** Daily trains leave North Station (tel. 617/227–5070) for several north shore communities, including Salem, Beverly, Gloucester, Rockport, and Ipswich.

**By Bus** Service to most towns is poor. The MBTA (tel. 617/722–3200) has buses to some of the more southern locations. Greyhound Trailways (tel. 617/423–5810) service to Maine and eastern Canada includes a stop in Newburyport. Travel time is one hour one-way.

## Guided Tours

**The Gray Line** (275 Tremont St., Boston 02116, tel. 617/426–8805) has a 4½-hour tour to Salem, with a stop for pictures in Marblehead, from mid-April through mid-October on Monday, Wednesday, Friday, and Sunday.

**Brush Hill Tours** (109 Norfolk St., Boston 02124, tel. 617/986–6100 or 800/647–4776) offers tours four days a week to Salem and Marblehead from late April to early October.

## Exploring the North Shore

*Numbers in the margin correspond with points of interest on the North of Boston map.*

**①** **Marblehead,** with its ancient clapboard houses and narrow, winding streets, retains much of the character of the village founded in 1629 by fishermen from Cornwall and the Channel Islands. Yet today's fishing fleet is small compared to the armada of pleasure craft that anchors in the harbor. This is one of New England's premier sailing capitals, and Race Week (usually the last week of July) brings boats from all along the Eastern seaboard. But the men who made Marblehead prosper in the 18th century were merchant sailors, not weekend yachtsmen, and many of their impressive Georgian mansions still line the downtown streets.

While parking is difficult in Marblehead, you must walk through the narrow, winding streets to appreciate fully their charm. Your best bet is to park wherever you can and leave your car. There is a 30-car public lot at the end of Front Street. If you choose on-street parking, watch the time to avoid being ticketed.

Begin your walking tour at the town's Victorian municipal building, **Abbott Hall,** which was built in 1876 and houses A. M. Willard's painting *The Spirit of '76,* one of America's treasured patriotic icons. Many people, familiar since childhood with the depiction of the three Revolutionary veterans with fife, drum, and flag, are surprised to find the original in an otherwise unassuming town hall. *Washington St., tel. 617/631–0528. Open Tues.–Thur. 8 AM–9 PM, Mon. and Fri. 8–5, and (June–Oct.) Sat. 9–6, Sun. 1–5.*

The **Robert Hooper Mansion, Mansion House,** and the **William Lee Mansion** (181–187 Washington St.) were built in the mid-18th century to house successful shipowners and merchants. All are privately owned and not open to the public.

The **Jeremiah Lee Mansion** of 1768, one of the finest examples of Georgian architecture in America, contains original Colonial furnishings and decoration, much of it imported. The mansion is now headquarters for the Marblehead Historical Society. *161 Washington St., tel. 617/631–1069. Admission: $2.25 adults, $1.25 children 10–16. Open mid-May–mid-Oct., Mon.–Sat. 9:30–4.*

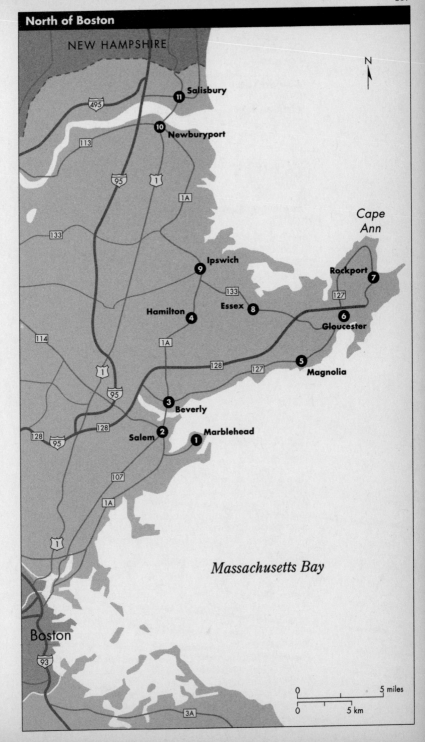

The Marblehead Arts Association has a gallery in the **King Hooper Mansion,** an early 18th-century building with slave quarters, ballroom, and garden. *8 Hooper St., tel. 617/631–2608. Admission for tour: $1. Open Tues.–Sun. 1–4:30.*

A corner of **Lafayette House** at Hooper and Union streets was removed to permit Lafayette's carriage to pass by on the narrow street when he visited in 1824.

**St. Michael's Episcopal Church** (26 Pleasant St.), built in 1714, is the second oldest standing Episcopal church in the country. The bell, rung by patriots until it cracked, was recast by Paul Revere.

**Crocker Park,** off Front Street, offers a fine view of Marblehead Harbor.

The **General Glover House** at 11 Glover Square was the home of the country's first general of the Marines, who led his troops rowing George Washington across the Delaware.

**Fort Sewall,** at the end of Front Street, built during the Revolutionary War, offers an excellent harbor view (and public toilets).

**Old Burial Hill,** off Orne Street, is where many of the town's first settlers—and more than 600 Revolutionary War casualties—are buried.

**Elbridge Gerry,** one of the signers of the Declaration of Independence and a vice president of the United States under James Madison, lived at 44 Washington Street. His name is remembered in the term *gerrymander.*

The **Old Town House,** at the intersection of State and Washington streets, was built in 1782 and is known as Marblehead's Cradle of Liberty.

When you've retrieved your car, drive out to **Marblehead Neck** to see the outer ocean. You'll have a good view of Marblehead Light from nearby **Chandler Hovey Park.**

**②** To reach **Salem,** head back inland on Route 114 and follow Route 1A. Settled in 1630, the town is known for the witchcraft hysteria of 1692, a rich maritime tradition, and the architectural splendor of its Federal homes. The frigates of Salem opened the Far East trade routes and provided the wealth that produced America's first millionaires. Numbered among its native sons were Nathaniel Hawthorne, the navigator Nathaniel Bowditch, and the architect Samuel McIntire.

The witchcraft hysteria began not in the present-day seacoast town but in Salem Village, now a part of nearby Danvers. When a West Indian slave named Tituba told fireside tales of sorcery and voodoo to a pair of impressionable girls, their subsequent nightmares were taken as a sure sign of enchantment. They accused Tituba of acquainting them with the devil, and soon no one—especially unpopular old women—was safe from the hysteria that gave rise to the term *witch hunt.* By the end of 1693, 19 persons had been hanged and one pressed to death in Salem (no one was burned at the stake). The witchcraft trials came to an abrupt halt when the wife of Governor Phipps and the saintly Mrs. Hale, the wife of a minister, were accused.

Nearly 300 years later, the mad behavior of clergy-ridden settlers still groping their way out of the Middle Ages has produced a tourist industry:

The **Witch House** is the restored home of Jonathan Corwin, judge of the witchcraft court; preliminary examinations of accused persons were held here. *310 ½ Essex St., tel. 508/744–0180. Admission: $3 adults, $1.50 children 5–16. Open mid-Mar.–June, daily 10–4:30; July–Aug., daily 10–6; Sept.–Nov., daily 10–4:30.*

The **Witch Dungeon Museum** stages a live reenactment of a witch trial and offers a tour of a recreated dungeon. *16 Lynde St., tel. 508/744–9812. Admission: $3 adults, $1.75 children. Open May–Oct., daily 10–5.*

The **Salem Witch Museum** uses a multisensory "time machine" to recreate the hysteria that surrounded the witch hunts. There's also a tourist information center here. *Washington Sq. N., tel. 508/744–1692. Admission: $3.50 adults, $3 senior citizens, $2 children 6–14. Open daily 10–4:30.*

The 100 years following the Revolution were brighter ones for Salem. This was the home port of the sea captains who made fabulous fortunes in the China trade, and here they built fine Federal-style mansions that tell us a great deal about the way they lived. The **Essex Institute Museum Neighborhood** maintains several homes that typify this and earlier eras; a museum with an excellent collection of toys, clocks, costumes, and period rooms; and original documents from the witchcraft trials. *132 Essex St., tel. 508/744–3390. Museum admission: $6 adults, $5 senior citizens, $3.50 children 6–16. Combination ticket for museum, houses, and guided tour are available. Museum open June 1–Oct. 31, Mon.–Sat. 9–5, Sun. and holidays 1–5; Nov. 1–May 31, Tues.–Sat. 9–5, Sun. and holidays 1–5. Closed Thanksgiving, Christmas, and New Year's Day. Houses open June 1–Oct. 31, Mon.–Sat. 9–5, Sun. 1–5. Hours for the museum, houses, and library change often, so it's best to call ahead.*

**Chestnut Street,** within a few blocks of downtown, boasts a magnificent architectural harmony circa 1800 and is a National Historic Landmark. The merchant princes who lived here created one of the most beautiful streets in America. The **Stephen Phillips House** is a handsome example of an early 19th-century sea captain's house, crowded with authentic Early American and English furnishings, Chinese export porcelain, and Oriental rugs. *34 Chestnut St., tel. 508/744–2028. Admission: $1.50 adults, 75¢ children under 12. Open May 28–mid-Oct., Mon.–Sat. 10–4:30.*

Among other houses of note are the **Pierce-Nichols House** (80 Federal St.), a National Historic Landmark, designed by Samuel McIntyre; the **Cotting-Smith House** (138 Federal St.), a late 18th-century home with furnishing from the days of Salem's busy trade with the Far East; and the **Pickering House** (18 Broad St.), the oldest house in the country to be occupied continuously by the same family.

The **Peabody Museum,** the largest museum on the North Shore and the oldest (1799) continuously operating museum in the country, is a treasure house of maritime history as well as of Oriental art and artifacts. The Asian Export Art wing, opened

in 1988, shows works of the 14th–19th centuries made for export. *East India Sq., tel. 508/745–1876. Admission: $5 adults,
$4 students and senior citizens, $2.50 children 6–16; $10 fami-
lies. Open Mon.–Sat. 10–5, Thurs. 10–9, Sun. noon–5. Closed
Thanksgiving, Christmas, and New Year's Day.*

On the waterfront, the **Custom House** of 1819, now the **Salem
Maritime National Historic Site,** covers 9.2 acres and includes
several buildings from Salem's years as an international seaport in the 18th and 19th centuries. Nathaniel Hawthorne
worked here as a young man. *174 Derby St., tel. 508/744–4323.
Admission free. Open daily 8:30–5. Closed Christmas and
New Year's Day.*

Another celebrity on the waterfront is the **House of Seven Ga-
bles,** built in 1668, which was an inspiration for Hawthorne's
novel. The admission fee includes an introductory audiovisual
program and a guided tour of the Gables, of Hawthorne's
Birthplace (built in 1750), of the Hathaway House (1682), the
Retire Beckett House (1655), and period gardens. *54 Turner
St., tel. 508/744–0991. Admission: $6 adults, $2.50 children 6–
17. Open July–Labor Day, daily 9:30–5:30; Labor Day–July,
Mon.–Sat. 10–4:30, Sun. noon–4:30. Closed Thanksgiving,
Christmas, New Year's Day.*

**3** Heading north from Salem on Route 1A, you cross the harbor
bridge and enter **Beverly,** celebrated as the birthplace of the
Continental Navy. Here, in 1775, the schooner *Hannah* was
armed and sent out to menace British shipping; she returned
with her first prize on September 7, just two days after her
commission. The **Beverly Historical Society and Museum,** headquartered in the **John Cabot House,** has exhibits documenting
the foray, period rooms with costumes, and maritime, military, and children's collections. *117 Cabot St., tel. 508/922–
1186. Admission: $2 adults, $1 children 6–12. Open Wed.–Sat.
10–4, Sun. 1–4. Admission fee allows entrance also to the Hale
House and the Balch House; both open mid-June–Labor Day.*

**4** Route 1A continues north through the "hunt country" of **Hamilton,** a town settled in 1638 and named for Alexander Hamilton. General George Patton, Jr., is a famous native son.
Hamilton is home to the U.S. Equestrian Team and the **Myopia
Hunt Club,** with its famed polo fields. *Rte. 1A (exit 2N off Rte.
128), tel. 508/468–7956. Admission: $5 adults, free under 12.
Matches Sun. at 3, late-May–mid-Oct.*

## Exploring Cape Ann

*Numbers in the margin correspond with points of interest on
the North of Boston map.*

To reach Cape Ann, bear right at Beverly onto Route 127. This
shore road will take you through Beverly Farms, Pride's
**5** Crossing, Manchester-by-the-Sea, and **Magnolia,** where many of
Boston's Brahmin families built their summer retreats. Head
down Hesperus Avenue in Magnolia for a look at **Norman's Woe
Rock,** made famous by Longfellow in "The Wreck of the Hesperus." The best view is from **Hammond Castle Museum,** a superb recreation of a medieval castle built as the home of the
inventor John Hays Hammond, Jr. The castle houses his collection of Roman, Medieval, and Renaissance art. *80 Hesperus
Ave., tel. 508/283–2080 or 800/649–1930. Admission: $5 adults,*

*$3 children 6–12, $4 students and senior citizens. Open Tues.–*
*Sun. 9–5. The castle has group tours and functions quite often,*
*so it's best to call ahead.*

Hesperus Avenue rejoins Route 127, which crosses the
Annisquam River and takes you into the old fishing port of
**6** **Gloucester.** When you enter the city by this route, virtually the
first sight you see is a statue that symbolizes Gloucester and
memorializes the Gloucestermen who have gone "down to the
sea in ships" for the better part of four centuries. Commissioned by Gloucester's citizens in 1923 in celebration of the seaport's 300th anniversary, the statue of a mariner at the wheel,
his eyes on the horizon, is dedicated to the anonymous souls
who do the work of the world. And dangerous work it often is;
hardly a year or two goes by without word of a Gloucester boat
and its crew lost at sea.

Workaday Gloucester is downtown, near the docks. The **Cape**
**Ann Historical Association** shows paintings and drawings by
Fitz Hugh Lane, as well as antique furniture and silver, in a his-
toric house. *27 Pleasant St., tel. 508/283–0455. Admission: $3*
*adults, $1.50 students and senior citizens, free under 12. Open*
*Tues.–Sat. 10–5. Closed Feb.*

For a different look at the city, head a short distance off Route
127 to the artists' colony on **Rocky Neck,** and to **East Point,**
where magnificent mansions stand above the granite shore.
The **Beauport Museum,** a historic house and museum created
by the interior decorator Henry Davis Sleeper, offers a guided
tour of 26 unique rooms furnished with American and European decorative arts. *75 Eastern Point Blvd., tel. 508/283–0800.*
*Admission: $5 adults, $2.50 children 6–16, $4.50 senior citi-*
*zens. Open mid-May–mid-Oct.*

**7** Route 127 continues to **Rockport,** at the very tip of Cape Ann.
The town derives its name from the granite formations, and
many a Boston-area structure is made of stone from the town's
long-gone quarries. Today Rockport is known primarily as a
tourist's town, one that has not gone overboard on T-shirt
emporia and the other accoutrements of a summer economy (although this may not seem to be true on a Sunday afternoon).
The best time to visit Rockport is during the off-season, when
many of the shops are open, the crowds are gone, and one can
see the place for the lovely New England seacoast town it is.
Walk out to the end of Bearskin Neck (the strudel shop along
the way is worth your attention) for an impressive view of the
open Atlantic and the nearby lobster shack affectionately
known as "Motif No. 1" because of its popularity as a subject for
amateur artists.

The **Rockport Art Association** displays changing exhibits of
paintings and sculpture and is the site of the Rockport Chamber Music Festival and summer painting workshops. *12 Main*
*St., tel. 508/546–6604. Admission free. Open weekdays 10–4,*
*Sat. 10–4, Sun. 1–5.*

The **Sandy Bay Historical Society and Museum** highlights local
history with Early American and Victorian rooms, granite and
fishing exhibits, costumes, toys, paintings, decorative arts,
and a library. *40 King St., tel. 508/546–9533. Admission free.*
*Open June 1–Labor Day, daily 2–5.*

Route 127 continues along the north coast of Cape Ann, affording fine ocean views as it winds its way to meet Route 128. Don't stay long on Route 128; turn onto Route 133 and head for the old shipbuilding town of **Essex,** famous for its clam beds and a 300-year construction tradition. The **Essex Shipbuilding Museum,** housed in an old schoolhouse of 1835, with a burying ground and a hearse house nearby, tells the fascinating story of the town's heritage and how the boats were built. *28 Main St., tel. 508/768–7541. Admission: $2 adults, $1 students, $1.50 senior citizens, free under 12. Open May–Oct., Thurs.–Sun. 11–4; Nov.–Apr., by appointment.*

Today Essex is a popular antiques center with a full afternoon's worth of shops on its main street. A number of places offer fried clams, which were invented here at Woodman's. The **James N. and Mary F. Stavros Reservation,** 74 acres of woodland, fields, and saltmarsh, presents spectacular views of the Essex marshes from the top of White's Hill. *Route 133. Admission free. Open sunrise to sunset.*

## Exploring Ipswich, Newburyport, Salisbury

*Numbers in the margin correspond with points of interest on the North of Boston map.*

Four miles north of Essex, the unimposing town of **Ipswich,** settled in 1633 and famous for its clams, is said to have more 17th-century houses standing and occupied than any other place in America. More than 40 homes in town were built before 1725. A *Walking Tour Guide of Historic Ipswich* is available at the **Chamber of Commerce information kiosk.** *Crane's Beach Rd. Open June–Labor Day, daily 10–4.*

The **John Whipple House** on the Ipswich Common at the intersection of routes 133 and 1A, a brooding, almost medieval dwelling built around 1638, is a fine example of 17th-century architecture. Owned by the Whipple family for almost 200 years, the house is filled with antiques—and the herb garden has more than 60 varieties. *53 S. Main St., tel. 508/356–2811. Admission: $3 adults. Open May–mid-Oct. Wed.–Sat. 10–4, Sun. 1–4.*

The nearby **John Heard House & Franklin Waters Memorial,** built in 1795, is a China trade mansion with Chinese and Early American furnishings and a restored carriage collection. *40 S. Main St., tel. 508/356–2811. Admission: $3 adults, free under 13. Combination ticket for this and the Whipple House: $5. Open May–Oct., Wed.–Sat. 10–4, Sun. 1–4.*

The turnoff onto Argilla Road leads to one of the finest beaches in New England, the **Crane Memorial Reservation,** 1,400 acres with more than 5 miles of white sand, dunes, and excellent swimming. There are bath houses, a snack bar, and lifeguards. *Argilla Rd., tel. 508/356–4354. Parking May–Labor Day, weekdays $6, weekends $10; Sept.–Apr., daily $3.25, weekends $3.75. Open 8 AM–sunset.*

Next door is **Castle Hill** (Arguilla Rd., tel. 508/356–4070), a 59-room Stuart-style mansion overlooking Crane Beach that was built for the plumbing fixtures baron Richard T. Crane, Jr., in 1927. Concerts and other cultural events are held here in the summer, and there are house tours.

Continuing north from Ipswich on Route 1A for 12 miles will
take you past the salt marshes of Rowley and Newbury to
**Newburyport.** Here Route 1A becomes High Street, which is
lined with some of the finest examples of Federal-style (rough-
ly, 1790–1810) mansions in New England. You'll notice "widow's walks," which afford a view of the port and the sea beyond,
perched atop many of the houses. Like those in Salem, they
were built for prosperous sea captains in this city that was once
a leading port and shipbuilding center.

While Newburyport's maritime significance ended with the
time of the clipper ships (some of the best of which were built
here), an energetic downtown renewal program has brought
new life to the town's brick-front center. Renovated buildings
now house an assortment of restaurants, taverns, and shops
that sell everything from nautical brasses to antique Oriental
rugs. The civic improvements have been matched by private
restorations of the town's housing stock, much of which dates
from the 18th century, with a scattering of 16th-century homes
in some neighborhoods.

The **Greater Newburyport Chamber of Commerce** has an interesting selection of brochures on, among other things, house
tours, charter boat fishing, and art galleries (there are several
good ones in town). They can also tell you about "Yankee Home-
coming" at the end of July: eight days of parades, concerts,
fireworks, sidewalk sales, and races. Those who plan to be in
town then will need to make reservations for accommodations
well in advance. *29 State St., tel. 508/462–6680. Open weekdays
9–5.*

Newburyport, Massachusetts's smallest city, is easy to walk
around in, and there is all-day free parking down by the water.
A stroll through the **Waterfront Park and Promenade** gives a super view of the harbor and the fishing and pleasure boats that
moor there. Walking to the left as you leave the parking lot will
take you to the **Custom House Maritime Museum.** Built in 1835
in Classic Revival style, it contains exhibits on maritime history, models, tools, and paintings. The audiovisual show is presented hourly. *25 Water St., tel. 508/462–8681. Admission: $3
adults, $2 children 6–16, $2.50 senior citizens. Open Apr.–
Dec., Mon.–Sat. 10–4, Sun. 1–4.*

*Walking back toward town, you pass through* **Market Square**
and **Inn Street Mall,** an ensemble of early 19th-century brick architecture built after the fire of 1811. The carefully restored
square once hosted a bustling outdoor produce market; today
it's a favorite meeting place and the center of many summertime activities. There's a pleasant "tot lot" on Inn Street.

The city's public library, the **Tracy Mansion,** was built in 1771.
Nathaniel Tracy played host to such luminaries as George
Washington, John Quincy Adams, and Lafayette before the
building became a library in 1865. *84 State St., tel. 508/465–
4428. Open in summer, Mon.–Thurs. 9–8, Fri. 9–5; in winter,
Mon.–Thurs. 9–8, Fri.–Sat. 9–5.*

Across the street, the **Dalton House** (95 High St.) was built in
1750 for a merchant whose son was the first senator from Massachusetts. The exterior is blocked to imitate cut stone; the interior displays Yankee craftsmanship.

The wooden spire of the **Unitarian Church** is one of the most beautiful in New England. The interior was designed by local ships' carpenters. *26 Pleasant St., tel. 508/465-0602. Open weekdays 9-noon. Sun. service at 10:30 except July and Aug.*

At the corner of School and Federal streets stands the **Old South Church** of 1756. It has a famous whispering gallery and a bell cast by Paul Revere, and the evangelist George Whitefield is buried here. *Tel. 508/465-9666. Call for appointment. Sun. service at 10:30 in winter, 10 in summer.*

On High Street, the Federal-style **Cushing House** (1808), now the home of the Historical Society of Old Newbury, was built by the city's first mayor. It boasts 21 beautifully furnished rooms, a collection of artifacts, a carriage house, and a French garden. *98 High St., tel. 508/462-2681. Admission: $3 adults, 50¢ children. Open May-Oct., Tues.-Sat. 10-4; Nov.-Apr., call for appointment.*

A few blocks up on the left is the **Superior Courthouse,** designed by Charles Bulfinch. Daniel Webster practiced law here.

A causeway leads from Newburyport to **Plum Island,** a narrow spit of land harboring a summer colony (rapidly becoming year-round) at one end and the **Parker River National Wildlife Refuge** at the other. The refuge has 4,662 acres of salt marsh, freshwater marsh, beaches, and dunes; it is one of the few natural barrier beach-dune-salt marsh complexes left on the Northeast coast. The birdwatching, surf fishing, plum and cranberry picking, and swimming are wonderful. A very popular place in the summer, especially on weekends, the cars begin lining up at the gate here before 7 AM (only a limited number are let in). *Tel. 508/465-5753. Admission: $5 per car (or $12.50 for a Duck Stamp, which permits free admission to all Federal Wildlife Refuges; or $25 for a Golden Eagle Pass, which permits free admission to all Federal sites). Open ½ hr before sunrise to ½ hr after sunset.*

**❶❶** The last town in Massachusetts before you reach the New Hampshire border is **Salisbury,** just across the Merrimack River from Newburyport but light years away from the upscale, brass-and-brick character of its neighbor. Salisbury's claim to fame is Salisbury Beach, a picture-perfect survivor of the great age of boardwalk honky-tonks, pizza joints, Skee-ball arcades, ferris wheels, and kiddie rides. You've seen a lot of authentic Americana since leaving Boston; before heading back down Route 95 or continuing north, why not take in a little more, circa 1955?

## Dining

North Shore restaurants have long been noted for fresh seafood. While lobster and scrod still hold sway, along with the ubiquitous fried clams, more sophisticated menus have begun to proliferate.

The restaurant price categories are based on the average cost of a three-course dinner (à la carte) for one person, food alone, not including beverages, tax, and tip.

| Category | Cost* |
|----------|-------|
| Very Expensive | over $20 |
| Expensive | $12–$20 |
| Moderate | $8–$12 |
| Inexpensive | under $8 |

*per person; add 5% tax*

The following credit card abbreviations are used: AE, American Express; CB, Carte Blanche; D, Discover Card; DC, Diners Club; MC, MasterCard; V, Visa.

**Beverly**  **The Capri.** Here are some of the best pizzas on the North Shore, along with capable Italian specialties. *418 Cabot St., tel. 508/ 922–9776. Dress: informal. AE, MC, V. Moderate.*

**Essex**  **Woodman's.** Woodman's is a historic landmark, the place where the first clam was deep-fried. Fish and lobster are served "in the rough." *121 Main St. (Rte. 133), tel. 508/768–6451. No reservations. Dress: informal. No credit cards. Inexpensive.*

**Gloucester**  **White Rainbow.** Creative and classic cuisines are served in a romantic candlelit setting. The bar serves appetizers, light fare, and desserts. The building is a registered landmark. *65 Main St., tel. 508/281–0017. Reservations suggested. Jacket and tie required. AE, CB, DC, MC, V. No lunch. Expensive.*
**Captain Courageous.** Popular with local residents, the restaurant's dining room provides an excellent view of Fisherman's Wharf and the harbor. The menu features seafood, steak, and prime ribs. Outdoor dining is possible in warm weather. *25 Rogers St., tel. 508/283–0007. Reservations accepted. Dress: informal. AE, CB, MC, V. Moderate.*
**Old Fire House Restaurant.** Home-style cooking is served for breakfast and lunch in a firehouse built in 1850. Try the anadama bread. *1072 Washington St., tel. 508/281–6153. No reservations. Dress: informal. No credit cards. No dinner. Inexpensive.*

**Marblehead**  **Rosalie's.** Rosalie's reputation rests on homemade pasta, tender veal, and consistently good renditions of the Northern Italian repertory. *18 Sewell St., tel., 617/631–5353. Reservations suggested. MC, V. Expensive.*
**The Landing.** This is an English-style pub down on the water with views of the harbor that caters to the boating and yachting set. Dinner can be elaborate and costly, but lunch can be as simple as fish and chips or burgers. *81 Front St., tel. 617/631–1878. Reservations suggested on weekends. Dress: casual. AE, CB, DC, MC, V. Moderate–Expensive.*

**Newburyport**  **Scandia.** The small, intimate restaurant specializes in new American cuisine; its seafood is always good, especially the chowder. The critics have consistently voted Scandia one of the best on the North Shore. *25 State St., tel. 508/462–6271. Reservations suggested for dinner. CB, DC, MC, V. Expensive.*
**Michael's Harborside.** A casual waterfront restaurant and pub specializing in seafood. Michael's has excellent daily specials. *Tournament Wharf, tel. 508/462–7785. No reservations. Dress: informal. AE, CB, MC, V. Moderate.*
**The Grog.** A Newburyport institution housed in a fine Federalist structure, The Grog offers American, Mexican, and Cajun food in an informal, publike atmosphere perfect for families.

The cabaret downstairs has live music on weekends. *13 Middle St., tel. 508/465–8008. No reservations. Dress: informal. MC, V. Inexpensive.*

**Rockport**  Rockport is a "dry" town; no restaurant serves alcohol.

**Yankee Clipper Inn.** The chef creates international fare with ingredients that are distinctively New England. Breads and pastries are baked on the premises. You are welcome to bring your own wine. *96 Granite St. (Rte. 127), tel. 508/546–3407. Reservations required. Jacket and tie required. AE, CB, MC, V. No lunch. Expensive.*

**Peg Leg.** Lobster, fresh fish, chowder, steaks, and chops are the fare in one of the town's older restaurants overlooking the ocean. Children's portions are available. *18 Beach St., tel. 508/546–3038. Reservations accepted. Dress: informal. Closed Nov.–Apr. AE, CB, DC, MC, V. Moderate.*

**Salem**  **Chase House.** Lobster, mako shark, halibut, swordfish, haddock creole, and steak are served in a 100-year-old restaurant with a cozy, traditional atmosphere. The Chase House caters to bus tours, and there is outdoor dining on a canopied deck. *Pickering Wharf, tel. 508/744–0000. Reservations accepted. Dress: casual. AE, CB, DC, MC, V. Expensive.*

**Roosevelt's.** Fresh local seafood, steaks, prime ribs, Cajun dishes, and an award-winning salad bar. Lighter fare is served in the Rough Rider Saloon. *300 Derby St. (Rte. 1A), tel. 508/745–9608. Reservations accepted. Dress: informal. "Early bird" dinners until 7:30. AE, DC, MC, V. Moderate.*

**Harry's Lobster Shanty.** Daily specials, fried clams, fish and chips, and sandwiches. On warm days there's an outdoor cafe. *Salem Marketplace, tel. 508/745–5449. No reservations. Dress: informal. AE, CB, MC, V. Closed Feb. and Mar. Inexpensive.*

## Lodging

Plenty of accommodations are available on the North Shore, from overnight motels along Route 1 to cozy inns and oceanfront motor hotels on Cape Ann. The following rates are based on double occupancy; remember that summer rates along the coast, and particularly on Cape Ann, will be higher.

| Category | Cost* |
|---|---|
| Very Expensive | over $95 |
| Expensive | $70–$95 |
| Moderate | $55–$70 |
| Inexpensive | under $55 |

*double room; add 9.7% state tax*

The following credit card abbreviations are used: AE, American Express; CB, Carte Blanche; D, Discover Card; DC, Diners Club; MC, MasterCard; V, Visa.

**Gloucester**  **Best Western Twin Light Manor.** The estate compound has 63 oversize guest rooms in two English Tudor manors, a coach house, and oceanview motel units. All rooms have color TV, direct-dial phones, and climate control. Some rooms have fireplaces. *Atlantic Rd., tel. 508/283–7500 or 800/528–1234.*

*Facilities: oceanfront dining, 2 swimming pools, play area, recreation room. AE, CB, DC, MC, V. Expensive.*

**Captain's Lodge Motel.** The spacious rooms have color TV and phones; kitchenette units are available on a weekly basis. Between Gloucester and Rockport. *237 Eastern Ave., tel. 508/ 281–2420. Facilities: coffee shop, heated pool, tennis court. AE, CB, DC, MC, V. Moderate.*

**Blue Shutters Inn at Good Harbor Beach.** The restored New England Inn is right on the beach; all rooms have ocean views. Rentals are made by the week, June through August (unless there are vacancies). Nightly rentals are available throughout the rest of the year *1 Nautilus Rd., tel. 508/281–2706. 11 rooms, 6 with private bath. Large common room. Suites and deluxe efficiencies available. No credit cards. Inexpensive.*

**Ipswich**   **Whittier Motel and Lounge.** The Whittier is your basic motel, conveniently located in Rowley, north of Ipswich, in the geographic center of the North Shore. Rooms have color TV and air-conditioning. *Junction Rtes. 1A and 133, tel. 508/356–5205. Facilities: lounge, outdoor swimming pool. MC, V accepted only to hold reservations. Moderate.*

**Newburyport**   **Garrison Inn.** The Garrison, a recently restored and reopened inn of 1809, is on the National Historic Register. The common rooms are decorated with antique reproduction furniture. Suites have lofts with spiral or colonial staircases; all rooms have color TV with complimentary HBO. *11 Brown Sq., tel. 508/465–0910. 24 rooms. Facilities: restaurant, Colonial pub. AE, CB, DC, MC, V. Expensive.*

**Essex Street Inn.** An old building in the downtown area was renovated recently to create an elegant hotel facility. All rooms have air-conditioning and are decorated with antique furnishings. Suites have fireplaces and whirlpool baths. *7 Essex St., tel. 508/465–3148. 21 rooms. AE, CB, DC, MC, V. Expensive.*

**Rockport**   **Seacrest Manor.** The Seacrest, a small, charming inn, prides itself on gracious hospitality and excellent service. Set on two acres, the inn offers some ocean views. All rooms have color TV, AM/FM clock radios, nightly turn-down service, and fresh flowers year-round; the decor is a combination of contemporary and antique furniture. A full breakfast is served for guests every morning, and tea is served in the afternoon. *131 Marmion Way, tel. 508/546–2211. 8 rooms, 6 with bath. No credit cards. Expensive.*

**Salem**   **Stepping Stone Inn.** A Greek Revival home built in 1846 has been restored, each guest room being refurbished in 19th-century style. All rooms have private bath and color TV with two movie channels. A full breakfast is served for guests every morning. *19 Washington Sq. North, tel. 508/741–8900 or 800/ 338–3022. 8 rooms. AE, CB, DC, MC, V. Very Expensive.*

**Clipper Ship Inn.** The Clipper Ship is a family-oriented motel in the heart of the city's historic district. All rooms have color TV and air-conditioning; some kitchens and efficiencies are available. *40 Bridge St., Rte. 1A, tel. 508/745–8022. 56 rooms. AE, MC, V. Moderate.*

# Index

# Personal Itinerary

**Departure**  *Date*

*Time*

**Transportation**

**Arrival**  *Date*          *Time*

**Departure**  *Date*          *Time*

**Transportation**

**Accommodations**

**Arrival**  *Date*          *Time*

**Departure**  *Date*          *Time*

**Transportation**

**Accommodations**

**Arrival**  *Date*          *Time*

**Departure**  *Date*          *Time*

**Transportation**

**Accommodations**

*Personal Itinerary*

**Arrival** *Date*       *Time*

**Departure** *Date*       *Time*

**Transportation**

**Accommodations**

**Arrival** *Date*       *Time*

**Departure** *Date*       *Time*

**Transportation**

**Accommodations**

**Arrival** *Date*       *Time*

**Departure** *Date*       *Time*

**Transportation**

**Accommodations**

**Arrival** *Date*       *Time*

**Departure** *Date*       *Time*

**Transportation**

**Accommodations**

*Personal Itinerary*

**Arrival** *Date*      *Time*

**Departure** *Date*      *Time*

**Transportation**

**Accommodations**

**Arrival** *Date*      *Time*

**Departure** *Date*      *Time*

**Transportation**

**Accommodations**

**Arrival** *Date*      *Time*

**Departure** *Date*      *Time*

**Transportation**

**Accommodations**

**Arrival** *Date*      *Time*

**Departure** *Date*      *Time*

**Transportation**

**Accommodations**

*Addresses*

| | |
|---|---|
| *Name* | *Name* |
| *Address* | *Address* |
| | |
| *Telephone* | *Telephone* |
| *Name* | *Name* |
| *Address* | *Address* |
| | |
| *Telephone* | *Telephone* |
| *Name* | *Name* |
| *Address* | *Address* |
| | |
| *Telephone* | *Telephone* |
| *Name* | *Name* |
| *Address* | *Address* |
| | |
| *Telephone* | *Telephone* |
| *Name* | *Name* |
| *Address* | *Address* |
| | |
| *Telephone* | *Telephone* |
| *Name* | *Name* |
| *Address* | *Address* |
| | |
| *Telephone* | *Telephone* |
| *Name* | *Name* |
| *Address* | *Address* |
| | |
| *Telephone* | *Telephone* |
| *Name* | *Name* |
| *Address* | *Address* |
| | |
| *Telephone* | *Telephone* |

## Addresses

| | |
|---|---|
| Name | Name |
| Address | Address |
| | |
| Telephone | Telephone |
| Name | Name |
| Address | Address |
| | |
| Telephone | Telephone |
| Name | Name |
| Address | Address |
| | |
| Telephone | Telephone |
| Name | Name |
| Address | Address |
| | |
| Telephone | Telephone |
| Name | Name |
| Address | Address |
| | |
| Telephone | Telephone |
| Name | Name |
| Address | Address |
| | |
| Telephone | Telephone |
| Name | Name |
| Address | Address |
| | |
| Telephone | Telephone |
| Name | Name |
| Address | Address |
| | |
| Telephone | Telephone |

# Fodor's Travel Guides

## U.S. Guides

Alaska
Arizona
Boston
California
Cape Cod, Martha's
  Vineyard, Nantucket
The Carolinas & the
  Georgia Coast
The Chesapeake
  Region
Chicago
Colorado
Disney World & the
  Orlando Area
Florida
Hawaii

Las Vegas, Reno,
  Tahoe
Los Angeles
Maine, Vermont,
  New Hampshire
Maui
Miami & the
  Keys
National Parks
  of the West
New England
New Mexico
New Orleans
New York City
New York City
  (Pocket Guide)

Pacific North Coast
Philadelphia & the
  Pennsylvania
  Dutch Country
Puerto Rico
  (Pocket Guide)
The Rockies
San Diego
San Francisco
San Francisco
  (Pocket Guide)
The South
Santa Fe, Taos,
  Albuquerque
Seattle &
  Vancouver

Texas
USA
The U. S. & British
  Virgin Islands
The Upper Great
  Lakes Region
Vacations in
  New York State
Vacations on the
  Jersey Shore
Virginia & Maryland
Waikiki
Washington, D.C.
Washington, D.C.
  (Pocket Guide)

## Foreign Guides

Acapulco
Amsterdam
Australia
Austria
The Bahamas
The Bahamas
  (Pocket Guide)
Baja & Mexico's Pacific
  Coast Resorts
Barbados
Barcelona, Madrid,
  Seville
Belgium &
  Luxembourg
Berlin
Bermuda
Brazil
Budapest
Budget Europe
Canada
Canada's Atlantic
  Provinces

Cancun, Cozumel,
  Yucatan Peninsula
Caribbean
Central America
China
Czechoslovakia
Eastern Europe
Egypt
Europe
Europe's Great Cities
France
Germany
Great Britain
Greece
The Himalayan
  Countries
Holland
Hong Kong
India
Ireland
Israel
Italy

Italy 's Great Cities
Jamaica
Japan
Kenya, Tanzania,
  Seychelles
Korea
London
London
  (Pocket Guide)
London Companion
Mexico
Mexico City
Montreal &
  Quebec City
Morocco
New Zealand
Norway
Nova Scotia,
  New Brunswick,
  Prince Edward
  Island
Paris

Paris (Pocket Guide)
Portugal
Rome
Scandinavia
Scandinavian Cities
Scotland
Singapore
South America
South Pacific
Southeast Asia
Soviet Union
Spain
Sweden
Switzerland
Sydney
Thailand
Tokyo
Toronto
Turkey
Vienna & the Danube
  Valley
Yugoslavia

## Wall Street Journal Guides to Business Travel

Europe
International Cities
Pacific Rim
USA & Canada

## Special-Interest Guides

Bed & Breakfast and
  Country Inn Guides:
  Mid-Atlantic Region
New England
The South
The West

Cruises and Ports
  of Call
Healthy Escapes
Fodor's Flashmaps
  New York

Fodor's Flashmaps
  Washington, D.C.
Shopping in Europe
Skiing in the USA &
  Canada

Smart Shopper's
  Guide to London
Sunday in New York
Touring Europe
Touring USA